I0479867

Finding Undetermined:
Hard cases for Coroners and Death Investigators

**An Analysis Based on Case Studies
And the Evolution of Modern Medical-Legal Death Investigation
In Fremont County, Wyoming**

Dedicated to those whose names are unknown,
Or questions still unanswered.

© 2017 Mark R. Stratmoen, All Rights, Reserved

Published by Lenore Wyoming Publications
522 East Park Avenue, Riverton, WY 82501

ISBN-10: 197431376X
ISBN-13: 978-197431376X

All references and quotes from *The National Association of Medical Examiners: A Guide for Manner of Death Classification, 1ˢᵗ Ed., 2002* are used by permission of the Association

Cover Photo: Tampered port of a medical delivery system
Back Photo: Pedestrian-vehicle collision circa 1941
Photo archives, Fremont County Coroner

About the Author:

Mark R. Stratmoen is currently the Coroner for Fremont County, Wyoming, and has been a certified death investigator since 1998. Before taking office in 2015, he also served as department administrator from 2004 to 2014, and as Chief Deputy from 2007 to 2014. Service also included being a member of DMORT (Disaster Mortuary Operational Response Team) under the Federal National Disaster Medical Service, Department of Health and Human Services, with deployment to work Hurricane Katrina in the New Orleans area in 2005.

Aside from the over 650 hours of State certified medical-legal training acquired up to this point, working in this area of Wyoming has involved experience in high altitude mountain recoveries, desert and remote area recoveries; air crash, fire incident, and water recoveries and investigations; vehicle collisions and traffic fatalities; industrial incidents; archaeological and anthropological recoveries and investigations; medical facility investigations; and the usual expected array of natural, accidental, homicide, and suicide deaths. This includes being the lead investigator on over 600 cases, including the lead on over 220 non-natural deaths.

He is also the author of *"Murder, Mayhem, and Mystery: Coroner Inquests in Fremont County, Wyoming 1885-1900,* © Mark R. Stratmoen, Pub. Lenore Wyoming Publications, ISBN-10: 146362932X

Table of Contents

Section IV: The Evolving Eighties

Section V: The Nearly There Nineties

Section VI: 21st Century Knock on the Door

Section VII: Better Late than Never in the 2010's
a. When the Cause of Death is Unknown or Undetermined.
b. When the Cause may be known but no defining choice exists between Manners.
c. Common Causes of Death that may result in Undetermined Manner.
d. Trends in Undetermined Cases.
e. Main Lessons to take away from this study.

Appendix A: Sample Coroner Report Form with Explanation
Appendix B: Record Retention, State of Wyoming
Appendix C: Coroner Statutes, State of Wyoming
Appendix D: Board of Coroner Standards

Suggested Bibliography

Preface

"Could not Be Determined" is a very unsatisfying phrase for the death investigator of any era. It leaves a person with the feeling that something was missed, that perhaps one more test, one more witness, or some unknown piece of evidence would shed a final light of explanation for the circumstances behind the demise of the subject at hand. Yet, in spite of all modern advances, technology, or research, it is the very nature of the mysteries of living, that there will always be some mystery at the end. Some things in investigations, in spite of the impression given by the media, television, or theatrical productions, simply won't be solved to a tidy conclusion, with 'happily ever-after' or the thump of the gavel of final justice bringing closure.

There are innumerable books on most of the manners of death. Medical texts cover and research the natural conditions, procedurals cover homicides, prevention and analysis studies look at accidents and suicides. Historical research looks at many of the more notable circumstances and incidents of the past. And while there are also a lot of books on theories and attempts to solve the major riddles or unsolved deaths of history, few address the day-to-day cases an average death investigator may encounter.

Death investigation is a continually evolving profession and skill. This text is a presentation and discussion of cases ruled "undetermined" in the files and database of Fremont County, Wyoming, in an attempt to educate and provide examples to the death investigator of the circumstances, issues, and reasoning that may lead to the conclusion of an undetermined manner of death. Like it or not, while statistically they are only a small percentage of the cases you will encounter in your career, you will have them, and find them frustrating.

By looking at a number of cases in historical sequence, you can get a feel for the evolution of the process of investigation and the past pitfalls, which hopefully will give a better awareness of how to do your job in current times. The principles of that investigation have basically remained consistent over time, but the implementation has changed drastically in detail and method. This study will also discuss how even the routine administration aspects of your job, can affect the outcome and results. Especially in the light of the fact that despite what you may not be able to solve now, the case may be revisited and solved by a later investigator even years down the line. What you do can have repercussions long after you have retired and left a department.

As a note on public records and confidentiality, persons related or familiar with circumstances may recognize a possible situation or case that is covered in this text, especially as we get closer to modern times. These cases are presented to educate and assist the skills of investigation, not to indicate any disrespect to the deceased. It should be noted that Wyoming Statute 7-4-105(f), passed in 2011 by the Wyoming Legislature, does allow the coroner to use the materials from cases for training purposes provided the identity of the decedent is not published, so later cases will have names and some other identifying data left out. There is also the fact that prior to legislative changes in 2011 all coroner files were legally public record, and that included graphic photos and autopsy reports. In many older cases versus current law, identity may and had been previously public. Also, both in the past and today, inquests are the exception to confidentiality as that entire process and all the information presented is considered by law as public record. Regardless, here we are interested in explaining the process and education, not graphic display, so all photos of known individuals from cases are not going to be included.

This study is also not the same as an individual investigator or reviewer would do on a single case. In those circumstances, the investigator would have access to all the complete documentation, records, photos, reports, and other materials of the actual case file. For obvious reasons, my role in this study is to provide summaries of what materials are available, and analyze them in the context of educational purposes, not to provide access to the complete file in detailed reproduction. This study is to enhance the investigator's understanding of undetermined cases in general and help them when they encounter similar circumstances. In a restricted classroom situation, the optimal lesson would be to present cases in full and let the student test conclusions based on the details of all the evidence in photos, reports and other materials.

I do offer my opinions where I feel warranted, and the student or reader is free to disagree. We work in a reality of approximations and probabilities, after all, and a different viewpoint may certainly be valid, if you can justify it based on the evidence.

Mark R. Stratmoen, Fremont County Coroner, Wyoming

Introduction

First, we need to establish the parameters of this study, in the context of numbers of cases, what a coroner case is in relation to all deaths, what other unknowns may be encountered in the performance of investigations, and what is, exactly, the standard for ruling a case as 'undetermined'.

a. Total numbers:

As of July 1st, 2017, the coroner database has 7,826 cases on file, going back to the year 1885. Of that total, in regards to 'manner' of death, 63.5% are ruled natural (4,968), 21.5% accident (1,683), 7.1% suicide (555), 4.4% homicide (342), and 1.6% (124) are undetermined. The balance includes 1.2% unknown (96), 0.5% non-human (42), and several cases not Fremont County jurisdiction. A few recent cases are pending investigations with the manner of death not yet determined, so the total at this point is not quite 100%. This does give an idea of how often the typical investigator will encounter a case that ends up as undetermined.

In modern times this coroner's office averages about 50% of the deaths in Fremont County as being coroner cases, with the balance being attended and/or anticipated deaths certified by a physician, and not our jurisdiction. This only accounts for the last two decades, however, of the above numbers, as prior to that, the farther back historically you go, the worse the record keeping, with many probable cases or county deaths not accounted for. In deep history, only a few, such as those that had inquests and were filed with the State Archives, survived to be counted in the database totals.

b. Definition of a "Coroner Case":

By law as of 2017, the following is the statutory definition of what is considered a "coroner case" in Wyoming:

W.S. 7-4-104. Definitions.
> (a) As used in this chapter:
>> (i)   "Coroner's case" means a case involving a death which was not anticipated and which may involve any of the following conditions:
>> (A) Violent or criminal action;
>> (B) Apparent suicide;
>> (C) Accident;
>> (D) Apparent drug or chemical overdose or toxicity;
>> (E) The deceased was unattended by a physician or other

licensed health care provider;

(F) Apparent child abuse causes;

(G) The deceased was a prisoner, trustee, inmate or patient of any county or state corrections facility or state hospital, whether or not the death is unanticipated;

(H) If the cause is unknown, or cannot be certified by a physician,

(J) A public health hazard is presented; or

(K) The identity of the victim is unknown or the body is unclaimed.

(ii) "Coroner's office" means all personnel appointed and elected to the office of coroner, including the county coroner, deputies and assistants;

(iii) "County coroner" means the elected or appointed officer of the county whose task is to investigate the cause of death in a coroner's case.

(iv) "Anticipated death" means the death of an individual who has been diagnosed by a physician acting within the scope of his license as being afflicted with an illness or disease reasonably likely to result in death, and there is no cause to believe the death occurred for any reasons other than those associated with the illness or disease;

(v) "Unattended" means the deceased had not been under the care of a physician or other health care provider acting within the scope of his license within sixty (60) days immediately prior to the date of death.

Statutes vary widely from state to state, and some jurisdictions use a Medical Examiner system, or a blended system of a Medical Examiner and coroners. Whether a Medical Examiner or coroner, however, the principles of medical-legal death investigation are the same, although the implementation and skill set needed in the personnel, and how responsibilities are divided, can vary widely among employees of the various systems. Even in a State such as Wyoming, there is a wide variation in how the different county offices operate and approach their responsibilities, as some smaller population counties may only have a few cases a year, versus the larger population counties may average over two hundred. To those in metropolitan areas, even this will seem small, but remember Wyoming only has around 590,000 people, the smallest in population of the 50 states. It is the nature of death, however, that the percentages appear to hold when compared by population, so even in Fremont County, we encounter the same types of cases as larger population areas, just not in as great of numbers.

Also keep in mind the context that we are the tenth largest state in square mile area. Fremont County itself is slightly less than 10,000 square miles with a population of only around 45,000; in area larger than several eastern states. At that, though, we get all the usual types of deaths that you would find in an urban area, mixed in with those that would be unique to an environment that includes rural, desert, mountainous areas, and the factors that go with it. Not every investigator in the country gets to deal with a deceased that was killed and eaten by a bear, or fell off a 14,000 foot high mountain. Again, the principles remain the same, but the implementation of investigation may be quite unique compared to what a lot of investigators experience in their careers.

c. Odds and ends:

1. The Fremont County Coroner Office will assist other counties if needed or requested, and today those cases will be logged in the database, even if not our jurisdiction, due to the amount of time or documentation required, as a form of record-keeping. While inconsistently applied, this was sometimes also recorded in the past. Four cases on file not discussed here are since 2006, and it should be noted that this does not represent all past assistance, as previous administrations often did not keep files on such cases, or they were entered in the database as something else. Also, some may have been assigned another manner of death depending on the preference of previous coroners. A few ended up listed as undetermined in manner, and will come up in the discussion.

2. Non-human listings in the database are for those cases where the remains, if any, are verified as being as animal or other origin. For the most part, our office on occasion gets asked to verify the nature of bones found by the public in assorted situations. Since time, energy, and often, expense is used to accomplish identification, the case is assigned a number and added to the database for tracking. Another circumstance would be where there is a suspected unknown burial or gravesite, and an investigation determines animal origin or nothing there. Small graves can be anything from someone's pet dog, to a missing child and need to be checked out. However, this is only a modern listing implemented for tracking in 1999 after I started with the department.

Of the 42 non-human cases, nine are suspected or reported grave sites. These include two sites that were examined as possibly being related to cases of missing persons where a body had not been found in the case, and ended up 'dry holes'. One was a site that actually had a headstone marked "the kid" and a drawing of a rat – turning out to be a pet cemetery. One was a community college archeology dig that turned out to be a natural deposit of piled rocks – grade for the class an 'F'? Five others either revealed nothing or contained animal bones.

The balance of 33 non-human cases for the majority of instances were verified animal remains, most commonly game animals. One was a grizzly bear femur – bear bones can look surprisingly human – and one a portion of an Alaska seal skull displayed at an auction of collected artifacts. With few exceptions, under Wyoming law, the public cannot possess non-related human remains, so auctioneers get nervous over stranger items. Another item was listed on an auction list as "medicine man skull", which turned out to be a coyote skull on a stick. Two cases in 2006 were piles of scattered antelope bones that the finders were sure belonged to a person missing for about 20 years, and one tongue found in a car wash was probably left behind by a game animal hunter. One case in 2013 was not even bone, but odd shaped cement nodules left behind after a house fire. To be sure, some of this seems silly, but we would rather have people report and find out it is nothing, than have a case missed because it was unreported. In any circumstance, if you suspect human origin, the law here requires a report to authorities, or otherwise you face possible fines and jail time.

3. There are 96 cases listed in the database as 'Unknown' rather than a specific manner of death. In older files, mostly from the 1950's, 60's, and 70's, all we have is a case listing for individuals with no case file information. This status accounts for 73 of the unknowns. Another 19 have case files, but minimal information with no indication of manner of death. Three cases are missing persons where no body was found – two of which have been reopened in recent history several times without specific resolution but have extensive follow up information. One case was a probable false report of remains in a landfill where nothing was ever found by investigation. A good number of the unknown listings could probably be completed as to manner of death if the names and dates were matched with a search of the Wyoming historical archives and vital records if available. This would be an extensive and time-consuming project to try and match the 92 of the 96 cases for which that would be a possibility, going back into records from forty to sixty years ago at the State level.

d. 'Undetermined' in General:

The above three categories account for 142 of the 266 cases on file that are not classified as Natural, Homicide, Accident, or Suicide. These 266 cases represent 3.4% of the 7,826 cases, the balance of which are assigned a definitive manner of death. The remaining 124 of that small percentage are ruled 'undetermined' and represent 1.6% of the total number of cases.

A case is ruled as undetermined for one of several reasons. The first instance would be if, in spite of a thorough investigation and even including a forensic autopsy, a cause of death cannot be determined. While rare, such cases do occur. If the cause of death could not be determined, obviously the manner of death remains undetermined. The second case would be where the cause of death is determined by investigation and/or autopsy, but the facts of the case do not clearly define the circumstances, or enable the investigator to eliminate all but one manner of death to a reasonable certainty. For example, defining whether a death was an accident or suicide, homicide or suicide, or such. For the most part, the difficulty comes in clearly leading to a non-natural manner, rather than a natural one. Generally, it is fairly easy to arrive at a basis for natural death versus a non-natural one, for obvious reasons, but in certain circumstances, caution must accompany that statement. For example, the investigator cannot forget that in the incident of a vehicular crash, if the driver died of, or suffered a non-survivable cardiac event prior to the collision, the death could be ruled natural rather than an accident from sustained injuries. The varieties and complications of determining manner can be a detailed tapestry of clues and direction.

The surety for the investigator in ruling a manner of death is not cut and dry, nor black and white – quite often it is shades of grey and a matter of judgment. The definitions for the main manners are fairly simple:
  a. Natural: exclusively a medical reason for death with no other cause or factors.
  b. Accident: a non-natural cause or event that precipitated death without planning, anticipation, or intent.
  c. Suicide: self-inflicted, intentional act on the part of the deceased that caused or led to the death.
  d. Homicide: in these circumstances, 'homicide' is a neutral term in that simply, one person killed another. The legal criminal considerations of 'degree' or 'intent', or 'premeditation', etc., do not apply. However, it can be considered as a manner in any case where another person's volitional or 'intentional act', violation of the law, or negligence resulted in a person's death, whether that act was directed towards a particular person or not.
  e. Could Not Be Determined: Either there is no clear single manner indicated by the evidence, or, the evidence could indicate more than one manner without defining it to a single manner within a reasonable certainty.

The judgement call has been adequately summarized in *The National Association of Medical Examiners: A Guide for Manner of Death*

Classification, 1st Ed., 2002:

a. Undetermined (less than 50% certainty)
b. Reasonable medical or investigative probability (greater than 50:50 chance, more likely than not)
c. Preponderance of medical/investigative evidence (for practical purposes, about 70% or greater certainty)
d. Clear and convincing medical/investigative evidence (90% or greater certainty)
e. Beyond any reasonable doubt (essentially 100% certainty)
f. Beyond any doubt (100% certainty)

As noted in this publication, "cause and manner of death" are opinions... seldom, for the purpose of manner of death classification, is 'beyond a reasonable doubt' required as the burden of proof. In many cases, 'reasonable probability' will suffice." The reality of investigations is that unless a death is witnessed, or occurs under medical care where the issues and circumstances are definitively known, the investigator is basing a conclusion on degrees of probability. Luckily, in most cases, that degree is usually at 70% or greater probability. That small percentage of those cases that cannot be defined with certainty, however, while only a few cases, can be the most challenging and frustrating for the investigator.

As for the 124 undetermined manner cases for Fremont County, 40 can be separated out as cases regarding bones that were identified by forensic anthropology as being human remains. A majority of these sets of remains are those from the older historical or prehistoric period, found within the county by various circumstances. In a vast area such as Fremont County, humans have been burying their dead for centuries, ranging from those that did not survive travel on the Oregon Trail to back to ancient aboriginal crevice burials in sacred areas. Over the course of time, these sites will work their way to the surface, or be disturbed by animals (or humans), and once they pop up, become a case for the coroner's office.

The first task for the investigator is to determine that skeletal remains are not a medical-legal case, that is, contemporary enough (usually 70 years old or less) to warrant investigation, either as one of the numerous open missing persons cases, or the remains of some unknown recent death. The age of the remains is usually determined through forensic anthropology, archeology methodology, and context of the scene evidence. Of these first 40 cases under consideration, all were determined not to be of medical-legal significance. Once that is the case, other investigative procedures come into play.

Out of 40 sets of skeletal or human bone remains, 24 were determined to be Native American. Federal law now generally determines the disposition procedure in those cases, mostly set by the location found, whether Tribal, Federal, State, or private land. Ten sets were turned over to the Human Remains Repository at the University of Wyoming, which is authorized to hold them for processing of repatriation to the appropriately determined tribe. Eight were directly repatriated back to a local tribe by the coroner's office. Six were examined on site and reburied immediately at the request of the tribe. The critical importance of following procedures and the law when dealing with Native American remains cannot be overstated, as aside from a simple matter of respect, errors can cause a world of legal difficulties.

Eight sets were determined to be non-native, and also turned over to the Repository. These included Oregon Trail sites, as well as those such as an old medical specimen from the early 1900's found in someone's storage shed. Two were sites of cremains burials where fragments or teeth were determined as human, also reburied on site. One was a case of a reported skull from a reliable source, but a search of the rural area failed to locate it. Five cases are older files where the information was too incomplete to determine the disposition.

It is important to note that in the case of older skeletal remains, while the cause and manner will in a large percentage be undetermined or unknown, there are those occasions where manner can be determined with a reasonable investigative probability. A few examples:

a. In November of 2007, a hiker goes missing in the mountains. General area of probable route and destination are known, so an extensive search and rescue operation is mounted that continues for about a week. This includes air resources, search dogs, and a large number of personnel. Due to the time of year, weather changes, and rugged nature of the area, probable survivability for the individual approaches zero as time passes, and the search is called off to avoid high risk to responders. A search resumes in June of 2008 once the snow clears from the mountains, not in hopes of rescue, but to try and locate remains. In a remote area, possible skeletal remains are found along with personal effects at the base of a cliff. Personal effects indicate a match to the missing person, and forensic anthropology indicates fall trauma is involved in the death. Enough DNA is obtained from the long bones for comparison to known relatives, and a match is positive. A skull is not present in the first find. Initiating circumstances are not known, and could be a predator confrontation or other mishap leading to an accidental fall off the cliff, which may have been a survivable height. Psycho-social background of the individual indicates suicide highly unlikely. Keeping in mind that the fall may have been survived and hypothermia or exposure an additional possibility, the cause of death is left as undetermined. In this case, however, the manner of death is ruled accident, as there is a greater than 50:50 investigative probability that the fall or its complications led to the death. Note that under these circumstances, the certifier could have also ruled the cause of death as a "probable trauma from a fall" with probable hypothermia as a contributing factor. This would be a reasonable probability in consideration of the forensic evidence and better match the ruling of an accidental death – my preference, but I did not certify this case. As an additional note, in 2012 a human skull is found in the same general area. While too old at this point to extract usable DNA, University anthropologists complete an overlay of known photos on images of the skull to establish a reasonable certainty of a match, and establish no evidence of fatal head injury – further supporting the earlier conclusions.

      b. In 2008, a set of remains are found in a remote area by a cattle rancher. Scene examination reveals they were partially scattered from a nearby crevice burial by animal activity, and a fairly complete skeleton and numerous artifacts are recovered indicating Native American origin. Anthropology exam determines the remains to be 100 to 150 years old, with death occurring when the individual was around 50 years of age and of local tribal affiliation. Details on the remains also show extensive growths and scarring on the skeleton of either tubercular or cancerous origin (possibly both). No evidence of immediate fatal trauma or injury is seen, although there are indications of a pretty rough life due to healed previous trauma. The skeletal state of the disease process is also highly indicative of the illness being near the terminal phase. At one point in the upper cranium, while alive the disease process had eroded a 50 caliber size hole through the bone, so the forensic anthropologists were critical in revealing the differentiation that this was a natural process and not a 150 year old homicide. So within a reasonable probability, the cause is known, and the manner determined as natural. The remains were returned for reburial by the tribes.

      c. In 2007, a rural landowner requests removal of an unknown small grave that has no documentation as to origin or time frame of the occupant. The grave is excavated using archaeology techniques, and the skeletal remains of a small infant and fragmented cedar casket are recovered. Burial is most likely from the 1920 to 1930's, and the age of the infant at death is either premature or close to birth in time frame. Again, no evidence of trauma or non-natural death is seen. The exact cause is unknown, but the manner is probably natural, especially in consideration of the infant mortality rates of the region and period of history – a reasonable investigative probability. The infant was reburied in a local cemetery. Again, the manner and cause is a judgement call on the part of the certifier within the realm of reasonable probabilities.

The same anthropology and archaeology procedures and techniques are valuable also for investigation of more recent remains that are skeletonized. It is the superior methodology for finding and collecting evidence in skeletal medical-legal cases that need cause and manner determined towards a resolution or adjudication, and answers.

e. Missing Persons:

Once the forty bones cases are cleared out of the 124 undetermined cases, that leaves 84 cases to consider. Two are missing person's cases where, while no bodies have been found, the evidence is fairly clear that a homicide occurred in each, and considerable investigator time has been spent over the years on both cases. As originally certified as undetermined, however, without the bodies, the cause remains unknown and manner undetermined due to the physical lack of concrete evidence. Also, again, this is just record-keeping, as they are not officially an actual case, nor can be certified with the State, until an actual body is found or certified by court order. The decision to rule or determine manner in a time consuming case that has no body, but uses a lot of investigative time and effort, is a discretionary one. The coroner's medical-legal skills are useful to law enforcement in searches or examinations of possible scenes, as often in missing person's cases, dead ends and false leads are numerous. For the most part, if a case has a wide margin in question or theory of whether or not the person is actually deceased or not, I file it as unknown. If there is a reasonable certainty the individual is dead and just not located, I file it as undetermined. Those can be changed and updated over the years as cold cases are reexamined or reopened.

This does not include cases where a party petitions the court for a declaration of presumptive death. When individuals have been missing and are believed dead, next-of-kin may petition the District Court for an Order of Presumptive Death. The Court will weigh the facts presented, and may issue such an order. The order will designate an effective date of death. This procedure is frequently used in cases where no evidence of life activity on a person missing for a good number of years can be proven, or where a body is never recovered, but an event, such as a fall into a river, is witnessed. Legal counsel on behalf of the family must provide all documents that support Court's declaration.

    a. Upon the ruling of the Court that an individual is declared dead, an order is issued. A certified copy of that order must be presented to the coroner in order for a death certificate to be completed.

    b. When such an order is received by the coroner, it is directed to an investigator who will perform a search to ensure that the decedent has not already been reported and listed as a case. If not, the investigator will prepare a case file. Generally, the circumstances and court may indicate a particular manner, or it will be certified as undetermined.

    c. The death certificate then is completed with State Vital Statistics through a Registrar. A date of death should appear on the court order, and if not, the date of the order will serve as the date of death.

f. And Finally...

That now leaves us with 82 cases where there were actual bodies, and the manner is listed as undetermined. Considering that is just a bit over 1% (1.05% to be exact) of the total cases on file for Fremont County since 1885, that is not bad. Based on an average of around 150 cases per year these days, that would mean one or two cases per year will defy complete explanation. That does not make it any less frustrating, but at least establishes a bench mark to go by... if the number grows much higher than average, then the coroner needs to consider an analysis of why that would be. It could be related to an unknown public health and safety issue, or some other heretofore unrecognized issue or cause. A lot of unexplained or undetermined deaths could indicate a real problem, obviously.

A further division of types of undetermined cases can be made on the 82 where bodies were available for examination. Of those, 21 have the cause of death listed as undetermined or unknown, thus the manner would logically follow as undetermined also. Another 16 have some sort of trauma indicated as a cause, and 21 have alcohol, drugs, or other substance indicated as a cause or associated factor. Five have ill-defined lung or cardiac issues, three have fire related death trauma, three list liver and /or kidney failure, three drowning, and two each sepsis and hypoxic injury. Single causes include a birth issue, anaphylaxis, hypothermia, malnutrition, and Creutzfeldt-Jakob disease. Some include combinations of these listings, and all will be more defined and adjusted as we study the individual cases.

Age relation to undetermined shows some interesting trends:

Fremont County Coroner - Undetermined Manner Cases												
1885 - 2016 (as of 10/28/16)												
Age	0	1	2-5	5-17	18-25	26-35	36-45	46-55	56-65	66-75	76-85	86-95	95+
cases	6	3	3	3	6	11	19	13	7	3	1	0	1
Note: younger age cases separated for newborn, infant, child determination												
In 7 of 83 cases, age is not known												

Infants, newborns, and children can often be difficult investigations, if for no other reason than physical size. The spike towards the middle of the average life span may be attributable to the rates for more common manner of deaths of a non-natural type being larger for those age groups (**see CDC National Vital Statistics**). The ability to differentiate between natural and non-natural death would generally seem more apparent than between different types of non-natural circumstances, but we will see if that holds when analyzing the cases.

CASE REVIEWS

First, a note on our numbering system and reasons: Fremont County Coroner's Office case numbers are assigned a bit oddly. At the time a database was started in the late 1990s, the office staff at the time just assigned the last two digits of the year followed by a three digit case number. For example, in 1998, the cases ran from #98001 through #98183. In a quirk of millennial madness, the office staff in the year 2000 only gave a three digit year followed by a three digit case number. So, in the year 2001 we end up with case numbers from #201001 through #201217. When I took over as administrator, I went through all 7,000 or so case files to make sure they were in the database, and had to assign numbers that would not conflict with the existing system. For the unnumbered 1800s, I assigned a four digit year with two digit case number. So I ended up with a number like 188902 for the second case file from the year 1889, and kept that system through the year 1900. Starting with the year 1901, we could go with #1001, 1002, 1003 etc., consistent with the current and existing system. The most logical solution might have seemed to have been to change the numbering system to a four digit year with three digit case number so everything was the same, but that would have meant either reassigning or reentry of the thousands of case numbers already in the system at the time. Anyone who has wrestled with existing databases to try and change the basic parameters of a template for data will appreciate that the slight inconsistent numbering system work-around was much easier than the more logical assignment. The work-around solution will be good for a while, and what office staff will do in the year 2099 will be up to them.

Also, in early inquest transcripts, many of the written misspellings were left in as found, in order to retain the historical flavor of the original documents.

Section I: The Historical Seeds of Method

In a study I did of all cases in the files from early statehood and county existence, I found that early coroners were often amazingly good at what they did in terms of investigations, although the political and social realities of the times could have a great impact on how independently their conclusions had validity. Often the coroner was the only death investigator available, with law enforcement having little experience in the matter. For sure, compared to today, a lot would be missed as far as deaths, due to the presumptions and assumptions of the times. For example, a lot of natural deaths were probably unattended but presumed one thing or another, and accidents on ranches or farms were a part of life as a hazardous occupation and not investigated in the detail we do today. Still, there are some good points to be made and lessons learned for the modern investigator by looking at the more historic undetermined cases.

[Note: Case Reviews #1 through #4 are excerpts from *"Murder, Mayhem, and Mystery: Coroner Inquests in Fremont County, Wyoming 1885-1900,* © Mark R. Stratmoen, Pub. Lenore Wyoming Publications, ISBN-10: 146362932X]

Case 1. #188702 (1887): The case of James Harwood, date of death 03/13/1887 with the location of the incident at Riley's Saloon in Lander, Wyoming Territory around 6:45 PM. The acting coroner in this case is Frank E. Coffey, Justice of the Peace.

Transcript of Case: (Summary)
The hand is an extreme flowing script on the document, and very hard to read. There is some indication in the testimony that the deceased frequented an establishment called the "China House" for women and recreation. Local Dr. Ullman examined the body and could not find a specific cause of death or trauma according to his testimony. Some suspicion was expressed by witnesses of opium use along with excessive drinking by the deceased. Evidently he was found collapsed in the bar "on his face". The jury verdict listed "cause unknown".

Commentary: The elected coroner, Dr. James Irwin, is not present or available for reasons unknown. By statute at this time, the justice of the peace is authorized to act as the coroner in his absence. There are accomplished professionals and civic leaders present, some of whose handwriting I have seen in other resources to be excellent. However, whoever was selected to transcribe this case had very poor script, or possibly was in a great hurry to write, either from inexperience to the situation, or by natural tendency. Transcribing oral testimony can be a difficult talent.

It also should be noted that not every death gets an inquest, then or now, and county commission records in the print media for the 1880's and 90's indicate that the coroner did have other cases, as he was paid for issuing a certification. For a majority of this time period, it appears that the coroner was paid for services when they occurred, and not a salary like other elected officials. Payment was usually expenses and wages for a formal inquest, fees for services on a more 'run of the mill' case. Even today in Wyoming's less populated counties, the coroner receives only minimal wage, has no staff, and little equipment, as the case load is sparse for the year and requires only incidental services on rare occasions. Less than half of the 23 counties today have a population base large enough to warrant a full, or close to full time coroner with some staff.

In any case, from the information as available, the identity of the poor fellow is known. Dr. Ullman could find no obvious natural process or trauma, although an accidental overdose could be possible in the absence of modern toxicology testing. Unfortunately even today in Fremont County, the number of deaths from a mixture of alcohol and natural or synthetic opiate type drugs is far higher than the national averages. These figures are regularly a part of the public record provided by the coroner's office, and compare local to national statistics provided by the U.S. Center for Disease Control. Even in a modern case it may be difficult to determine if the overdose is from accidental combination of amounts, suicidal and intentional combination, or homicidal provision of the substances by another party. Detailed toxicology and analysis of the circumstances and witness testimony would be critical in defining the difference. The jury verdict does not mention a specific manner of death, only that the cause is unknown. In such circumstances, or the inability to differentiate the possibilities, even if you knew it was an overdose, the manner would be listed on a death certificate today as "unable to determine". Even today, with all the modern forensic tools available, and the best forensic pathology examination, we may have one or two of these types of "undetermined" cases a year. Sometimes a mystery remains a mystery.

If nothing else, this case shows that human behavior towards recreational indulging remains the same in some ways over the course of time, in spite of over 120 years of technological and social change.

Case 2. #188904 (1889): The case of an unknown male, found on 04/21/1889 on Alkali Creek about 12 miles east of Lost Cabin Post Office. Inquest by Coroner William A. Feiser.

Transcript of Case:

Verdict: We the undersigned Jurors impaneled and sworn to inquire how and in what manner, and by whom or what cause the dead body of a man found on Alkali Creek about twelve miles East of Lost Cabin post office in Fremont County Wyoming Territory came to his death, do return the following verdict. We found the body in a state of decomposition and so badly defaced as to render a positive statement as to what manner the deceased came to his death. The body had on a shirt and vest, and pants, overalls, overcoat and hat, found also a saddle blanket, boots and stockings. Nothing was found in the pockets by us. We found the body to be that of a small man with sandy hair and supposed to have been about 35 to 40 years of age. We found no means by which we could determine in what manner the deceased came to his death.
[signed] W. B. Trosper, Samuel Long, Chas. Cobb, J. A. Couch, J. D. Russell, James Irwin M.D. Forman; Alkali Creek Fremont County Wyoming Territory; April 21st 1889

Commentary: This case has no witness testimony, and probably none were known other than the person who found the body, and they are not mentioned. All the information, both in the file, and about the case, is contained in the verdict, and an extensive list of expenses for all involved. The distance of twelve miles east of the town of Lost Cabin along Alkali Creek would actually mean that the event might have occurred just over the boundary in Natrona County. Technically, out of the Fremont County Coroner's jurisdiction, although even if they were aware of that detail, it was closer for Fremont to deal with it than someone out of the town of Casper. These days the investigators would contact the agencies of jurisdiction and either secure the scene until they arrive, or work it on their behalf if desired. Terrain and geography sometimes make that necessary, and in this case, slow communications would have delayed the mission from Natrona. My assumption is that without the accurate mapping and GPS we have, they may have been aware it was close to the county line and thought it was Fremont, or did not consider the detail significant. There may also have been concerns in relation to other events of the time that are not hinted at that warranted a quick response. This case occurs a little over two months prior to the 'Cattle Kate' lynching.

Cause and manner are undetermined. Taking Dr. Irwin on the expedition shows good judgment, as he would have noted major trauma or gunshot wounds even on a decomposing body. The body being "defaced" either refers to the degree of decomposition, or scavenger activity. Defaced by blunt force trauma or weapons such as a knife, again, would most likely have been noted by the physician. Generally, homicide, except by asphyxia, should have been obvious. Natural death, such as from a cardiac or other health issue, is possible. Suicide from a toxic substance, is possible – not a gunshot in this case as that would have been obvious. Accidental death from dehydration or other environmental factor, is possible. The interesting point in the verdict is that nothing was found in the pockets, nor any weapons on the deceased. That may indicate that someone robbed the person and then abandoned them to wander, perhaps lost. More than three or four days without water and you would be in trouble in this country. Weather that time of year probably eradicated tracks or signs from the original incident, or the route the deceased took to get where he lay.

By modern standards, if a person was robbed and abandoned to die later, that could be considered a homicide, just as sure as if the perpetrator pulled a trigger. We will never know in this case – it may just have been a traveler who kept everything on his horse and lost it, only to die trying to reach civilization. In consideration of the times, I would lay odds it was a person who was intentionally "dry gulched" (ambushed) due to the lack of found property, but we have no clear evidence. It also would be realistic for someone to come along after the fact and "collect" what would be useful from a person who so obviously does not need his goods anymore.

Today in a similar situation, coroner staff would also mount an expedition with vehicles, scene equipment and other investigative tools. The body would be recovered for forensic autopsy and examined in detail. The degree of decomposition, unlike most TV shows, would not give too accurate a detailed range of how long a body had been out, due to a multiplicity of environmental factors. A body can be out two weeks or two months in some situations, and almost appear the same, depending on circumstances and micro-environment. Also today DNA, dental exam, and even fingerprints (if the hands are mummified and not damaged) could possibly be obtained. All in all, the verdict shows a pretty good investigation for what they had to work with at the time, even if brief.

The expense list shows that an expedition suitable for that era was mounted in this case, and the duration was five days, which probably included travel time by wagon. Everyone gets the expense of 190 miles travel, probably 95 miles from Lander, there and back. Coroner Feiser gets 15 cents per mile, everyone else, 10 cents per mile. He also gets 5 days at

$6.00 per day, everyone else, 5 days at $2.00 per day. Constable James Couch gets $2.00 in addition for summoning the jury. William Trosper and Dr. Irwin get an extra $5.00 per day each for providing transportation for the jurors, I would guess at least a wagon from each one for the seven people and their gear. James Russell gets a total of $9.20 extra for "furnishing victuals for jurors". The total cost for the investigation and recovery was $293.70, which would have been billed to the county. The cost in 2008 dollars would be around $6,857.90, which actually would be reasonable today for the wages, travel, fuel, food, and other investigation expenses for a five day recovery.

It is unknown if the body was buried at the site, or brought back for internment in a town. In these inquests, usually the latter is the case, although a couple of cases specifically mention burial at or near a scene. I think, however, for such an expedition I would ride my own horse, rather than the wagon, just in case they brought the body back. The high altitude fresh spaces of the rangelands of Wyoming can only go so far in compensating when an investigation of this type tries to 'clear the air' on a case.

Case 3. #189405 (1894): Another case of an unknown male found on 04/17/1894, listed as being seven miles southwest of Rongis, Wyoming, a small town near the old Oregon Trail and stage routes that no longer exists today.

Transcript of Case:
Rongis Wyo. Ap.17th, 1894, Witness Mr. M. Rigby: Evidence given in case of the body found dead 7 miles S.W. of Rongis. Found the body unknown 14 April in a gulch seven miles southwest of Rongis body with overalls underclothes with coat also shotgun and revolver also a purse containing money at once notified the coroner [signed] Mason Rigby <break>
Rongis, Fremont Co. Wyo. April 17th, 1894
We the jury, empaneled by W.A. Fieser, coroner of Fremont County, make the following report on the dead body found about seven (7) miles south west of Rongis, Fremont County, Wyo.: The cause of death unknown to the jury.
We found the following effects on and around the remains, viz:
one (1) Coat – single breasted sack – dark checkered.
one (1) Pocket comb in case
one (1) Shot gun – breech loading – No.6240 – manufactured by Bacon Arms Co. Norwich, Conn.
one (1) pr. Cotton flannel drawers.
one (1) pr. Brown overalls – size about 38x29.
one (1) Skull & other bones of the body. Complete set of under teeth, and four (4) teeth extracted from upper jaw.
one (1) Pistol – 5 shooter – 32 Cal. – Smith & Wesson
one (1) Pocket knife – 2 blades – curved handle – makers – Clark Bros., Sheffield
one (1) ten dollar greenback.
one (1) five dollar greenback
one (1) two dollar greenback
one (1) ten dollar gold piece – 1886
five (5) half dollars.
three (3) 25 c. pieces
three (3) 10 c. pieces
three (3) 5 c. pieces – two dated 1887
one (1) brass check – engraved "cabinet 40 Phil"
[signed] Eli A. Signor; John Zillig; Wm. Marshall, foreman

[Detailed expense sheet included: Signor received $5.00 for burying the body; all three jurors received $0.15 per mile travel for 14 miles; pay for one day each juror and witness at $2.00 per day; C.M. Morrison $5.00 for "tram conveying jury"; Coroner Feiser billed four days duty at $5.00 per day and 134 miles travel at usual rate.] [Written note by Coroner Feiser certifying the Inquest]

Commentary: Only one witness testimony, the person who discovered the remains. No papers or other documents in the file other than as noted. None of the goals of an inquest are attained in this case, which sometimes happens. 'Undetermined 'would be the present day manner for a case like this, where the cause is unknown, or the evidence does not lead to a definitive selection between the other manners of death available. Sometimes the answers are not defined, even with a forensic autopsy and all the other tools available to the modern investigator.

Identity is here also left as an unknown. These days that is usually a rarer case than ones where cause and manner cannot be determined, again, since our resources are better. Take the descriptions of the property as presented. Clothing is detailed and described. Weapons information is given, including the serial number on the shotgun. The body is skeletonized, and some basic information given on the dental work. In that regard, someone was knowledgeable and observant, as the signs of extraction during life are different than teeth that just fall out through weathering of the skull. Money is noted, including some of the dates of issue. And finally one "brass check" that was engraved is described.

If this evidence was presented today, the following could be done with the resources we have. Although none of this would guarantee identification, the odds are increased. The bones of the skeleton would be transported to a forensic anthropologist, who could determine sex, size, approximate weight and age, race, possible traces of disease process, and examine in detail for any signs of trauma or weapons. The clothing would be examined for possible source, additional signs of trauma or injury, and listed as part of a missing persons 'john doe' description. The weapons through serial numbers could be traced to a manufacturer and perhaps a point of purchase, trade or sale, and be part of the 'john doe' description with the other miscellaneous items. The money, especially with more detail on dates and serial numbers, would at the minimum give you a date that you know the person did not die before, as with "1887" above. It would be highly unlikely that a passerby would place good money on a corpse, so that says this person has been dead less than seven years for sure. Considering terrain, climate, recent weather, condition of the remains, lack of being scattered by scavenger animals, my impression would be less than a year, but microenvironments can do some odd things in this part of the country.

Today dental work could be examined, X-Rayed, and charted. DNA samples obtained from the bones and filed for comparison. Everything would be photographed in detail, and the whole works... filed away [for later comparisons]... Databases and technology are always advancing, and a lack of success now may become tomorrow's solved case.

Then we have the "brass check". A brass check is in the times a term used for a receipt token, usually purchased for a specific amount of cash, and then used for services. An example would be in a facility where the manager or owner wants to centralize the money dealings while services are rendered. Like something similar to a gambling house, bordello, or some public facility, or storage. Modern casinos do the same thing when you are purchasing their proprietary chips to gamble with. Another use was to issue them as a means of barter receipts to be redeemed for goods later. This was a use on the Shoshone Reservation for a time. Such an engraved item could maybe be traced to a facility, and with the general description obtained by analyzing the other evidence, a direction towards an identity could be obtained. Even in those sparsely populated times, someone along the nearby trails and stage stops may remember such an individual. Perhaps that was even tried with what they did know at the time, but we can only guess.

The absence of information is often also as helpful as what information you have. If we can assume these were observant and intelligent investigators, they would have noted any obvious signs of gunshot in the clothing, or blood stains, or blunt force trauma to the bones. While that does not eliminate asphyxia, it does rule out most of the more common methods of assault. A knife slipped between the ribs could possibly only be noted by marks on the skeletal remains by a forensic anthropologist, but blood patterns on the clothing should have indicated something of that nature that would have been seen here if present. The presence of so much cash probably rules out robbery. Each item considered and analyzed can narrow the range of possibilities for identity, and the fatal event.

Since the remains were found in April, it could be someone who got lost in bad weather and perished over the winter period. However, it does take some time for insects, rodents, birds and environmental factors to deplete the flesh, and the process slows the colder it gets. We do not know to what degree that process was completed, how 'clean' the skeleton was, but it would not happen much in the dead of winter, nor be completed to any degree in early spring, so I would guess with the other factors as outlined above, the body was there for at least six months, less than a year. All in all, they did document quite a wealth of evidence, they just did not have all the tools to process it. Just an opinion. Still unknown.

Case 4. #190001 (1900): The case of Orin Parker, found on 06/02/1900, near Leckie, Wyoming, another stage stop no longer in existence. Inquest conducted by Coroner: J.W.H. Schoo.

Transcript of Case:
State of Wyoming, County of Fremont } SS:
Mr. J. Johnson being duly sworn testifies as follows:
Q: Do you know this man Parker.
A: Yes sir.
Q: Where did you last see him?
A: The last time I see about the 14th to the 17th of May. He left our place to go to Meeks and that's the last time I see him. Dead about the 2nd of June. The last time I see him alive was at my place about the 17th of June. All the money I ever see him have was when we buried him and his pocket was cut open. It contained $5.05 or five dollars, five cents. He was lying with his face down and when he shot himself, he fell forward on his face and we turned his body over to the right and the revolver fell out of his right hand. I was the first one that picked the revolver up after it fell from his hands. It was the 16th or 17th to the 2nd of June that I did not see him.

Q: Was it agreeable for all parties there to spend the money that he had for drink.
A: Yes sir.
Q: Is this revolver and scabbard the one he had.
A: Yes sir. [signed] John Johnson

Mr. Stevens being duly sworn testifies as follows:
Q: Mr. Stevens do you know anything about this man.
A: Came from Washington to Joel Walters place on Big Sandy
Q: State where you next saw him.
A: He was laying on his stomach with the right side of his head lying on the ground, both hands under him and the gun in his right hand. The belt and scabbard as near as I can tell was lying about four feet from his feet.
Q: Who was there when you found him?
A: John Johnson, Jim Jenson, Joesh Hansen, Henry Williams, one of the Dollard boys.
Q: Did you proceed to investigate.
A: Yes sir. We all examined the body.
Q: How long do you think he had been there?
A: About seventeen days (17 days).
Q: About when did you see him alive?
A: About the 10th day of May.

Q: Did you see any money about him.

A: He showed me just an evan sixty dollars at Washington's.

Q: You may state to the jury Mr. Stevens, what kind of money it was.

A: It was green backs.

Q: Mr. Stevens you may state the denominations of the money if you saw any of them.

A: One ten and two fives & two twenties, & that is exactly the amount that he showed me.

Q: Do you know any place he had been since you last seen him.

A: He came right to Mr. Leckie's and paid his bill.

Q: How much money did he have when you buried him?

A: Five dollars in Silver.

Q: Mr. Stevens, who got that money.

A: Jim Jeanson.

Q: Was it agreeable for the company to spend that money for beer and whiskey.

A: Yes sir.

Q: Did you find any empty cartridges lying about him.

A: No sir, only the empty one in the gun. [signed] Peter Stevens

Mr. J. Hansen being duly sworn testifies as follows:

Q: Do you know this man Parker.

A: I have seen him.

Q: Was you at the burying of this man.

A: Yes.

Q: [missing]

A: He laid on his stomach with his hands under him with a pistol in his right hand.

Q: When did you see this man Parker alive?

A: It was sometime in May but I don't remember the date.

Q: Did he have any money that you know of.

A: Yes sir, it was green backs.

Q: Did you ever hear him make any threats of violence against anybody.

A: No sir.

Q: Did you ever know of him having a qurral with Mr. S. Leckie or Mr. J. Johnson.

A: No sir.

Q: Did you see any blood on his slicker.

A: No sir.

Q: Do you think he had been turned over by anybody.

A: No sir.

Q: Do you reconize that revolver, scabbard, and belt.
A: It looks like it.
Q: How much money did he have on him when you found him?
A: He had $5.00.
Q: How long do you think he had been dead?
A: About 15 or 16 days.
Q: How long was it from the first time you saw him till the last time.
A: I do not know.
Q: Do you know anything more about this case.
[A:] No sir. [signed] Joseph J. Hansen

Mr. J. Jensen being duly sworn testifies as follows:
Q: Do you know about the death of Mr. Parker.
A: I was over in the Pasture after some horses with one of the Dollards and he came up and told me there was a man lying dead over there in Long Draw, and I asked him to go along over with me to the place and see if I know the man. And I seen that it was Parker and I said I would go over and see the Justice of the Peace, and I went over to New Fork that day, but he told me he had nothing to do with it, and I came back the next morning, and I came over and got Peter Stevens, J. Johnson, and Joe Hansen; and as we went down we meet the horse round-up and took Henry Williams and one Dollard, and one or two more, I do not know. And after, they turned over the body.
Q: How was the body lying?
A: He was laying streched out, laying a little on the right side of his face. His hands was under him.
Q: Did he look like he had been turned over.
A: No sir.
Q: Mr. Jensen do you recognize that revolver and scabbard and belt.
A: Yes sir.
Q: Did you see any blood on his slicker.
A: No sir.
Q: How long do you think he had lain there?
A: About 14 or 15 days.
Q: When did you see him the last time?
A: Down to J. Johnson's about the 12th of May.
Q: Were you there when they got the money.
A: Yes sir, I was there. We spent the money for beer.
Q: How much money did he have?
A: $5.00
Q: Did it seem agreeable to all the men there to spend the money.

A: Yes sir.

Q: Did you know of him having a qurral with Mr. Leckie or J. Johnson.

A: No sir.

Q: Do you think you know any more about this case Mr. Jensen.

A: No sir.

Q: Which hand did he have the revolver in?

A: Right hand.

Q: On the day he left you did he make any threats of violence about anybody.

A: No sir.

Q: Mr. Jensen, was he powder burnt.

A: I could not say for sure because he was black.

Q: Was the hole tore where the bullet went in.

A: No sir.

Q: You are sure that is Parker.

A: Yes sir. [signed] Jim Jensen

Mr. S. Leckie being duly sworn testifies and says:

Q: Do you know this man Parker.

A: I knew him since last fall.

Q: Did you see him this Spring.

A: Yes sir, he staid with me for 42 days.

Q: When did you see him the last time?

A: The 18th of May or the 19th.

Q: When you saw him the last time did he have any money.

A: Yes, he gave me $17.73.

Q: Did you see him with any more money.

A: He had some money, but I did not know how much. He spent about $4.00.

Q: What time did he leave your place?

A: About dusk.

Q: Did he mention a place where he was going.

A: To J. Johnsons and Pete Stevens.

Q: Mr. Leckie, did you hear of him any more after he left.

A: Yes sir, the next day down to J. Johnsons.

Q: Did you have any trouble with him.

A: I never had any trouble with him but once, over a little bill, and after I explained it to him, it was all right.

Q: Have you ever saw the deceased since the day I was here (J.S. Pope).

A: No sir. [signed] Sam Leckie

Dr. W.H. Maghee being duly sworn as expert witness testifies as follows:

[A:] I held the post-mortem and found the direction of the bullet; entered under the left ear, and the direction upward and to the right side, passing out through the skull about two inches above and a little behind the right ear. There is no other visible signs of injury. There was no signs of powder burn because the body was so badly decayed. It was impossible to distinguish one part of the body from the other. The left side of the neck there was a greater destruction than on the right side of the neck.

Q: Would that cause instant death, the way the bullet went.

A: Yes.

Q: Do you think that if that man was sitting or standing, could anybody deliver that shot on the ground that he was on.

A: No, it is impossible. [signed] W.H. Maghee, M.D.

State of Wyoming, County of Fremont}SS:

We the jurors in holding an inquisition at Leckie in Fremont County on the 30th day of June 1900 before J.H.W. Schoo, Coroner of said county, upon the dead body of one Parker lying here dead by the jurors whose names are hereto subscribed, the said jurors upon their oaths do say, that said Parker came to his death by a gun shot wound delivered by his own hand accidentally or otherwise unknown, in testimony whereof we the undersigned, set our hand and seal the day and year aforesaid. [signed] Jos. M. Boulter; J.S. Pope; A. Bybee

<break>

State of Wyoming, County of Fremont}SS:

To the Honorable Court, of the Second Judicial District of Said County and State.

Report of John W.H. Schoo, Coroner, of the County of Fremont, State of Wyoming, reports the inquisition held over the dead body of Orin Parker at Leckie, Wyoming, on the 30th day of June, A.D. 1900.

Whereas, it was represented to me, John W.H. Schoo, coroner of said County, on the 18th day of June A.D. 1900, that a male person was found dead at the Big Draw, on the Big Sandy, in said County, supposed to have come to his death by violence, casualty or undue means; whereupon, I soon thereafter summoned a jury of three good and lawful men, of the neighborhood, to-wit: Jos. M. Boulter, J.S. Pope, and A. Bybee, of Leckie, Wyoming, to inquire how and in what manner, and by whom, or what he came to his death. And as soon as the said jurors assembled at the said place where the said dead body was lying, I appointed Jos. M. Boulter, one of them, as foreman, and in presence of all the rest, administered to them the following oath: "You do solemnly swear that you will diligently inquire into, presentment make, when, how, and by what means, the person whose body lies here dead came to his death, according to your knowledge and the evidence given you, So help you God."

Whereupon the said jurors after the examination of the said dead body, and hearing the testimony of Peter Stevens, John Johnson, Joseph J. Hensen, Jim Jensen, Sam Leckie, and W.H. MaGhee, who were summoned as witnesses, returned the following verdict, to-wit: "Leckie, June 30th, 1900. We the jurors in holding an inquisition at Leckie in Fremont County on the 30th day of June 1900 before J.H.W. Schoo, Coroner of said county, upon the dead body of one Parker, lying here dead, by the jurors whose names are hereto subscribed, the said jurors upon their oaths do say, that said Parker came to his death, by a gun shot wound, delivered by his own hand, accidentally, or otherwise unknown, in testimony whereof we the undersigned, set our hand and seal the day and year aforesaid. Jos. M. Boulter; J.S. Pope; A. Bybee."

I, John W.H. Schoo, Coroner, in and for the County and State aforesaid, do hereby certify that the foregoing is a true statement of the proceedings had before me, of and concerning the death of said Orin Parker.

Given under my hand and seal this 30th day of June, A.D. 1900. [signed] J.W.H. Schoo (Seal)

Commentary: Instead of an inquest held at or near the day of death, here we have one that occurs a good period after the fact. From the testimony it appears that the body was originally found around the second of June and had at that time been dead for about two weeks. It was reported to the Justice of the Peace in the town of New Fork, who for whatever reason refused jurisdiction in the case. A group then returned to the scene, examined the body, removed what cash was there and then buried it. The general agreement was then to spend the money on beer. How exactly this news got to Coroner Schoo on the 18th is not stated. Either one of the participants, or someone they talked to while enjoying themselves, eventually got word to Lander on the other side of South Pass on the source of the beer money. Travel from Leckie in what is now Sublette County over the Wind River Mountains at the pass to Lander would certainly have taken some time and effort. Coroner Schoo then has to make arrangements to go back over the mountains, gather the witnesses, and commence an inquest. By this time it is probably about five or six weeks after the death, four weeks after the body was originally found the first time. Since Dr. Maghee did an examination, the body would have been exhumed from the location of burial and transported to Leckie. Everything does come together on the 30th of June.

While there is no time limit on when an investigation can be called, it obviously can be more difficult the more time that passes. Also in this case, the coroner and jury do not have the option of seeing the scene as originally presented at the time of discovery. In the 'Q&A' format of recording, we can better see how Coroner Schoo seeks to gather the evidence, confirm the stories and seek confirmation among the witnesses. Powder burns would have indicated a close contact gunshot wound, but the weathering and decomposition at the time found (black) would have hidden ready sign. By the time the good doctor has a look, the decay has progressed further towards obscurity. Blood on the slicker could have indicated position when shot. The fast pumping of the heart in a head wound of that magnitude would leave a spatter pattern in a downward direction on a person standing, even if he fell fairly quickly. Such a pattern usually survives for considerable time on clothing, even when exposed or buried. The variations possible to avoid getting blood on the slicker are numerous, and we do not know to what detail it was examined. Coroner Schoo's last question about "the ground that he was on" is unclear as to the point he is trying to make. He could be talking about the terrain he was on, the relative position of the body, or how the wound was inflicted. Another variable would be if the deceased was mounted on a horse at the time of the injury, as that introduces a whole separate quantity of possibilities.

The gun is noted as being in the right hand by all, with one spent cartridge in the chambers. No other cartridges were seen in the area, but we do not know the extent of the area searched or the quality of the effort. One shot spent could have been from a single self-inflicted firing, or all that there was time for against an assailant with a rifle at a distance. The questions about Mr. Leckie and Johnson may not imply any particular suspicions, but just be to check out the most recent known associations. The inquiry as to the hole being "tore" when first seen could help with range, but unfortunately the witness and questioner did not mention what side of the head they were referring to, which would have helped when we look at Dr. Maghee's testimony. As a whole, initial indications may show a suicide, but the doctor's words throw a wrench in that conclusion. Maghee indicates the direction of travel of the gunshot as being from left to right. If he misspoke, I am surprised there were not more questions to clarify this, but they might not have been recorded and occurred during deliberations. While it is possible, and has been seen in modern cases, to hold the gun in the right hand and shoot yourself in the left side of the head is awkward and unusual. There is just no evidence to eliminate another person as the source of the shot. Without more information on the size and caliber of the weapon, we cannot be sure that the "greater destruction" of the left side, which would be more consistent with a close contact exit wound, indicates a right to left pathway for the projectile. A key examination these days would be to examine the beveling on the holes in the skull which would give a directional path with certainty. To be fair, with the age of the corpse, examination on a decomposed body was probably difficult at the time, and greater destruction of tissue by insect scavengers begins and advances more at the point of the most tissue injury, or natural entrances into the body. Position and trajectory remain foggy.

The fact that the cowboys who originally found the body reported it to the Justice of the Peace (which could be verified), relieves them to an extent of responsibility when the official refuses to do anything about it. They at least return to bury the body decently, and figured they might as well quench their thirst for their trouble. This may seem outlandish or improper to modern sensibilities, but times were tough, and cannot compare to our views. There is a particular justice and practicality for the time to not allow something useful to go to waste. The moldering Mr. Parker was at least good for a beer, and one hopes they at least toasted a round to him on his passing.

The verdict of the jury recognizes the deficiencies in coming to a definitive conclusion by stating that Parker "came to his death by a gunshot wound delivered by his own hand accidentally or otherwise unknown", allowing for the possibility of a homicide or suicide as well. In those cases, the official notation on the death certificate would read "undetermined". Cause is known, and the manner stated as it should be for the evidence available. This may be another death related to the conflicts in the area at the time, but we have no evidence to know one way or another.

Case 5. #2005 (1902): Titled "Inquest – No Body Found" on the written papers for this case, filed with the Clerk of District Court on October 6th, 1902. The enclosing envelope states "Inquest Upon Some One or Something – No body found. Soda Lake Matter. 9-29-1902". The Soda Lakes are located in rural Fremont County, east of Jeffrey City, and north of WY Hwy 789 and the Sweetwater River. This is also along the Oregon/Emigrant Trail areas. On the included subpoena copies, J.W.H. Schoo is identified as the coroner: George Hittle, Frank Kerwin, Peter Gwen, & S.D. Meyers are summoned to appear as jurors at E.P. Steele's on the 29th of September at 9 AM. Constable is noted as P.J. Burch. Additional summons as witnesses are to John Seaton and John Steele.

Mr. Seaton, after being duly sworn is asked: "What time did you find this body?" He answers, "About noon we were hunting and came down to the lake, saw an object laying in the water, looked like a hunting coat. We examined it to tell what it was and found that it was a human being. We left it laying at the edge of the water." Testimony signed by John Seaton. Mr. Steele after being duly sworn testified as follows: "We was out hunting and came down to the lake about noon of the 16th [September] and then went up along and we seen something that looked like a hunting coat. We examined it and found it was a human body then we went on home." Question: "Who did you inform?" Answer: "John Vible, the Justice of the Peace." Testimony signed by John Steele.

Verdict of the Jury:
State of Wyoming, County of Fremont }SS
Soda Lake Sept. 29 - 1902
We the Jury being summoned and duly sworn heard the testimony of John Steele and John Seaton state as follows: We the Jury have made a thourgh [sic] search for the body and failed to find it.
        (signed) Foreman, Geo. A Hittle. S.B. Meyers. Frank H. Kerwin

State of Wyoming, County of Fremont]SS –
I, J.W.H. Schoo, coroner of the County of Fremont in the State of Wyoming, being informed on the 24th day of Sept. 1902 that a dead body was found at Soda Lake in said County, I there upon proceeded to said place, summoned and empannelled [sic] a jury to inquire into and by what means and manner said person came to his death, and also subpoenaed witnesses to testify before said jury, and after being duly sworn as required by law, return the above verdict which is as follows: (written repeat of the above verdict followed by a statement of certification, signed and dated the 6th day of October, 1902).

Commentary: This is from a handwritten document of the Inquest with no notation as to the recorder or transcriber. This in a sense is an early case of documenting whatever comes to official attention for the record, regardless of there being an actual body, or specific jurisdiction, much as we would do today for a continuing cold case missing person, or assist to another county. Here a partial reason is also that with an official record, bills for expenses and wages and travel for the coroner can be submitted to the county commissioners for payment to cover the effort. Just as today where no body was found, if the witnesses seem credible, the file would be set as undetermined. As to the circumstances, from the limited information it appears the body was seen in the water. These particular small features and lakes are of variable depth depending on time of year, and it is unknown what condition they were in at the early times we are talking about. The location is also along the well-traveled trails and wagon routes in southern Fremont, so the body could have belonged to a resident, traveler, or other unknown subject. If a body was indeed floating and then sank before officials could get to the location, it was probably of recent origin in a short time frame prior to the witnesses seeing it. A body that had been under water and rising later as it decomposes, would have stayed on the surface for a while at that point. In drowning, or when otherwise placed in the water soon after death, once a body sinks, at that altitude and probable water temperature it would stay down for a week, or even weeks before resurfacing, if at all, depending on circumstances. Resources for searching underwater were limited at the time, mostly a rowboat and grappling hook to drag below the surface, and no mention is made of whether or not those efforts were employed.

Did anyone report a local missing person? Did anyone periodically recheck the area to see what popped up? Times are still pretty rough in this period and it is impossible to say what circumstances would have led to such an incident.

Case 6. #7004 (1907): The only paper on the case is a typewritten verdict which is as follows –

State of Wyoming, County of Fremont, S.S.

At an inquisition holden [sic] on the Homestead belonging to one Butterfield, on the former Shoshone Indian Reservation, County of Fremont, on the 31st day of December, A.D. 1907, before me J.H. Schoo, Coroner of said County, upon the body of an unknown person lyeng [sic] dead, by the jurors whose names are here unto subscribed, the said jurors upon their oath do say, that the body is that of an unknown Indian, and that the time of death and the cause of death cannot be arrived at by this jury.

In testimony where of the said jurors have here unto set their hands the day and year aforesaid.

(Signed) Chas. F. Smith, R.A. Horton, A.J. Olson
Attest: (Signed) J.W.H. Schoo, Coroner
Filed Jan. 3rd 1908, Ralph Kimball, Clerk

Commentary: Standardization of death certificate information as far as manner of death was established in 1910 as the *U.S. Standard Certificate of Death*, and is for the most part an American invention to promote consistency in reporting and records. It is not considered a legally binding opinion. In modern times the basic format is recommended by the Center for Disease Control, National Vital Statistics, and occasionally tweaked for improvement. It is up to the States to adopt a particular format, and most follow the CDC's recommendations. Manner of death includes natural, accident, suicide, homicide, and 'could not be determined'. A few jurisdictions also allow a manner of "complications of therapy", but this is not common.

For most Inquests, the verdicts for record keeping, such as in this example, are noted as 'undetermined', even though the term itself was not sometimes common to the legal language of the times, especially prior to the national standard produced in 1910.

Case 7. #9003 (1909): Inquest on the death of James Murty was held on August 26th, 1909, by J. W. Calloway, Justice of the Peace, in Thermopolis, WY. Subpoenas included in the file list a R.W. Hale for "medical testimony", Jery Ryon [sic], Carl Emsley, A.P. Goonrin, and Frank Tracy as witnesses; H.S. Cover, A.W. Bebb, and R.G. Haskin as jurors. A photocopy of a newspaper article is in the file, which states:

"MAN FOUND DEAD – James Murty, a stone cutter who formerly worked here and who returned recently after an absence of some time, was found dead Thursday morning behind the stables at the race track on the outskirts of town. He had been seen there the previous day, but was alive at that time. A stranger found him and informed Robert Brydon, who immediately informed the authorities. The body was brought to Holdrege's undertaking rooms. Coroner Schoo could not be reached by phone, so Justice J.W. Calloway empaneled a jury composed of A.W. Bebb, H.S. Cover, and R.G. Haskin and held an inquest. After examining a number of witnesses, the jury returned the following verdict:

Thermopolis, Wyoming, August 26, 1909. We, the jury duly empaneled, sitting in inquest over the dead body of Jas. Murty, do find that there is no evidence of foul play or marks of violence on the body of the deceased, and that the cause of death is to the jury unknown. Signed, (jurors listed).

Deceased had no relatives in this part of the country and little is known of him. A few cents in money and some small articles were found in the pockets. The body was buried yesterday at the expense of the county."

Commentary: Of note, the subpoenas are written that they were served by Horace Tyrrell, special constable by "reading to him" or "them". A signed typewritten copy of the above verdict is included, on stationary with the header of "Fred E. Holdrege & Co. – Furniture, Pianos, and Undertaking Supplies – Second Hand House Furnishings". Also included is a hand written proceedings certification note by Justice Calloway.

Hot Springs County, with a county seat of Thermopolis, was not formed until 1911, and at this time the area was still a part of Fremont. Statutory procedures at the time allowed the Justice of the Peace to perform as coroner in his absence. Both JPs and constable positions were eliminated in the later 20th century. The local business that was a furniture builder and seller often multi-tasked as an undertaker in communities, as they were most adept at building coffins as a side task, so this situation would not be unusual. While there is no transcript of the actual testimony, the subpoenas indicate at least a cursory medical exam, and what witnesses that could be found. By noting "no evidence of foul play or marks of violence" a lot (but not all) of possibilities of accident, suicide, or homicide appear to have been eliminated. Unknown natural causes, such as heart conditions or other disease processes, in this period could be indefinite to discovery, even with the best medical exam of the times. Therefore, this is best left as an 'undetermined' case.

Case 8. #10009 (1910) Coroner's Inquest on Alex Martinson. Typed transcript of the proceeding is as follows:

The State of Wyoming, Fremont County: SS, In Justice Court, before Chas. F. Smith, J.P. and acting Coroner, Shoshoni, Wyo., Sept. 19th, 1910. Coroner's Inquest on the body of Alex Martenson, at Boysen, Big Horn Canyon [Wind River Canyon today], Fremont County, Wyoming.

In the matter of the Coroner's inquiry upon the body of Alex Martinson, deceased,

Monday, September 19th, 1910, having this day received notice that the above named person came to his death in an unknown manner, the undersigned, Chas F. Smith, a Justice of the Peace in and for Fremont County, Wyoming, having been duly appointed to act in this behalf, by the County and Prosecuting Attorney, during the absence of the regular Coroner to become acting Coroner for Fremont County, did proceed to the Black Tunnel Camp, in Big Horn Canyon, a distance of 18 miles from Shoshoni, with S.O. Morrison a deputy sheriff in and for said Fremont County,

Upon arriving at Black Tunnel Camp, the following persons; J.J. Martin, C.E. Brenniman, and Carl Anderson were by me appointed to act and become the coroner's jury herein, the said members of this jury being duly qualified voters of this county,

Whereupon the said jury, being first duly sworn as required by law, did on this day view the body of the deceased, and then and there examined the following witnesses; John Jacobson and Alex Nord.

At the conclusion of the examination the jury rendered the following verdict;

Boysen, Wyo., Sept. 19th, 1910

We the undersigned Coroner's jury being duly empaneled by Chas F. Smith, Justice of the Peace and acting Coroner to investigate the cause of the death of Alex Martinson, do find, that said Alex Martinson came to his death – the actual cause being unknown to this jury. We the jury, by the evidence given before us at this inquest exonerate the accused Chas Swanson from being guilty of any evil or malicious intent of causing the death of said Alex Martinson.

J.J. Martin, C.E. Brenniman, Carl Anderson

The remains being turned over to his friends and fellow workmen and by them shipped to Denver Colorado for burial.

(Signed) Chas F. Smith, Justice of the Peace and acting Coroner

The State of Wyoming, County of Fremont: SS – I Chas F. Smith a Justice of the Peace in and for the County and State aforesaid, and Acting Coroner in the above entitled inquest do hereby certify that the above and foregoing is a true and correct transcript of my Docket in the above inquest as the same appears on page 135 of my said Justice Docket.

(Signed) Chas F. Smith, Justice of the Peace and Acting Coroner

The papers were noted as filed on September 22nd, 1910 with F.W. Thomas, County Clerk. I have taken the liberty of correcting mistyped and misspelled words throughout the above text, which are numerous and frequent. For example, 'coroner', whether typed or handwritten, is spelled 'coronor' in all cases, and in several instances the typist either struggled or was dyslexic with the keyboard. The following hand written testimony was attached to the certification document.

Testimony of John Jacobsen concerning the death of Alex Martinson on the night of Sept. 18th, 1910:

Q: What is your name?

A: John Jacobson.

Q: Where do you reside?

A: Camp Mile 30.

Q: Are you acquainted with Alex Martinson, the man that was killed last night?

A: Yes, have known him for over a year.

Q: Where were you last night about one o'clock?

A: At the saloon on the hill with Alex Martinson and Charlie Swanson.

Q: Was Martinson and Swanson drinking?

A: Yes, they were drinking a good deal and were talking and laughing a good deal, calling each other names, but not in any way as to indicate any hard or ill feeling towards each other.

Q: Did you go home with them and what time was it that you went home?

A: We went to Camp about 1:30 o'clock. I went in front and they came behind me, they were talking all the time. I looked around to see if they were coming when I saw Swanson throw a rock at Martinson, striking him on the head, Martinson fell down and never spoke a word, I tried to raise him up but he was limp, and I think he died when he fell.

Q: Was there any ill feeling between the two men, Martinson and Swanson, that you know of?

A: No, they were best of friends.

(Signed) John Jacobson

Testimony of Alex Nord concerning the death of Alex Martinson on the night of Sept. 18th, 1910:

Q: What is your name?

A: Alex Nord.

Q: Where do you reside?

A: Camp Mile 30.

Q: Are you acquainted with Alex Martinson, the man that was killed last night?

A: Yes, I know him over a year and worked with him.

Q: Are you acquainted with Charlie Swanson?

A: Yes, I know him over a year and worked with him all that time.

Q: Were you with these men last night?

A: No, I was in the camp.

Q: Do you know of any ill feeling existing between Martinson and Swanson?

A: No, they were the best of friends. I never heard them have any words or quarrel.

     (Signed) Alex Nord

Commentary: That is the extent of the papers and information found in the file for this case. Obviously there is considerable lack of specific information as to any other side conversations or discussion with the jury in regards to their conclusions. Evidently, while the direct testimony above indicates head trauma following shortly thereafter by death, there must have been some question as to the exact cause or circumstances. Yet they are sure enough to specifically note they "exonerate" Charles Swanson of ill intent. On the face of the limited information, one would think they might rule an accident as the result of drunken horse play, or by today's interpretation an unintentional homicide, yet the ruling specifically notes the actual cause as being unknown, and therefore, undetermined. As with a lot of older documentation, there just simply is not enough information to question or overrule the jury's conclusion.

The "Black Tunnel Camp" mentioned would have been a work camp set up to blast and create tunnels through the sheer portions of Wind River Canyon near Boysen Dam for the Burlington Railroad passage made during this period. A tough and dangerous job that involved well over a thousand workers, and hazardous enough that two camp hospitals were maintained for injuries during the work, There are other cases of accidental death in the coroner files for the period, mostly due to falls or explosions.

Here for this period of time we can consult the Wyoming State Archives on-line and search the Wyoming State Library's digital newspaper database for any further public information on this case. For the death of Mr. Martinson, two sources are found, both of which print the same article text on this incident: *Riverton Republican #15, September 30, 1910,* and *The Wyoming State Journal, Vol. XXIX, #7, September 23, 1910.* The text of the article is as follows: "Laborer Killed At Black Tunnel Camp –

While returning from a drunken spree at the blind pig saloon near the Burlington works in the Big Horn canyon, Alex Martinson was struck on the head with a rock thrown by his companion Charles Swanson. It seems that three men, Martinson, Swanson, and John Jacobsen, were nearing their cabin in the canyon at midnight, all being pretty loaded with liquor – Swanson and Martinson had been cutting up all evening, wrestling and calling each other all sorts of fancy names in jest. Martinson was in the lead when Swanson hurled a rock at him, hitting him on the head. Martinson fell and never rallied afterwards. The [town of] Shoshoni authorities were notified and an inquest over the body was held by Justice Smith in the absence of Coroner Schoo. The coroner's jury exonerated Swanson and turned the body of the dead man over to his friends, who shipped it to Denver, Colo., for burial. Swanson was turned loose." Other than the colorful period way of describing the incident, the article does not reveal any additional information. I am not so sure about having a drink at any facility called the "blind pig", however.

It is interesting to note also that in looking at the two front pages of these publications, that three other deaths are noted in articles. One is a body found on an island in the Wind River near Kinnear that was "evidently deposited by high water" with identification "impossible" due to the condition of the body, but the remains "are thought to be those of the companion of Loyd McGetrick who was drowned one year ago this spring in the Wind river near the Dry Creek ford." Second is the death of a four year old in Dubois after a sickness of "only a few hours duration", with nothing suspicious indicated in the article. Third, a shooting in the South Pass area was investigated by Coroner Schoo and Sheriff Stough, and occurred during a heated argument over a borrowed plow. Four bullet wounds, "any of which would have caused death", were inflicted during an incident where witnesses stated both men had pulled their revolvers. The suspect turned himself in and was bound over to the next term of District Court.

None of these cases are included in the ten cases we currently do have on file for 1910, and these days all three would have been coroner jurisdiction; an unanticipated child death, a shooting, and an unidentified body in the river. Even in 1910, while the sudden death of a child without suspicious circumstances might not have been unusual considering the fatality rates for kids during that period, the other two certainly were coroner jurisdiction under the statutes of the time. That just shows how incomplete the records are, either having been lost, not filed, or otherwise unnoted. That leads to the next point, explaining why we now jump from the year 1910 to the year 1945.

Regarding this gap in the records: there are 462 inquests listed in the State Archives for the period from 1901 to 1959, only a few of which are in the Fremont County Coroner files or database. The Archives inventory lists those only by name and year, so it is unknown how many of those were "undetermined" in manner. Based on average percentage of 1.6%, we could presume that about 8 of the 462 cases would be undetermined, however, keep in mind that only inquests are required to be filed with the Clerk of District Court. There is no way to know the actual number of cases that were worked by a coroner in any year as most were not logged or tracked in official files that have survived. An in depth study of all available county commission minutes, which were published in local papers, might reveal how many cases were billed to the commission by each coroner in a given year (they were at that time paid by the case), but even that arduous task would not give any information as to cause and manner of unlisted cases, unless noted in some additional article on an event.

We do have all available archives from 1885 through 1910 on file, as we were requesting each decade copies for a while to fill out our records, but in 2009 the Archives stopped filling those requests for free due to budget and staffing shortfalls. Anyone can make an appointment to go through and pay to copy such documents in person at the State Archive facility in Cheyenne, but our coroner's office does not have the budget or staff time to do that either. So, there is a 35 to 50 year gap of incomplete files in our records for the time being. In the 1960s through today, record keeping has improved enormously over time, and, as required by State Statute, all records belong to the State of Wyoming and are passed (or supposed to be) to succeeding administrations. Also, starting with the next case from 1945, most inquest documents are typed in detail by court reporters on legal size paper, which gives a more complete record to analyze. Case files from that time that did not include an inquest, however, still have varying degrees of information and completeness, increasing and working towards appropriate documentation standards and the excellent reporting and recording that is the policy today.

Consequently, we jump from what was still pretty much a 'wild frontier' way of resolving things to a post-World War II sensibility of progress, both in investigative methods, and procedural coverage in how manner and cause are approached.

Case 9. #45001 (1945) In the Matter of the Inquest over the Body of Charles H. Murray, deceased. This case represents the first undetermined case that actually has an inquest transcript somewhat in the modern format we would expect today. It consists of 48 pages of testimony, plus a certification sheet from the jury and one from the court reporter. The listed coroner for 1945 is E.E. Davis (served as coroner from 1929-1952), however the inquest was called and convened by Floyd G. Payne, a Deputy Coroner (served as coroner 1953-1954). Mr. Payne called the inquest to order in the office of L.A. Crofts, the County and Prosecuting Attorney, and Mr. Crofts, rather than a coroner or deputy, runs the proceedings. This would not necessarily by unusual for the time, or in other jurisdictions, but would not be the way I would conduct it today, in order to maintain independence of the investigation and its appearance.

In an opening statement to the jury, Mr. Crofts notes that the inquest is held at the request of the Federal Reservation authorities: "...government authorities, through the Superintendent, have requested that the State, in this case having the machinery for such purpose, conduct this hearing...". Jurisdiction of State and County authorities, even now, over sovereign tribal areas, is usually only by request or grant by tribal officials.

Testimony by a "Deputy Special Officer of the Indian Service" is first, detailing the report of the body found in a closed garage on June 28th and initial response by the officer, the Superintendent, and reporting party. He notes a strong decomposition odor and describes what is either blood or decomposition purge fluids near the body. Decomposition would have been only moderately started, as the deceased was recognizable to the witnesses. The fluid is described as dry. After verification of the death, the parties left and the officer secured the door with his handcuffs. The County Attorney and Sheriff were contacted to assist in the investigation. The clothing of the deceased is described, his work history, lack of law enforcement encounters, personality and lack of drinking habits. He is described as being in the front seat of a car that had the ignition switch in the 'on' position, with an empty gas tank. The garage and contents are noted, location, and the officer notes he took photos, but that they had not been developed yet. Family situation is described, and the deceased's home was inspected. Nothing unusual was found at the home, no note, medications or poisons, no evidence of struggle or fighting. The body was recovered by the coroner's office, and an autopsy arranged. The initial conclusion of the officer in testimony is a suicide, and he notes he was informed that the coloration of the deceased was consistent with carbon monoxide poisoning, and he noted the body was cold and in rigor. The officer is asked if the deceased had any insurance, which is unknown. The jurors have no questions for the witness.

The next witness is a nurse employed at the Ft. Washakie hospital, who is a neighbor of the deceased. She testifies to how long she has known the family, notes that the deceased had been discharged from the Navy eight or nine months; describes a lack of any conflict with the family. She verifies health issues of the wife of the deceased, and that the wife was admitted to the hospital on the 24th of June, and was still admitted there on the 29th of June. She reports the wife had not heard from her husband and wanted to go home. The deceased's wife asked the witness to go in the house to retrieve the car keys and come and get her, and when the witness did, she discovered the body in the garage. She immediately left, and saw the individual that eventually reported the death to the officer. He verified the death and then went to report it. The scene, position of the body, and circumstances are described in detail, and lack of recent disturbances in the neighborhood. Deputy Payne and the jurors ask several questions to elicit more detail.

The next witness is the individual that was notified by the nurse, verified the death, and reported it to the officer. He also is a game warden and reservation officer. His testimony confirms that of the first two witnesses, and it is also noted he lives nearby the same location. He reports no noted trouble that the deceased had with character, finances, job, marriage, or other individuals, and no noted despondency or drinking. His opinion is also that of a suicide. The jurors also ask the witness questions as to details of the case.

A local physician is the next person to testify. He reports on his notification and examination of the body at the mortuary (Fremont County had no morgue at the time). He notes the subject had been dead at least 24 hours, and the cause as asphyxia by carbon monoxide poisoning. He verifies the illness of the wife, and notes no particular injuries to the deceased. He notes the deceased was very concerned about his wife's health issues, and was at the hospital with her a good portion of the time during her hospitalization. The jurors ask questions of the physician about the level of concern, and he notes that the deceased was as concerned about the conditions leading to the illness, as he was about the illness itself. The inquest record then notes that a "lengthy discussion" was held off the record in that regard – an unusual occurrence considering all proceedings except jury deliberations should have been on the record. At that point the inquest is adjourned for two days pending the ability of the wife of the deceased to testify.

On resumption of the inquest, the wife testifies that they had been married for 12 years, She notes she was in the hospital in Lander, WY, that her husband was visiting her there a lot, and did not seem unusually disturbed or "dissatisfied", worried, or depressed with anything. In regards to his "habits" concerning the car, she notes he liked to sit in it while running and play the radio. She notes their children were staying in another town (Riverton) with his mother while she was hospitalized. She is asked about whether or not there were any known valuables in the vehicle (no), or if there were any known conflicts with other people (also no). No physical, work, or financial issues noted. Her opinion is that being lonesome, he might have gone to listen to the radio in the car and fallen asleep. She states being concerned when she could not get ahold of him from the hospital, and more worried when she found out he missed two days of work. She notes they had a ten thousand dollar life insurance policy kept up from the Navy, and that she was the beneficiary. She describes his community involvement and unlikely possibility of suicide.

Another local is called to testify that was with the deceased around 48 hours prior to the discovery of the body. He notes nothing unusual and can account for his whereabouts in the intervening time. The sheriff then testifies. He details the investigation and notes the lack of evidence of foul play, suspicious activity, or involvement of any other persons. The jurors then have more questions for the deceased's wife, who notes that her husband did often have a "nervous disposition" at the thought of no one else being home, and on those occasions spent a lot of time with the car, working on it. The jurors then recall the physician with more detailed questioning on the nature of carbon monoxide poisoning. He notes that CO itself is odorless, colorless, and tasteless, and often builds up with the victim being unaware. He notes the deceased was aware his wife's condition was improving. In answer to a question, the doctor notes the other substance that leaves a similar coloration is cyanide, but that the post mortem showed definitely it was carbon monoxide. After that, the inquest record notes more off the record discussion between the physician and jurors, then adjourns for deliberation.

The certifying document then states the ruling of the coroner jury that the individual came to his death on June 28th, 1945 by carbon monoxide poisoning from his automobile. A particular manner of death is not noted on the document.

Additional notes in the file record that a copy of the inquest transcript was sent to the Veteran's Administration at their request; and a letter from the County Attorney to the U.S. Attorney. In that letter, the County Attorney states that the jury declined to determine either accident or suicide. He also notes he "had a feeling that something out of line occurred in connection with the death". He notes on the date of the letter he is writing that he received a call from the widow of the deceased, who told him she had just learned that the wife of the Federal officer that was first notified originally of the body, was with the deceased "...late into the night before the body was found, and that the parties were drinking heavy..." at the deceased's home. She also gives the name of another individual supposedly involved. The County Attorney notes it is not his place to proceed with further investigation as it is Federal jurisdiction, and while he cannot think of any reason someone would wish to "dispose" of the deceased, he notes that other individuals on the Reservation do not believe the incident was accident or suicide. He also cannot see any reason why the named individuals would withhold information, although he could understand why the wife of the officer might have "reason to keep her movements quiet."

The final note contains a list of expenses for the inquest, including $35.00 for the doctor's autopsy. $31.50 for the court reporter, $4.00 each for three jurors and $3.00 for two witnesses, totaling $81.50 for the procedure.

Commentary: The situation outlined in the County Attorney's letter, considering the condition of the body, shows he was dead for longer than the night before he was found, either did not occur as indicated, or not on the evening indicated. It also does not fit the personality of the deceased as described by the witnesses in detail. Unfortunately, there is no record of toxicology on the remains, which would have confirmed or eliminated such a story. For this period of time, toxicology would not have been a standard part of the exam.

**Note: Generally cases older than 70 years (before 1950) are no longer considered to be of medicolegal significance due to the fact that any persons involved in a non-natural case would be most likely also dead, or not in any position to be affected, prosecuted, or otherwise related to any changes in information revealed by reopening a case to further examination. The previous cases are of historical value only. Subsequent cases from this point on, however, while they can be presented for educational purposes by law, will not have the names of the deceased included in this analysis, out of sensitivity to those surviving next of kin. In some cases as time approaches the present, other details may be left out if the case holds the possibility of being reopened for further investigation. Undetermined cases may simply be unknown in manner or cause, or hold the possibility of being an unsolved homicide, and are therefore today treated as a homicide by policy as far as records & information retention.

While cases since the statutory change in 2011 are restricted by the confidentiality laws as to what information is public and released by the coroner, any case that has an inquest is different. Inquests are public proceedings, with the information and evidence filed with the Clerk of District Court, and eventually the Wyoming State Archives. As such, all inquest information is considered public record if obtained through the District Court or Archives.

Section II: The Uncertain Sixties

10. #65008 (1965) The only information in this file, dated 7/26/1965, is an autopsy report. Autopsy was performed on a 40 year old female on 7/28/1965 at 10:00 A.M. at the "Darr Funeral Home" in Lander WY, on authority of Coroner Lee. The pathologist is a Dr. D.L. Becker from Memorial Hospital in Casper, WY.

In the mid-20th Century, especially in rural Wyoming, autopsies were performed by medical pathologists rather than certified forensic pathologists. This was due to availability of medical pathologists, and the still developing field of forensic specialty pathologists that was not available anywhere near this part of the country. The difference in approach, training, education, and skill of the forensic pathologist in current times is significant in terms of death investigation, and using a non-forensic medical pathologist would be inappropriate for a modern case. Specialists are the name of the game in modern forensic investigation.

While there is no coroner report of the investigation, the autopsy does have a 'clinical summary': "History of episodes of depression for many years. In recent years has taken sleeping pills intermittently and had sometimes drunk more alcohol than usual, although was not considered alcoholic." Last seen Monday 26th after stating she was going out of town "to think things over". "Found dead early A.M. 27th lying half in and half out of Jeep in the countryside out of Lander, Wyoming." Subject is 5 ft. tall and estimated 110 lbs. in weight. External exam showed an old abdominal surgical scar but no other significant findings. Internal exam was normal except for the lungs, which showed bilateral congestion with moderate to marked edema, worse in the lower lobes. No stomach contents seen. Laboratory toxicology showed no alcohol, trace of carbon monoxide, negative for the more common sedative drugs, trace amounts of amphetamine, but nothing in any significant amount as to cause death, although most of these tests are presumptive, not quantitative. Microscopic examination of tissues showed hemorrhagic pulmonary edema. The pathologist's comments note that the coroner found no evidence of physical violence, and that in the absence of any other physical cause, he must assume the death is natural although the "causes remain unexplained".

Commentary: In spite of what may be insinuated in the clinical summary, there is no physical evidence of suicide whatsoever. Accident or homicide also seem highly unlikely, and the physical exam leaves no clear picture of a natural cause with the pathologist only presuming that in the absence of any other indications. Without any detailed investigation reports or medical history, and not knowing what may have been missed with the lack of a true forensic exam, this case is best left as 'undetermined'. Under modern standards, if the cause is unknown, the manner is usually undetermined, rather than saying it was natural in the absence of any other indication.

Case 11. #66028 (1966) Another case where the only documentation is the autopsy report. Subject is a 54 year old sheepherder that was noted to be missing on 10/15/1966, and found dead near his horse and herd of sheep around 4:00 P.M. that same day near "Sweetwater Crossing, WY". Autopsy completed two days later by Dr. James Thorpen of Casper, WY, at a local funeral home. The clinical summary notes that there was no sign of violence or foul play, and that the deceased was known to be a "vigorous, hardworking individual". Other than some small abrasions to the lower lip and left cheek, no trauma or injury are reported. The only markedly abnormal portion of the physical exam is that the lungs are both exhibiting "marked consolidation with firm hemorrhagic parenchyma... abundant frothy fluid...". Other than confirming the issues in the lungs, nothing else is significant on the microscopic exam. Toxicology shows negative for all tested substances, with the urine negative for ethanol, but positive for methanol at 0.075, a significant finding. Diagnosis is listed as methyl alcohol poisoning with associated pulmonary and cerebral edema, moderate liver cirrhosis, and some kidney/adrenal damage.

Commentary: Here is a case where a thorough investigation, or at least the documentation, would be handy. It is not that unusual in a person who is a chronic alcoholic of limited means, to consume methanol, rather than the drinking type substance ethanol, if desperate for intoxication. In a majority of those cases it is the intoxication that is sought from the methanol (which is similar to ethanol), even if the toxicity of the methanol is known. Rarely is methanol seen as a method of suicide, and like most substances, if intent is involved for that end, the level would be much higher. Deaths from a single or chronic use of methanol are most often ruled accidental, especially if the social and medical history of usage is known. The liver damage seen is indicative of chronic alcohol abuse, and the lung and kidney damage probably connected to the immediate effects of the methanol. Other than the general solitary nature of ethnic sheepherders and commentary in the clinical notes, we know nothing about this individual. Today a sociological and psychological profile could be obtained from interviews with his employers and co-workers to perhaps narrow the circumstances. At least there is no physical indication of suspicious activity or event, and the deceased was found in his working situation near his horse. With more information to confirm, we could probably reach a better than 70% certainty that this is accidental rather than an undetermined death.

Case 12. #67001 (1967) 58 year old male noted as having been found dead in bed on 1/9/1967, with an autopsy performed on the embalmed body on 1/10/1967 by the aforementioned Dr. Becker of Casper. Toxicology noted as having been drawn prior to autopsy, but only alcohol is run on the blood – drug screen was on urine obtained from the embalmed body. Again the autopsy report is all that there is in the file. No reports from Coroner Lee, and the file folder itself in Lee's handwriting says "accidental OD". The clinical summary states the man was found dead in bed with no signs of violence, and no medical history is available. At a height of 5'9" and recorded weight of 145 lbs., the physician calls him "moderately thin". The gross physical exam reveals severe atherosclerotic cardiovascular disease with 85% occlusion in one vessel. Bilateral severe congestion and edema is seen in the lungs, most notable to the posterior side. No other gross abnormalities are seen, and the microscopic exams are consistent with the basic findings. Toxicology is negative for alcohol, positive for phenothiazine and barbiturates, but the positive findings are not quantified as to level, nor specifically identified. The physician states that by the "morphologic and chemical findings" the death is due to "poisoning by the drugs mentioned above". He further says "whether this was suicidal, homocidal [sic], or accidental I cannot tell."

Commentary: This case is a great example of the difference between a modern medical legal investigation and one from 50 years ago. Documentation is terrible, with no justification as to why Coroner Lee wrote "accidental OD" on the case folder. Current reporting would not only detail the scene and body evidence, but also should document the process and justification leading to a conclusion. The coroner can change the conclusion of the pathologist based on the totality of the investigation (the pathologist only knows what is initially told him), but for legal reasons and accountability he had better note why in a report. Without any evidence and documentation to the contrary, we now have to discount the coroner note and only go by what is presented. Modern files would also have a copy of the death certificate as filed with the State, to show what the official ruling was. This could be obtained from the State Archives/Vital Records if really a critical point.

Toxicology today, aside from a better and more complete scientific process, is in two phases: presumptive, which simply tells you what is present; and quantitative, which is automatically run on any positives to tell what the exact levels are. Without the quantitative levels, the simple presence of phenothiazine and barbiturates does not indicate if they were at trace, therapeutic, toxic, or fatal levels. Obviously, one cannot presume any sort of overdose by mere presence.

Also, the body was autopsied after being embalmed. I cannot say what the effects of embalming are on tissue fluids, whether it be the lungs, or urine in the bladder – that would be a subject for research prior to interpreting the physical findings. Bodies are rarely taken these days for forensic autopsy in an embalmed state unless exhumed or necessary by some quirk of the investigation. For example, we had one case that the embalming process brought out previously undefined bruising not visible in the initial external examination (something for you to keep in mind in assault victims), and the funeral director raised the alarm. The notation of fluid in the lungs as being posterior sided may be due to the fact he died on his back in bed and positional, or some dynamic to the embalming process – I cannot tell at this point.

The severe lung congestion, while a result or symptom of many conditions, including overdose, could also be indicative of pneumonia, and today, cultures would be run to define or eliminate that possibility. Depending on degree of congestion, it could also be an artifact of the dying process. The cardiac atherosclerosis appears by description severe enough to be a natural cause of death in and of itself, especially if the body is stressed by another illness. There are certainly indications this may have been a natural death, and there are also no medical records or summaries presented to give that aspect of history that we would have obtained today.

To be fair, we have to keep in mind that this was not completed by an experienced forensic pathologist, and a lot may have been missed through no fault of his own. A forensic autopsy is a process of elimination along with discovery and examination, and there is simply not enough data here to eliminate anything, as even the pathologist of the time noted in his own way. The investigative process, methodology, and scientific testing and procedures available today were just not around in Wyoming at this time, and some processes had not even been invented or refined relative to death investigation. Based on the little we know, and the larger portions we do not know, this case is correctly listed in the database as undetermined.

Case 13. #67010 (1967) A roughly 50 year old "John Doe", 6' tall, approximately 185 lbs., autopsy date of 3/20/1967 by Dr. Becker at Memorial Hospital in Casper, WY. Clinical summary on the autopsy noted date found as 3/19/17, and suspected of being a Native American male missing since 2/4/1967, or about six weeks. Full body x-rays were completed and found no fractures or foreign bodies, examination did not reveal any significant or suspicious injuries either. In spite of the expected decomposition, and probably due to cold water submersion and weather for that time of year, some good information was obtained. Unrecognizable facial features, but a two letter set of block initials are tattooed 3 inches above the left wrist. Lungs, trachea, and bronchi are full of fluid and water. No evidence of prior illness or abnormality seen. Under 'other information' in the autopsy report, it is stated that the missing man "presumably this person, was reported to have been drinking heavily at a party on the Reservation", after which he left the scene alone. The radiologist report and actual x-rays are on file, and significant for first, the absence of significant trauma; and second, description of dental fillings and features. No toxicology was obtained.

Commentary and Identification: even for the times, if anti-mortem dental x-rays had been obtained, there is enough to have obtained a positive ID scientifically by comparison. The tattoo would have been presumptive, but supported the possible ID. Interviews with those present and investigation of circumstances the night the individual went missing, might add information on clothing or other evidence to add to the totality of ID. There is really no reason for this person to have remained a "John Doe", even then, and it is unknown, due to lack of reports and documentation, if ID was eventually achieved. These days a DNA comparison could be run against probable relations and sealed the deal.

The pathologist lists drowning as most likely, and in consideration of the recorded physical evidence, lack of trauma, time of year, probable temperature of the water, and report of intoxication despite lack of toxicology results, this case should have been listed as accidental drowning with a better than 50-50 probability. Hypothermia would have also been contributory as waters stay cold enough in Wyoming to induce hypothermia even in the summer season – certainly the status for February in any year. Once wet, you only have a few minutes before unconsciousness would lead to drowning or death.

Case 14. #68040 (1968) A 50 year old white male found dead in a local hotel room on 9/28/1968, noted as having stayed there for about two weeks. No autopsy on file, but there is an incomplete copy of the death certificate worksheet, a one page and pathetic coroner report, handwritten note from a funeral home in Montana, and copy of a toxicology report. Several old Polaroid photos of the scene are in the file.

The coroner report only has basic description parameters of the deceased, location, and notes the reporting party. Other than noting $22.56 in cash found, no details of the scene or body, sequence or progression of the investigation. The death certificate worksheet does list an ID, notes a wife whose residence is in Cody, WY. Burial is to be done in Montana. No manner or cause of death is listed. Occupation is listed as "equipment operator". The Montana funeral home note is a request for the personal property, but no listing or inventory is in the file relative to what was kept or transferred by the coroner's office, other than "done" written on the note. The note also lists the deceased as "veteran of #2".

The toxicology results slip states both urine and blood were sampled, with results negative for phenothiazines and 'barbital'. Presence of codeine phosphate is noted, yet elsewhere it states "no opiate derivatives", which is inconsistent. Blood ethanol is listed as 0.37, and urine ethanol as 0.41. As usual for this time period, there is no quantitative level on the codeine, so no way to know if this was a false positive or not.

The few (five) Polaroids, however, do give a good amount of information, in spite of the lack of written documentation. The individual is mostly on his left side on the floor in a semi-fetal position, with his head elevated on a low lounge chair. The lower cushion of the chair is lifted up against the back cushion. He is dressed in matching grey pants and shirt, and his eyeglasses are on. No evidence is seen of trauma, injury, blood or biologics in any of the photos. A general photo of the room partially shows the bed, with property and papers scattered across it, although the room does not look unusually disturbed. Off to one side is a travel trunk, and next to it is a bottle of whiskey on its side on the floor, and an ashtray with cigarette butts partially spilled. Several other articles of the grey clothing are seen next to the trunk, and these look consistent with the type of clothing an equipment operator of the time would have worn as work clothes. One photo shows the trunk opened, which contains more of the grey clothing, and at least seven more bottles of whiskey.

There is no evidence seen or noted that would indicate any suspicious circumstance, and the toxicology on its own could be considered evidence of accidental ethanol toxicity. However, without an autopsy or medical history to eliminate the possibility of some underlying physical issue or event, a natural death aggravated by the intoxication cannot be excluded. This case is best left as undetermined in manner of death.

Case 15. #69033 (1969) This 33 year old Native American male was found "dead in his quarters" on 8/18/1969, according to the autopsy clinical summary, lying on his back "with no signs of violence" The summary also notes no known medical history but history of ethanol abuse. No coroner report, but there is a certified copy of the death certificate. Autopsy was performed two days after the body was found and embalmed. Findings on this 5'6", 145 lb. individual are evidence of severe fatty changes in the liver with early portal cirrhosis, no other significant issues noted. The pathologist notes that no blood was obtained for toxicology, but urine showed "strong traces" of barbiturates and an ethanol level of 0.112. Diagnosis is the cirrhosis first, with history of chronic alcoholism and recent ingestion of alcohol and barbiturates listed after. The pathologist also notes the immediate cause of death is a "matter of conjecture".

Interestingly enough, the death certificate is certified by a physician from Indian Health Service, who notes on the paper that he attended the deceased "only one day". The manner is listed as undetermined. The cause of death listed for this 33 year old is "acute alcohol ingestion and cirrhosis (duration: unknown)", due to "poverty, lack of education & job (duration: 33 years)", due to "cultural deprivation (duration 33 years)". While the IHS physician appears to have wanted to make a social statement, the death certificate is not really the place to do that, and today would not pass through vital records as listed in that manner. Being undetermined, the certification should have been completed by the coroner in any case, not a physician with little history with the patient.

The ethanol level of 0.112 would in modern times not be considered high enough for a cause of ethanol toxicity, as that is not even twice the legal limit of 0.08, and would not even be notable in a chronic alcoholic. Without quantification the influence of drugs is unknown as stated before. If the liver damage was severe enough to cause death, in spite of being the result of chronic and long term ethanol abuse, the standard is to consider that a natural death from a disease process. So there is both the possibility from the limited evidence of either a natural or accidental death from overdose, thus undetermined it should remain.

Section III: The Inconsistent Seventies

Case 16. #73012 (1973) The file on this 54 year old Native American female contains an autopsy report, toxicology report, woefully inadequate coroner report, authorization for autopsy, and copy of the death certificate. The death certificate has no indication of the manner of death that was ruled, and lists "acute alcoholic intoxication" as the cause, with "barbiturate intoxication" as a contributing factor. While the State Vital Records could be searched for how the manner of death was certified at the time, by current standards the death would be undetermined based on the information available. The one sheet coroner report only has basic demographic information, but does indicate "DOA Memorial Hospital" and has a note "left home at about 5 pm & came back home passed out about 6:30 pm & was DOA 7 pm". The death certificate lists approximate time of death as about 6:30 pm with a pronounce time of 7:10 pm, and location at the hospital, so evidently the patient was transported from home to that location. The autopsy reports as a clinical summary, "Yesterday this woman and her husband began drinking early in the day in or near Riverton. They returned home on the Reservation and later this woman went out again with friends and resumed drinking. Late in the afternoon the friends brought her back home and told the husband that she had 'passed out'. She was carried in and placed on a couch. An hour or so later the husband found she was dead."

Several issues here, just to start: first, the time frames of the autopsy note and the coroner note do not coincide. While an ambulance would most likely not have transported to the hospital if determined dead at home, it is possible she was transported via personal vehicle and arrived DOA at the hospital. In either case, the narratives are not accurate. Second, while one might assume her friends carried her in passed out with death occurring later, we have had incidents where drinking partners assumed a person was passed out but in reality they were already dead when carried in and dropped off at home, and the friends just were too drunk to notice, or were trying to divest themselves of the issue. If all parties were intoxicated and the transport was by personal vehicle to the hospital, the subject may have been dead some time, and just carried to two different locations before that was figured out. It has happened.

The medical autopsy – remember these are still not considered forensic – does not indicate any other physical issues that could cause death, nor any noted trauma or injuries. The toxicology indicated a blood alcohol of 0.304, high enough in some cases to induce ethanol toxicity, but in other cases we have seen people walking around and doing just fine at that level. The screen for barbiturates is positive for several types, but at this time is only presumptive with no quantitative levels, thus the medical interaction or effects between the drugs and alcohol cannot be determined, even though by history that could very well be a lethal combination. The conclusion of a cause of death from those involved at this time could be considered reasonable in consideration of the standards in the seventies, but falls far short for today's standards.

The inclusion of an authorization for autopsy signed by family members is interesting, as Wyoming Statutes give the coroner the authority to do one as part of an investigation whether anyone else approves or not, if he feels it is necessary (statutes regarding autopsy were basically the same in the 70's as they are now).

The cause, while not as defined as it would have been today, appears relatively sound based on what is known. As far as manner of death, now this would be considered an accidental death due to mixed ethanol and drug toxicity. Without better documented circumstances or history, however, we cannot eliminate other possibilities. For example, in some jurisdictions, if the drugs were illegally obtained and provided, and levels could be shown to directly cause death, some cases have been ruled and prosecuted as homicides. The described circumstances seem unlikely for suicide, but again, without more information, for our purposes, better left as undetermined. Perhaps the autopsy authorization was done because the family insisted on having one. In looking at case files from this time period, unfortunately one gets the impression that some cases are viewed as "just another drunk Indian" – sad, but true for the period, and certainly not the viewpoint of current situations, nor the way an investigation would be handled by my office or staff – that attitude is not tolerated one bit, even if I still run into it on occasion from other agencies or the public.

Case 17. 73016 (1973) ...And now for something completely different. The file for this Native American male concerns an individual whose remains were found 1/28/1978, "pronounced" in 6/2/1981, buried 6/13/1981, with a presumed date of death of 12/15/1973. Age is listed as 40 or 43, depending on the document, but by the date of birth listed on the death certificate, 40 is the accurate number.

For the first time, the file contains a wealth of information, unfortunately, the coroner report is not in that group. The single page coroner report is blank except for a date – "1/30/1978"... pretty pathetic. Luckily we have other documentation.

The pathologist's autopsy also contains a decent narrative (which should have been part of the coroner report) as well as anthropologic information, since the remains were skeletonized. The presumptive ID is stated and attributed to other information described later. The presumptive subject is known to have been treated in the past for alcoholism, tuberculosis, and as well often involved in fights. His lifestyle included sleeping out in "haystacks practically any time of the year". He was last seen on 12/15/1973 purchasing items at the gas stop/store in Crowheart, WY, a rural collection of a few buildings midway between Riverton and Dubois, mostly used as a Post Office box address and source of convenience store type supplies for the local ranches. The narrative notes that after the disappearance, searches were conducted in the local area and waterways, with no success until 1/28/78, when a "bird watcher" identified a skull in a ravine about a mile from the highway. The scene was examined by the pathologist, FBI, and coroner, locating scattered skeletal remains, clothing, and a wallet in the pants that contained an ID as well as receipts from the store purchases. The report notes "the clothing seemed in orderly array with socks tucked inside the boots... no recognizable blood staining of the clothing articles." Approximately 25 yards away are noted a "number of bones from quadrupeds... evidently... place of discard for cattle and big game carcasses." "The skull has configuration of eye sockets consistent with Asiatic or Native American racial origin. The pelvis and brow ridges are consistent with male sex." Reference is made that the coroner is retaining the remains for further anthropological exam (no report in the file), and notes a local dentist had treated the prospective subject seven years prior for a fractured mandible, although no x-rays from that period still existed. It is noted that the nasal septum is deviated to the left and consistent with a healed fracture. A non-depressed fracture to the right occipital bone is defined in detail. The dentition is charted also in detail, and include the statement that the "alveolar sockets of the central incisors #25 and #24 are filled with reparative osseous tissue." There is minimal residual tissue, no fillings in the teeth, and "no metallic fragments or disruptions of the skeletal bones are noted..." All recovered parts and findings are summarized in the face page of the report.

The date of this report is 12/1/81 as an attachment to the original report, and includes the following remarks: the case was presented informally at a forensic conference by the pathologist in 1979 "with various experts concurring with the interpretation of findings of the fractured skull and teeth as being related to temperature extremes and exposure to the elements. One participant offered to locate a photograph of the deceased if a free tooth from the skull could be made available and used by a medium. This was not attempted." ...interesting conference, and not something I have ever encountered at a forensic meeting, for sure.

There is a narrative letter from the coroner to the FBI dated 6/15/1978, roughly five months after the find, which does describe the prospective circumstances, life description and general findings of the discovery. It notes the subject was seen leaving the store in the company of other individuals, also at a time when he would have received his monthly per capita check and had available cash. He notes the likely occurrence of animal predation in scattering the remains. He encloses an x-ray report from a fight incident in October of 1969, but notes the actual x-ray is no longer on file at the hospital. Clothing remains are identified as similar to what the subject wore, as identified by the store owner when last seen. The clothing appears in his opinion "taken off and sort of piled up. His socks were in his boots kind of rolled up." The weather per National Weather Service for that area around that time was a coldest of 17 degrees F. above zero, with only a trace of precipitation for December. The coroner notes the delay in submission is due waiting for the snow to clear and conducting additional searches, and requests assistance in examination of the remains and clothing. He notes the jurisdiction as Reservation, with FBI and BIA as investigators. Urgency is requested as potential relatives want to claim the remains (no FBI lab reply is included in the file).

Medical records from 10/5/1969 from a local hospital are included in the file, describing trauma from a beating that occurred that date. X-rays note no fracture to the skull and head other than through the angle of the mandible on the right side and at the base of the condyle also on the right side – which may be significant, as the pathologist's report noted that the right condyle was missing. Weathering and predation might cause a bone to fragment at a point of previous injury, but unfortunately, there were no actual x-rays available to compare ante-mortem and postmortem configurations on the mandible. Old rib fractures are noted on the left side, but again, no ribs are documented as being found with the remains. Other findings include multiple lacerations and possible concussion, shock, intoxication. Treated and discharged to a care center for recovery after the dentist wired the jaw.

Other papers in the file include miscellaneous handwritten notes, a letter from presumed next of kin wanting to claim the remains, and copies of the Crowheart store receipts found with the remains dated 12/15/1973 for a purchase of Listerine and Anacin. Death certificate copies indicate filed as the presumed person, cause unknown, manner undetermined, and dates noted as indicated at the beginning of this case. One other note on the outside of the manila file folder says "bones & clothes in brown plastic sack in garage", in blue ink. This is crossed off in red ink, with a side note also in red "buried 1981". This is a rather unorthodox method of property and remains storage, and tracking of inventory and release. The coroner at the time was known for keeping skeletal remains at his home in the garage or basement, often for years, and while he had no physical office space, I think this was over the top, even for the times. Chain of custody requirements have definitely changed, as has how remains are respectfully handled.

Also, here a larger number of photos are included for an undetermined case. By way of reference, the first general case on file that contains photos is from 1938, with that sort of documentation being only intermittent for the next 30 to 40 years, as far as having survived in the files. This case includes ten Polaroids of the scene and find. Polaroids at that period were "the" technology, due to portability, immediate review, and simplicity of function, however, for durability of retention and documentation, a terrible technology. As they age, the colors fade and change, papers separate or stick together, and resolution for duplication is poor. These are in good shape at this time, considering their age, and do give a general overview of the originating scene, but are not of any detail or close proximity to add any information to what is, or isn't, contained in the written reports.

Circumstantial and presumptive evidence in this case is strong for an ID, even without a true anthropology exam that would have confirmed race, approximate age, stature, and other parameters to compare with known life features. The one thing about a forensic anthropology exam, however, is that their skill set is also much more attuned to examination of skeletal remains for tool or weapon marks, as well as age and source of trauma, whether from life injury, or postmortem animal activity. In modern times, we would do both anthropology and pathology, to have the advantage of the expertise of two different perspectives. As to cause of death, without specific indications on the remains of fatal trauma, that remains unknown. Certain homicides would go unnoticed if they involved only injury to the soft tissue, long gone. Accidental death due to hypothermia or drug or alcohol toxicity remains in play. Natural death from a physical process would never be known in these conditions. Even in a case today, with modern forensic capabilities, unless the bones tell a specific tale, or an event was witnessed or confessed, these cases are often a manner of undetermined.

Case 18. #74059 (1974) This case of a 43 year old Native American male has no coroner report in the file, although a narrative by the deputy coroner is included with the autopsy report and referenced in the clinical summary. This subject had sustained a head injury and laceration that caused notable swelling to the eyes and head. He was seen in the local emergency room, where he told the physician that he had fallen off a horse a few days before. The wound was not closed due to the age of the wound, skull x-rays were negative. He was released to the care of a niece who lived in the same home. Within the next 12 to 18 hours, he was found dead by the niece. Further interviews with the niece revealed that she hit him in the head with a frying pan a couple of days prior, and that the story of the fall from a horse was false. Autopsy notes the laceration and underlying edema, pulmonary edema, severe fatty liver, rheumatic heart disease, and cardiac hypertrophy. The diagnosis notes a possibility of cause of death as the pulmonary edema, or sudden death from liver disease, and states "I am unable to document a correlation between the head wound on 6/12/74 and the patient's demise on 6/16/74". Toxicology was negative. Cause on the death certificate is listed as the pulmonary edema, with the other items, including the head wound, as contributory. Manner is assigned as undetermined. Three photographic prints from the scene are also in the file, but do not reveal anything further of note. Today a proper forensic autopsy could perhaps have defined the cause more specifically, but for a medical autopsy the physician was pretty thorough. Even today, with the best examination and analysis, sometimes there is no answer, or more than one possibility, thus undetermined is a valid conclusion in the case.

Case 19. #76046 (1976) Very incomplete file on this 21 year old Native American male, considering the circumstances. The death certificate copy included does not indicate any manner or cause of death, but a note on the coroner report indicates it was sent to the autopsy physician for certification – an unusual step, as the certifier in a case should be either the coroner who investigated the case, or a personal physician in a natural death that is the treating doctor and familiar with the history. This is most likely not a natural death, so the coroner legally should have certified. The autopsy narrative indicates the individual was last seen the day before he was found floating in a local hot springs facility, fully clothed when found (including cowboy boots) with no indication as to how he got there. The physician notes also that the pool had a walled enclosure, and was lined with concrete. Within the boots and within the socks there is heavy dirt which is not found in the enclosure and source unknown. The time of year was late April.

Notes indicate a three person jury was selected for an inquest, but it is unknown if one was ever held – no copies are in the file of any transcript, and a search of the listings of what is in file with the State Archives do not show any for this person or date. Either it was decided not to hold one, or if held it was never properly recorded and filed as required by State Statutes. A folded envelope in a plastic baggie is in the file, with a written note, dated, of "material taken from feet of (name of deceased)". Such evidence, not properly collected, contained, or stored along proper chain of custody guidelines is most likely useless at this point, some 40 years later. One never knows, though, and we do not destroy or throw away such things when found, so it will remain in the file. The obvious thought process at the time would be to have tried to match and track down where it came from to document a previous location for the deceased, but with no follow through that time is long gone. The technology at the time of the death would not have been adequate for too much definitive information for matching up such evidence, which in any case, had also been soaking in the water for whatever length of time the body was there. Nice thought, but probably an exercise in futility.

The coroner report details the clothing, notes numerous tattoos, and personal effects found in the pockets the include "1 pocket knife, 1 beer can opener, 1 dice, 1 fingernail clipper, 30 cents in change". Body was found early afternoon by a life guard and facility manager, water temperature in the pool measured at 92 degrees. Very little narrative in the coroner report, so again, the most complete description of the event is in the pathologist's narrative.

At autopsy, there was no water or blockage found in the throat, lungs, or gastrointestinal system; all internal organs normal, no noted trauma or injuries. General condition is partially decomposed, which as far as time frame would be highly variable and accelerated due to the temperature and mineral content of the water in the hot springs pool. The physician did run CO, sodium, potassium, and hemoglobin levels on cardiac blood from both sides of the heart, levels found comparable and "elevated instead of depressed as would be expected if water had been inhaled and absorbed in the lungs." Carbon monoxide was around 7%, which would be what you might find in a tobacco smoker naturally. Ethanol content was a 0.144, not even twice what would be the legal limit today, and not unusual or an explanation for immediate cause of death. Cause of death is listed as "unknown, possible drowning". His summary notes "findings suggest that this man was dead before his body got into the pool" with "no findings grossly to suggest what the cause of death was...". In a note added from May he indicated authorities have been unable to provide any other pertinent information, and must assume drowning as a possibility in the case.

The idea of drowning seems a stretch for me in the case, as the physical findings documented would be extremely atypical for that – I would more likely agree that he was probably dead prior to hitting the water, rather than drowned. One must avoid grasping at a possibility just because nothing obvious is available as you usually will be wrong. The proper ruling unless you can hit at least a 50% probability is to admit the cause is unknown, and thus the manner is undetermined. Even considering intoxication and a stumble into the pool, drowning would have left different evidence. Also, without current definitive toxicology, who knows what else might have been involved. A 21 year old would probably not odds-on had some sort of natural event, such as a heart attack, and then fallen in, although certain arrhythmias would not have left a physical trace like an infarction would have. There is also the possibility of something occurring and then the body was dumped in the pool by others. There is simply too much lack of evidence from the documentation available, but the circumstances sure sound suspicious.

At this point we are also on the edge of what might be opened as a 'cold case' for further investigation. This would have, or should have, been an FBI case, having occurred on the Reservation, and it might be a possibility to check with that agency for any records. Interviews or other documentation, even if minimal, might shed light on what the deceased's last movements were or who he was seen by or with. Even for a Federal agency, however, investigations, documentation, and record keeping might be very inconsistent or incomplete for the time frame, but one never knows. Anyone of his age and peer group at this point would be in their 60s, if still alive, and have probably limited recall of the event unless personally involved in some memorable way. Thus, my saying we are only on the edge of a cold case consideration, especially without any indications that point to more firm suspicions or reasonable hope of progress. Older cases have been solved than this, but they usually start with more initial documented information and investigation. Keep that in mind as a possibility as we continue, however, as any undetermined case is like a homicide, never really closed. Advances in technology, investigation, and a new set of eyes on the evidence, may warrant a second detailed look into the matter.

Case 20. #76061 (1976) The next case involves a 17 year old female resident of what was known at the time as the Wyoming State Training School in Lander, a facility for the mentally disabled or brain injured. Clients have a wide range and degree of abilities from independent self-care to total care. By State Statutes, all deaths at a State facility, or those in the custody of the state or its political subdivisions, are automatically coroner cases. The principal being that the coroner's office is to be an independent investigative agency beyond any other authority or law enforcement, to ensure objective analysis and conclusions for custodial deaths.

There are three sheets of poorly copied papers in the file. Two are copies of a small notepad sheets that describe the name of the deceased, time of 6:45 p.m. "happened", and 7:08 "p. dead". The supervisor on duty evidently states another resident took her in a wagon from the residence to a pond, and then returned without her. Staff went to search, and found the deceased in the pond. The pond is described as "murky", "3 feet deep at most", and had a small dock on the east side, according to a small hand drawn diagram. There are no coroner or autopsy reports on file, and no documentation as to whose notes these are.

An unsourced clipping from a newspaper is on one of the copies that reports the age as 18 years, and gives a death time of 6:15 p.m. after "apparently falling into a pond on school grounds". The article attributes discovery of the body of the 11-year facility resident in the pond by the residential director at a time of "about 6:30 p.m.". It further states the deceased "had asked to take a walk around the school grounds about 6 p.m. after dinner. The house mother gave permission, as she had often gone for evening walks. When the girl didn't return in 10 minutes, as she had promised, a search for her began, ending with the discovery of her body in the pond, near the southern entrance to WSTS."

The last copied page is of the death certificate. Keep in mind that at this time, certificates were typed or filled out by hand, unlike the digital on-line process of today. One has to remember the effects of the changes in technology, no internet, no ubiquitous computers, and no smart phones. Forms were filled out by hand, or by typewriter, which actually has the advantage of some interesting non-standard comments in these cases, and still represent an 'official' record. On the certificate, identification details are given, age listed as 17 years, social security number listed as "none". Parents are listed, but the informant for demographics information is, and signed by, the Superintendent of the School. Date of death at the top is listed as 8/4/1976.

The interesting part is the hand-written medical certification. The cause in Part 1 is listed as "Suffocation, due to: Drowning-Aspiration of Water, due to: Found in pool of Water". Interval between onset and death for all three listings is "minutes". Part 2, "other significant conditions", lists "Severe mental retardation, Microcephaly, Dwarfism, Behavior problem". Autopsy is indicated as "no". Manner is listed as "?Accident?Homicide?" (these days on-line you have to pick one, which if you cannot decide, would obviously be undetermined). Date of injury is 8/3/76 and time of injury "Approx. 6 p.m.". "How injury occurred" shows "Found in fish pond – suspicious evidence she was pushed in by another student". The certifying physician lists that she had attended the deceased for 2 ½ years, last seen on 5/7/76, she did view the body, and pronounced at 7:08 p.m.

Lots of issues here in this case. One thing that might seem an issue to modern coroners, but isn't, would be the time frame for physician certification. Today's statutes state that the death is unattended (and to be certified by the coroner) if the physician has not acted under the scope of his license within 60 days prior to the death... and the time frame listed on the certificate since 'last seen' is about 90 days. One must be aware in looking at old cases of any statutory changes that may have occurred. The 60 day limitation is as of a legislative change in 2005 – prior to that the time frame was within six months, which would have been what was in effect in 1976. Thus the physician was within the scope of her license, <u>if it was a natural death.</u> That is the kicker here, that even in 1976, the physician should not have certified anything other than a natural death, it should have been the coroner. And since this physician signing is also the facility caregiver, there might be a conflict of interest or question of cover-up in the certification. At least the physician here expressed her reservations in the matter, so that probably is not an issue, at least for her.

Other listed facts do however, raise questions. The typed date of death indicates the 4th, and all other notes indicate the 3rd. The notes indicate the incident "happened" at 6:45, while the physician notes "approximately 6 p.m. Pronounce time is the same for both sources. The newspaper article also varies in times, but that variation could depend on their source of information. The most disturbing aspect is the evident conflict of narrative available. We have a handwritten note that another resident took her off in a wagon and returned without her, the physician statement that there is suspicion that other resident pushed her in, and the newspaper report of statements the deceased went for a walk and implying she fell in on her own. There is also an implication by what was said to the paper that the deceased was very independent in action and behavior, which may or may not have been accurate for the particular client, and again, contrasts with other notes such as the physician's listing of conditions and diagnosis. That does smell of a cover-up, at least in what information was released by the facility publically.

Without accurate, detailed, and complete reports on the part of the coroner, we will never know the truth, which is pathetic in this case. First, the coroner wrongly avoided his statutory duty for certification, and obviously, did not do his due diligence in the case of a non-natural death. Second, an autopsy should have been done to determine cause and check for any evidence of injury or other involvement. Even in the lower standards of autopsy at the time, evidence might have been obtained, and a cause defined, rather than just guessing at the cause due to the circumstances in which the body was found. Obviously, someone, for some reason, suspected the other resident may have precipitated the death, which would have made it a possible homicide. Interviews should have been obtained, recorded and included, with all the involved parties and staff. Mental deficiency does not preclude testimony, just the context and nature of consideration. This is all very disturbing, as the deceased deserved a detailed and thorough investigation regardless of physical or mental status, with probably a public inquest if there were questions of improper care, public safety in a state institution, or other malfeasance. To be sure, if another disabled resident was responsible, prosecution for homicide would be unlikely, but our job is not that end, but to find justice and clarity for the deceased in manner and cause... even at the cost of discomfort or accountability for a state facility. In fact, I would think that situation is even more important for such disabled residents, as the coroner is specifically tasked by law as the party of oversight in these types of deaths. Maybe even with detailed investigation, the manner would remain undetermined, but at least the effort would be there, and accountability for how the situation happened, and spur changes that might prevent similar cases in the future.

Today, any non-natural death at the facility would be responded to and investigated fully, including an autopsy. One must keep in mind that even if no criminal actions result, there certainly are civil implications, as well as accountability for the institution. A thorough investigation serves not just the deceased, but also staff of the facility, to verify lack or presence of accountability. In some cases it is just as important to show that there was not any malfeasance on the part of individuals, if that was indeed the case. The coroner has to remain an impartial set of eyes on such situations.

Natural deaths for individuals at such places often involve those with long and detailed medical conditions, good records of care, and in some cases recent hospitalizations. End of life subjects are often medically certified as hospice, which being an anticipated and attended death would not normally be a coroner case. Since one part of statute says that sort of natural death is not a case, and another part says it is, due to custodial nature by the State, our policy is at minimum to do the basics and review records to verify conditions, circumstances, and status of hospice. If well documented as natural circumstances, certification can proceed, and an autopsy or detailed exam is not needed.

In this case, however, I feel the State, the coroner, and the system all let her down.

Case 21. #77008 (1977) A 35 year old white male is described as having been found in early August in a residential apartment complex after neighbors noticed a "foul odor". The narrative is once again only included in the autopsy report, and is relayed by law enforcement investigators. The deceased had not been seen for several days, and was found in a closet adjacent to the bathroom, doors closed and closet light off. He was in a sitting position, slumped forward, with open pants lowered to mid-thigh. Apparent vomit was seen in several locations of the apartment, no noted blood, and no indications of struggle or violence at the scene. The decedent's car was reported "full of empty beer cans" and the apartment showed numerous used and partial containers of beer and wine. An opened letter dated from five days prior was in the area. The pathologist contacted the Sheridan VA hospital and located admission records from three years prior, with diagnoses listed of acute and chronic alcoholism, withdrawal seizures, and passive-aggressive personality type disorder.

The autopsy details the decomposition artifacts and notes set lividity patterns consistent with the found position. No evidence of trauma, injury, or ligature are seen. The oral cavity shows a good amount of probable vomitus material in the mouth and upper throat. Internal exam reveals an intact hyoid, clear trachea, empty stomach, and organs free of occlusion, disease process, injury or abnormality, except for "hepatic fibrosis". Neck dissection shows no hemorrhagic changes. X-rays are done and no indications of fractures or skeletal injury are found. Toxicology on liver tissue shows an ethanol of 0.01 and acetone, isopropanol, and methanol below reporting limits. No barbiturates are detected. The final diagnosis notes the ethanol level, mild cirrhosis, vomit in the mouth, and history of withdrawal seizures, but does not state a manner of death.

A listing of property includes wallet, cash, ID, traveler's checks, personal checkbook, watches, keys, discharge papers, and clothing. A typed coroner report is mostly "fill in the blank" information, but does note a date of death approximately 4 days prior to being found, time unknown, and manner as "natural causes". Photo prints are in the file, one showing original position in the closet, others with the body laid out, and some that are apparently to document the areas of vomit noted in the narrative. The certified death certificate states the cause of death as "acute alcoholism (probable)", due to "chronic alcoholism". The manner is listed as undetermined.

While still not up to modern standards, the documentation from the pathologist, is detailed and thorough. This is the first time we see an autopsy report that is starting to resemble that we would receive in a case today. Often investigations are a process of elimination, and the autopsy for the most part removes homicide and suicide as a manner, which leaves us accidental due to aspiration asphyxia or seizures, or natural due to the complications of chronic alcoholism. Without physical evidence of blockage in the trachea and lungs, one could surmise that the vomit in the mouth was present as a "last gasp" of dying, rather than the cause of accidental asphyxia. Decomposition would account for some natural process ethanol in the system, so the level at death was probably zero. In that case, based on history, withdrawal seizures are a definite possibility, commonly seen after someone comes off an extended session of binge drinking. Death from withdrawal seizures can also occur without asphyxia due to induced cardiac arrhythmias. Long term ethanol abuse related issues such as seizures, cirrhosis, and other complications, are forensically considered natural, even though they are self-inflicted over a period of time. Ethanol toxicity from high levels in the system is usually considered a single incident accidental overdose.

Money and property are present, so no robbery or other evidence of assault in line with the physical findings. Nothing else in the photos or papers indicates additional evidence. The placement in the closet is a question and unknown, but people do odd things depending on how they feel at the time. Based on what is known here, and considering what might not have been documented but experienced at the scene, an investigator could arrive at a natural death as a manner with more than a 50-50 surety – probably 60 to 70 %. I would not complain about that based on what is available, however, since the certificate was completed as undetermined, someone had enough doubt to feel more comfortable with that manner. The doubts or thought process are absent from the record, so in this case, it is best to leave it as undetermined.

Case 22. #77005 (1977) Here we have an ambulance report but again, no coroner report. EMS responded to a 49 year old white male who had been fishing along the river, noted "DOA – patient had heart trouble history, was pulled from the river while fishing with wife. CPR administered to no avail." Luckily we have an autopsy report which, also once again, is the only source of any narrative. The physician notes that information came from a phone conversation with the coroner, so evidently no one from the agency was present at the autopsy, which is not proper protocol in modern cases. In a forensic autopsy today, often the interplay and questions between the pathologist and the agency can help define findings in the immediate examination.

The narrative notes that the subject had a history of moderate alcohol ingestion while fishing with friends who are also noted to have been drinking, but were not interviewed. Someone reported hearing a splash and then finding the subject in the water. He was removed after floating roughly 60 feet downriver. Reports indicate he was deeply cyanotic in the face and upper chest, and CPR attempted unsuccessfully. On transport some blood was noted on the shirt and scalp lacerations were discovered. The coroner returned to the scene which revealed no evidence of struggle and no blood in the area he had been fishing. The event occurred in early September, and the doctor reviewed local hospital records from an admission in March of the same year. Diagnosis at that time was hypertension, grand mal seizures, and chronic obstructive pulmonary disease (COPD). The body shows the marks and features of embalming, but was not embalmed. Apparently, someone changed their mind and decided on autopsy after the process was started, but prior to the administration of fluids.

Two head lacerations are noted, one in the right frontal region and another posterior left frontal region, both less than one inch, fairly superficial with underlying scalp hemorrhage. Injury is determined to be recent. No other skin abnormalities are noted other than a superficial skin abrasion on the right upper arm towards the elbow. Tattoos are noted and described. The oral cavity is sutured shut (part of the preparations for embalming). Internal examination shows no gross abnormality of the chest or lungs; main vessels, or most organs. Cardiac abnormalities are detailed and are also noted in the conclusions. No injury or hemorrhage is noted inside the skull. Toxicology shows blood alcohol as zero, vitreous sodium is slightly low and potassium is slightly high. Detailed heart examination shows atherosclerotic cardiovascular disease with a 60% occlusion of the left anterior descending coronary artery. The balance of the microscopy is normal. An accompanying diagram detailed the head injuries which gives a good visual of location, clearly to the front and top of the head. X-rays of the head and cervical spine are normal.

The autopsy summary states "no definitive anatomic cause of death". The physician does note that while the cardiac occlusion is only moderate, there is a possibility of acute ischemia or arrhythmia that may have caused loss of consciousness and fall into the river. Or perhaps seizure activity caused the fall into the river and resulted in a vagal arrhythmia mechanism as a result of immersion. It is stated that no evidence of drowning is seen. The lacerations are considered to have occurred as a result of the fall in the river, or during recovery, and are not significant to the death.

The included copy of the death certificate states the cause of death as: possible cardiac arrhythmia, due to generalized atherosclerotic disease or possible death due to seizure activity. Manner is listed as undetermined, and signed by the physician pathologist.

This case is a good example of why the coroner should do his job and be the certifier... remember, the autopsy by a pathologist is just a part of the investigation, and as such, considered in the context of the entire investigation. Here we have a medical, not forensic, local pathologist, who is doing his best, and in comparison to today's forensics, issuing a detailed and complete report that holds up well against today's forensic standards in process and steps. Even if not board certified, he obviously is aware of and has studied the procedure, and does not do a simple medical autopsy, which just looks to verify a cause, but follows forensic principles to verify and also eliminate all other possibilities. For example, medical autopsies do not always open the skull and examine the brain, unless indicated by a disease process. Forensic autopsies always do so, regardless of circumstance, as that is a step that by evidence eliminates or confirms issues. The medical pathologist starts by assuming a probable cause of death, the forensic assumes nothing, and only eliminates by confirming nothing is there.

The conclusion of cause as listed on the death certificate is accurate for what the physician saw, and is backed up by his examination, however, absent any evidence of drowning, he is only saying undetermined in regards to choosing between two initiating natural causes. He is not a death investigator, and should not be expected to be. This is not a choice between types of non-natural versus natural death. Even absent decent reports from the investigators, the autopsy within a reasonable certainty eliminates assault (homicide), intent (suicide), and accident – the head injuries in no way were severe enough to cause the death from a fall, they were only collateral damage. So the manner of death here should have been natural, as that would be the circumstance for either of the two choices, arrhythmia or seizure, expressed by the autopsy.

We may never know, but the scene with careful examination may have had evidence of the mode of the fall. If the originating location can be found, and evidently it was since the coroner reported no signs of struggle, there might be different marks or indications that differentiate between how the body fell from position. Collapsing from arrhythmia versus the motions of seizures, for example. Depending on the ground surface, maybe nothing would be seen, but that should also be part of the report. If fishing, how was the gear positioned left on the shore? Interview the companions - what was the behavior that day of the deceased? Anything unusual, what conversations, any complaints, any change of routine or habits? Impending cardiac issues can leave clues in words or behaviors that an impending grand mal seizure would not, or be different in manifestation. If a person simply topples over directly into the water, that would more likely indicate sudden cardiac death – and it is noted by the pathologist that reports indicate he was deeply cyanotic in the face and upper chest – a classic sign of a cardiac event that would normally not be seen in a seizure. With no evidence of drowning, he was most likely dead before he hit the water or very shortly thereafter. Grand mal seizures can be dramatic, but are rarely a single cause of death... there is usually some associated mechanism. If he seized and fell, logically he probably would have drowned and had the associated evidence of that process.

Even without any other information that should have been included, the pathologist was thorough enough that we can eliminate a lot, and narrow down to better that a 50-50 conclusion. As an investigator, I would feel sure enough to probably a 70% certainty that this was a natural death due to a cardiac event due to probable arrhythmia due to hypertensive atherosclerotic cardiovascular disease. The seizure condition, and COPD would be listed in other significant conditions. We must always acknowledge that we are talking reasonable certainties in any case, unless an event is witnessed, but that is our job. We could be wrong, but odds are, we are not in this case based on what is known.

To be fair, modern investigators are termed 'medical-legal' and have a combination of skills and background, both medical and investigation principal knowledge, enhanced by experience. Being elected, in Wyoming at this time, anyone could end up a coroner, and often they were funeral directors, not investigators. Even law enforcement if assisting, did not have always the experience in death investigation, which is a specialized field.

Obviously as we are seeing, the skills in documentation are also not common. Luckily the pathologist is ahead of the coroner as far as good forensics. The 70s are only consistent in being inconsistent. So let's continue...

Case 23. #77026 (1977) This 63 year old white male died in mid-December, 1977. We again initially look to the autopsy narrative for initial information. The procedure took place the day after the recorded death. The doctor's notes documented diagnoses of chronic alcoholism, hypertension, and mild emphysema. The deceased had been "engaged in heavy drinking" for most of the day, and earlier had fallen at the home of a friend, breaking a "light table". "Following the fall his friend had noticed no external evidence of trauma, though his friend was possibly under the influence of alcohol himself." That evening, the deceased was driving his pickup truck "with high beams forcing another car to change course in the on-coming lane." That vehicle then turned and approached the deceased's vehicle from the rear. Both stopped on the side of the road, with the other driver described as "irate". The deceased struck him through the open window, with the response of being hit several times in the head, then pulled out of the driver's door partially onto the ground. The assailant had also been drinking. Those discovering the body found it with legs in the cab, and torso draped out onto the road in a head down position with neck flexed. Resuscitation was unsuccessful. "The account of the assault was not available at the time of the autopsy and the body was not photographed at the scene."

The pathologist obviously obtained further information as the investigation progressed. That would be consistent with today, as new information relayed can help in interpretation of the physical evidence, and the final autopsy reports are not written until weeks later, after labs, microscopy, and toxicology results are received. It is not noted specifically the source of the information in the narrative, and since it could obviously not have come from the deceased, it must have been from the assailant or another passenger in that vehicle, relayed through interviews. There are no notes as to any other witnesses. The physician is the same as in the previous case, and likewise here detailed and thorough in his examination along forensic lines.

The physical conditions listed include many issues. Left ventricular hypertrophy, a probable contributor to the hypertension. General atherosclerotic cardiovascular disease. Blood ethanol level of 0.30, with chronic abuse history. Emphysematic changes to the lungs. Physiologic atrophy of the cerebral cortex, most marked in the frontal lobes (which could be a disease process, age, or attributed to the chronic alcoholism). Injuries noted include multiple facial abrasions and contusions; hematoma of the right lateral face; lacerations of the ears; contusions of the temporal regions left hemorrhage of the calvarium; contusions and minimal lacerations of the left hand; contusions of the right knee. The report and diagrams detail all findings of the examination more thoroughly than the basic listings. No drugs were found, but at this time screening is still only for barbiturates. X-rays are all negative. There is an autopsy authorization from the wife of the deceased, which as previously stated, was not necessary for a coroner case, especially a suspicious death.

The pathologist's summary notes "the autopsy does not reveal a cause of death. However, the description of events fit with many of the autopsy findings." Contusions and abrasions correspond to striking with the left hand and a fall to the decedent's left out of the driver's side of the cab. Temporal contusions are speculated as having occurred either from blows, or possibly from the fall at the friend's house. He states the deceased "may have possibly been in a state of confusion and driving irregularly" and "may have also had dizziness depending on his tolerance for alcohol." "Possibly the blows to the head were sufficient to daze him or render him unconscious. A subsequent body positioning could then be the cause of death from [positional asphyxia]... respiratory movements would be compromised and flexion of the neck could easily produce airway obstruction. The cause of death is not anatomically demonstrable and the manner of death is undetermined."

An inquest ruling sheet is included in the file, but not the transcript. A check of the Wyoming State Archives listing shows the transcript was properly filed through the Clerk of District Court and then with the State, and is on file. Should there be a reason for further investigation, that transcript could be obtained. As it is, hand-written notes indicate that the alleged perpetrator of the assault, investigating deputies, the pathologist, and several other persons were on the witness list. Three 'head shot' photos of the injuries are in the file. The inquest ruling states the deceased came to his death "by receiving several blows to the head and being pulled forcibly from the pickup allowing victim to fall on his face and head on roadway. It is possible the death was caused by blockage of air passage. No attempt was made by assailants to determine if victim was alive or dead before leaving the scene". No manner of death is assigned by the inquest jury. The inquest was held roughly three weeks after the death.

A newspaper article, unsourced or dated, notes that sometime later the suspect in the case was sentenced to one year in county jail for malicious assault and battery. "It was never proven that [the deceased] died from the blows..." Figuring the usual delays and timeframes for judicial process, this trial would have been some time after the inquest was long over, and it is not mentioned what the original charges were. It is also not known how the identity of the assailant was revealed to authorities, but by piecing the information above together, obviously someone talked or confirmed the scenario stated, either in the inquest, or at the trial.

Here in this case scene photos would have been great, as they might have confirmed positional asphyxia within a reasonable certainty. In any case, this presents the coroner with a decision. Would the pathologist with more accurate information on how the body was found have come to a more certain cause in the case? Positional asphyxia is notoriously hard to prove without detailed evidence on how found relative to degree of obstruction, although in thinking of the description, a strong possibility, as the pathologist noted. It does not appear that the head injuries were a direct cause, and the intoxication with the other medical issues would be contributory. So, if an altercation leads directly to a position that induces death, is it a homicide on the part of the assailant? How culpable is the deceased's voluntary intoxication? What about the previous fall? I do not think the inquest transcript would shed much greater clarity on the situation, and it appears the inquest jury still had doubts, although were peeved that the assailant just left him there. And one must try and avoid fitting the evidence into a pre-conceived outcome or goal – that is the job of the judiciary process. I think here that undetermined is the only firm standing for manner since cause is not reasonably clear, although pretty close. That is the judgment call that a coroner is supposed to do, and some may disagree with a conclusion, but some things are best left to a criminal jury, especially if an inquest jury does not give a clear ruling. I rarely like ruling undetermined in any case, as I feel that the job is incomplete... but sometimes it is what it is, or isn't, and that is the correct choice. Ruling a homicide generally requires, or should require in my opinion, a higher degree of certainty, as we are supposed to be the independent death investigators, and someone else's life may be in the balance.

Again, remember that it is the coroner who should be certifying the death, not the autopsy pathologist. The inquest jury makes a ruling, that should be followed if definitive, but they only sign off on the inquest ruling, not the final death certificate. The coroner-investigator is the one that ultimately has the duty for State certification in these cases, and is the only one to have collated all the evidence, including what is presented to the inquest jury. The coroner has the right, and sometimes does, change the manner of death from the conclusion of the pathologist, if the totality of the evidence by the end of the case indicates that is what it should be. That is the coroner's responsibility, and in some of these cases it is improperly being passed off to the pathologist for some reason. That may have slipped by vital records in the past, but it would be rejected these days on any non-natural death.

Case 24. #78012 (1978) This 48 year old Native American male was found next to an active railroad line in late September by a passing rail worker. The body had been there some time as it was already partially decomposed. The 'fill in the blanks' coroner's report contains mostly demographics on the case and once again we are dependent on the pathologist's narrative for most information. He notes that scene investigation showed where the body had hit the rail bed shoulder, bounced, and came to rest, without any sign of movement once it landed. A wallet recovered from the clothing and subsequent fingerprint comparison established the identity of the deceased as a non-resident from Oklahoma. The body had no shoes; however shoes "similar to those the deceased was known to wear" were later discovered in an open freight car, which "contained no sign of violence."

Autopsy showed severe chest trauma on the right side and sternum, fractured left clavicle without other penetrating wounds, and notably a pneumothorax with internal bleeding that indicated the injury to the chest and shoulder occurred sometime prior to death. The pneumothorax is seen to have been caused by the internal clavicle fracture rather than the chest injury. Scalp lacerations and other surface head injuries showed minimal hemorrhage with only a small amount of blood from the head injuries at the site of the body, indicating they occurred post mortem from contact with the ground and the subject was probably dead when he exited the train car. Other physical findings include cardiovascular disease, severe tooth decay, and cirrhosis of the liver. No source of the chest trauma is identified, but considered consistent with either assault or falling. Toxicology was for the most part negative with a low ethanol level that could be accounted for as a decomposition artifact.

The physician's opinion is that the chest injuries could account for the death but are not necessarily incompatible with life. The manner of exit from the train car is unknown, and the body may have been discarded by other individuals present at the time. He states the manner as undetermined. Detailed description of the decomposition artifacts and condition, as well as insect activity, in that time of year would probably indicate a time frame of two to three days prior to being found, but that is very temperature and weather dependent. Polaroid photos that are included in the file contribute minimal information but do support that the body left the train car while the train was moving.

This case is interesting in the fact that the body location is a secondary scene, and rather than the body being moved from the primary scene, the primary moved away from the body. Or perhaps the injury occurred completely elsewhere and the rail car was also a secondary scene. Riding the rails can be a hazardous habit and we really do not know if the chest and shoulder injuries were inflicted or occurred accidentally. It is also possible that the individual died at the open door of the rail car and was jostled by the movement of the train off at that particular spot, rather than being tossed. The autopsy physician once again certifies the certificate with a cause of pneumothorax due to the fractured clavicle and anterior chest injuries, manner listed as undetermined. Since it cannot be determined that the injuries were either accidental or inflicted (homicide), I would not argue with the pathologist based on the information he relates.

There is also a letter from the coroner to the sheriff's office in which he states that while the physician certified as undetermined, he thinks it is a homicide, and it occurred as the result of an assault along the line somewhere between Billings, Montana and the scene – in fact he states his opinion "that this man had been dead for some time and that consequently that the death did not occur in Fremont County." He speculates that the involvement of authorities from Montana down through Basin, Wyoming would be wise. I disagree with the time frame – judging by the state of decomposition, if he had been "dead for some time" and decomposing on the train, there should have been evidence of that, if they had the right rail car. There would have been a time frame, perhaps 24 hours, before fluids would have marked the car, to be sure, and someone else may have noted an odor and pushed out the body. However, due to the peripheral effects of decomposition, if the body fell or was tossed from a moving train with decomposition in process, there would have been more external postmortem disturbance to tissue. My impression is from photos and description is that a majority of the decomposition occurred after landing. Speculation on time of death in decomposition is so environmentally dependent that ranges are only educated guesses, as many factors can accelerate or retard the process. A lot of skill sets, such as forensic entomology and others had not been studied at this time to lend any definition to the time frame from death. We also do not have any time frame for movement of the train along the line defined, or any other noted basis for suspicions to back up that opinion, nor any other documentation or reports. Basically, if it is not documented, such suspicions are baseless and useless. Again, there are other scenarios that could be just as valid.

Further, if the coroner does not like what the pathologist certified, he should have done his job and responsibility in that area, as well as providing documentation, rather than complaining about it.

Case 25. #79024 (1979) This case is the last undetermined case from the 70s. This decomposed body of a 38 year old Native American male was identified by x-ray comparisons to previous films of presumptive ID on record three years prior to being found in early June, noted as consistent dental work and frontal sinus mapping. In addition, there are old injuries to the skeletal structure and small metallic clips in the gall bladder area from previous surgery. As is the case for most of the incidents from the 70's, we have only the medical and pathologist's reports to go on.

Decomposition here is moderately advanced, with partial skeletonization of the face. Left ribs # 4 through 10 are fractured with "vital reaction"; fractured left 2nd and right 4th ribs without "vital reaction; displaced closed fracture to the right tibia with associated hematoma; abrasions to the flanks and right posterior contusions of the shoulder and knees; cirrhosis; obesity; remote or old fractures are noted and post- operative cholecystectomy. Toxicology is ethanol at 0.115, methanol at 0.093. Scarring is noted consistent with previous surgeries for noted old injuries and gall bladder. The balance of the exam is documented in excellent detail typical for this pathologist.

The pathology narrative is actually titled "field summary" and indicates that the doctor was at the scene after discovery of the body prior to removal. The body was evidently discovered by a cyclist along a rural road roughly 13 feet down a side embankment and in some sagebrush, with slide marks from the roadway to the body location. He surmises that the body location is not the point of original injury, and that the observed trauma is consistent with a pedestrian/motor vehicle incident such as a bumper strike on the right tibia and subsequent impact with hood, windshield, or roof creating the rib trauma. He notes no directional component to the tibia fracture and no directional scrapings on the soles of the shoes. Also, the bleeding and hematomas from the injuries indicate in his opinion that the subject was alive a few hours after the injuries. He is unable to determine if death occurred at the found location, or he was injured elsewhere and dumped there. The cause of death is undetermined "while several possibilities exist" although most likely from the chest trauma or related to it. He also speculates that exposure to a cold environment might have contributed, and yes, hypothermia is possible at any time of year in Wyoming depending on the weather at the time and location, especially at night. If the physician stated that, we must assume he had the local climate at the time in mind in addition to probable duration after injury and prior to death.

All that does induce an amount of uncertainty into the equation, and left to his devices, the doctor certifies it as death from the trauma due to possible pedestrian/motor vehicle accident/injury; manner is undetermined. Here his inexperience as an investigator under medical/legal principles (and lack of accountability from the coroner) fails to help him define things. He cannot be faulted for not being versed in the nuances of deciding manner of death. On top of that, a vehicular-pedestrian collision can very well depend on the standard of interpretation for an individual jurisdiction. Some medical examiners and coroners term all vehicular deaths as accidents, and let the legal and judicial system work out the details and justify whether or not it is a homicide. Others call all deaths at the hands of another a homicide, regardless of circumstance. My opinion is that both are a bit of a cop-out and the coroner bears some responsibility to those involved by regarding the circumstances in detail and making a judgement accordingly. We have had numerous occasions where a person is walking down the lane of travel on a highway at night, dressed in dark clothing and intoxicated, and get struck by a vehicle. If the driver is operating the vehicle legally and is not intoxicated themselves, in most cases the incident is due to no fault of their own but the responsibility of the deceased, and I will rule it accidental. If however, the driver is operating illegally, such as being legally intoxicated, then the driver must be accountable and I may rule a homicide, since but for being intoxicated, the driver may have been able to react appropriately and avoid the collision. When rulings have possible life-altering implications, flat standards do not to me seem appropriate when in the grey areas, especially since there are logical arguments for different perspectives. Making the hard decisions is part of the job. In this case, however, regardless of circumstance, the trauma matches a vehicle collision, and the driver left the scene and failed to render aid. We are pretty far over 50-50 on that based on the available documentation, and should not get confused by the pathologist's numerous speculations on scenarios of circumstance for the sequence of events. He was hit, and left, plainly said. Regardless of the situation for the driver, I would in that circumstance rule a homicide, especially since the injuries may have been survivable. I would not have left this undetermined as a manner of death.

Section IV: The Evolving Eighties

Forensics in the 1980s, like a lot of technology in the period, starts to accelerate in what is available for use in death investigation. DNA, for example, while first isolated as a substance in 1869 by Swiss physician Friedrich Miescher, it took a good century of science to define what exactly we were looking at and how to use it. Watson & Crick finally defined the structure in 1953, the use for profiling was initiated around 1984, and the first U.S. conviction based on that evidence was a Florida rapist in 1987. From there the idea of DNA has gotten public saturation through popular media, although miss-represented. Results do not come back in five minutes like a TV show, and coroner needs always take a back seat at labs to time oriented judicial cases. Our use of DNA takes a minimum of six to eight weeks for results, and while dependable, it is usually a method of last resort as far as identification goes.

Other forensics, like fingerprints, actually had been used as identification by the Chinese well over 2,000 years ago by impression on clay tablets. For the West, their uniqueness to individuals was noted about the 1780s with a suggested use in crime investigation in the 1840s. That application was not approached in an organized manner until around the 1890s, and had been refined and used dependable for the most part, ever since. In the same way, other skills, such as forensic anthropology, forensic dentistry, and general investigative procedures have all in some manner been around for centuries, but have become refined and accepted standards in the last few decades. Even toxicology, which you can see in the 1970s was only at a basic level, had been around for a few thousand years – the Greeks and Romans wrote extensively on the effects and lethality of different poisons and substances. Like a lot of things, that race always historically seems to be a quest between ingestion, or hidden application, and the skill at identifying what was used. One of the first notable recorded autopsies was on Julius Caesar in ancient Rome, and we are still learning the various potentials of that procedure even now. The story never ends, and we try to adapt to new uses and tools as time goes on. As with most things, adaptation in the Western areas like Wyoming, takes a while to catch up to other locales.

Case 26. #80064 (1980) As far as documentation, the 1980s start off in a terrible manner. This is a death in the local hospital emergency room of a 25 year old male on the 7th of January. There is no coroner report, but there is a police department form report that notes the basic demographics of the deceased, and even has space for narratives. Here is what is written: scene description, nothing; body description, nothing; trauma description, nothing. Events of death: location noted, and reported as a possible overdose, autopsy planned for the next day. The physician reports that the deceased had been seen in the ER with pain "under the rib cage" and hyperventilating, given valium, and sent home. No documentation of the time frame from that incident until the death, as the report also leaves the time of the call and death notification blank. The physician doing the autopsy is different from the one doing them in the 70s, and no copy of the autopsy report is in the file. There is an evidence list that vitreous, gastric contents, and bile were collected, and some handwritten notes that do not illuminate the case any further. A toxicology slip indicates the samples were run by the State Public Health Laboratory, and took around six week to get results that a heavy metal and drug screen was negative. In one week the following alcohol levels were received: vitreous – ethanol zero, methanol 0.15, isopropyl 0.01, acetone at 24... gastric contents showed ethanol at zero, methanol 0.05, isopropyl trace, and acetone at 41. That's it for the written record.

Noting at the time that law enforcement officers also served as deputy coroners, EMS personnel, volunteer fire, or other multi-hat duties in the community, that is the source of the police reporting form. Regardless of which hat is being worn, deputy coroner or police officer, the reporting is incredibly poor, whether the perspective of officer or death investigator is used. This case is in the file as undetermined, precisely because of that – we have nowhere to go with a manner of death, although even in this sad state of investigative affairs, there are clues. While the ethanol levels are zero, chronic alcohol abusers will occasionally turn to sources of methanol, commercial and cheap, for the buzz. This can have devastating health effects and in quantity cause death. The acetone levels could be indicative of ketoacidosis that might be seen in some sort of terminal diabetic event, or other health crisis. So it could be a natural or accidental event, just from that minimal information, although we are stretching here and the room for error looms large. We could do research into the vital records area and see what it ended up being certified as, but with no supporting information, we really could not justify that conclusion either. So in the file, undetermined both cause and manner will remain.

If you haven't figured it out already, documentation is one of the often neglected necessary skills of the job. Reports, properly completed in accurate detail, and filed and maintained appropriately, are crucial. In the area of death investigation, cases may be returned to at any time in the future, for trials that take place a year or two after the event, for civil procedures, for cold case consideration, or for information requested by descendants, among other reasons. Memory is too fluid and unreliable without the written documents to refresh and support it. Spend one long afternoon being cross-examined by a skilled defense attorney about an incident that occurred a year ago, and you will appreciate your skill at reporting – or not, and be made to look like a fool in court.

Case 27. #80072 (1980) For this October case of a 20 year old Native American male, we return to the "standard" of the 70s... a death certificate, one page fill-in-the-blank coroner report, autopsy report, and some peripheral information. Luckily we have the appropriately thorough pathologist again, and rely on his narrative for initial information. The cause of death is found to be aspiration pneumonitis with findings consistent with asphyxial death and hypoxia. Blood ethanol is at 0.29, numerous healed scars are present with more recent injuries to the face, head, and hands that are consistent with a recent fist fight. Injuries are consistent also with a blow to the face and resulting countercoup injury of the brain, which the physician states may have rendered the individual unconscious, but that cannot be determined anatomically. The focal subarachnoid hemorrhages are not considered the cause of death. All findings when reviewed are consistent with the conclusion stated, and injuries are also detailed in a body diagram. X-rays show no sign of fractures. The deceased was found on his back with airway and lungs notable for aspirated vomit; petechial hemorrhages are present. The pathologist notes it as undetermined in manner, due to the question of accidental asphyxia from ethanol intoxication versus issues from the fight. He also once again signs the certificate as to those conclusions with a time frame from fight to death as two hours.

The deputy coroner investigator also includes a copy of a statement from the brother of the deceased to a reservation agency officer, describing the circumstances of the fight. All parties were intoxicated at the time, so the narrative is somewhat disjointed. All parties ended up falling down and drinking some more, other than the deceased, whom everyone assumed had just passed out on the floor. After a bit, they discovered him unresponsive, and someone called the police. An unsourced newspaper article in the file does not add any other information other than documenting the basics of the incident.

Without any anatomical definition that the injuries were the fatal factor, one cannot assume a homicide. If the deceased was voluntarily intoxicated, the "passing out" could be attributed to either the alcohol or the blows, or a combination of both, and be accidental positional aspiration asphyxia. Undetermined appears justified in this case.

Case 28. #81011 (1981) Now we get to a good a meaty file for a change of pace. There are two coroner reports, several crime lab documents, an autopsy, death certificates, newspaper articles, a full inquest transcript, photos, miscellaneous handwritten notes and assorted papers. The case involves a 26 year old white male who died of a gunshot wound in late October. The situation is further complicated in that the incident occurred across the county line in Teton County, WY, but the subject was transported and died at a physician's clinic in the town of Dubois in Fremont County. One of the hand-written notes states that "under the law Fremont County does the coroner work and Teton County pays for it and they do the crime scene." Under current Wyoming Statutes [W.S. 7-4-201(d)] "If a coroner determines the injuries which caused the person's death were received in a county other than that in which the body was found, he shall transfer authority for the investigation and inquest to the coroner for that county" and [e] "The expense and costs of conducting the investigation or holding the inquest shall be paid by the county in which the injuries were received." That seems pretty clear, although it depends on the working relationship between the counties, as the coroner of originating scene jurisdiction retains the authority to decide if an autopsy or inquest is needed. It is not unusual with sick patients, wandering hunters or recreationists, and scattered medical providers and facilities, to have an individual be sick or injured in one county and end up elsewhere when they died. This generally works well within the state, but not always if a subject is transferred to a more specialized medical facility out of state. Sometimes the laws are different in other state jurisdictions, and they often do not really care about the law in Wyoming, and do their own thing. Here for all intents and purposes, it appears Teton and Fremont did a good joint investigation, with extensive documentation, the best we have seen so far in these cases.

Also keep in mind that at this time, the coroner and his deputies are all "occasional" employees that have other jobs and responsibilities – there is no full time staff for the office of the coroner. Sometimes their working skills coincide with death investigation (fire, EMS, law enforcement, funeral director) and sometimes are totally unrelated and dependent on whatever field experience or training they have gained.

First we have the initial responding deputy coroner report. The form used has now changed to a booklet that includes space for narratives; Handwritten input gives the basic demographics of the deceased, and indicates the call came in from the physician's office around 10:00 p.m. on the evening of the 31st of October, 1981. Present are the deputy coroner, a Fremont sheriff's deputy, and a Teton County sheriff investigator. The scene is not described other than noting it is at the physician's office in Dubois, but that is not the originating scene of the event. The originating scene description is a basic location noted as such that I could probably locate it today if you knew who was living where along a particular road and area in Teton county at that time. Body and trauma description are adequate and include entrance and exit wound details by rib numbers and measurements from body features. The event narrative is limited, but at this point we are at the initial investigation. No witnesses are noted, but next of kin information is detailed. Clothing is described and $75.10 in cash is noted. Body diagram templates are used to indicate entrance and exit, and other contusions and abrasions. The original toxicology slips are taped to this report, which would have been received later from the State lab, and indicate the blood alcohol was 0.21 and positive for cannabinoids, noting "no instrumentation available for its confirmation". A note on the back of the form gives the vehicle make and plate number, as well as the make, model, and serial numbers of the available weapons. All in all, for the times, a pretty decent initial report.

The next coroner report has handwriting from the coroner and coroner investigator (I recognize both) and possibly other handwriting. In other words, this form was used to collect assorted information as it was obtained. Narratives all have some notation, such as "scene description – not examined, body removed" which would be fine for an investigator that did not witness the originating scene. It is noted as a suspicious death, narrative of the injury description is included plus identification of the pathologist, a witness, and the decedent's brother is given. Under the incident narrative it states, "see Teton County Sheriff's Office investigation report", which is fine. Location of death and pronouncement are listed, and the names of the inquest jurors and detailed next of kin. Evidence collected and clothing are detailed, disposition of the body, and summary of the inquest verdict. A summary supplemental sheet is included with a short narrative relayed from the Teton County investigators as to originating circumstance, another listing of photos taken, and another list of more detail on evidence collected and photos.

Lab reports in addition to the toxicology noted above are in the file. These include gunshot residue testing, results of firearms and ammunition/bullet testing, and clothing analysis. Range of fire for the injury was indeterminate, and the weapon was found functional and not prone to accidental discharge. Chain of custody procedures are observed that were standard for the time.
Autopsy report is detailed and well documented along forensic principles, noting the entrance, exit, and path of injury, fatal internal hemorrhage, and

absence of any other physical or medical issues. In one odd note, the pathologist records that, as far as the clothing goes, a set of brown coveralls were removed in Dubois, but redressed by investigators prior to autopsy. This may have been to orient the pathways but probably should have been avoided as the more you handle bulk evidence, the increased possibility trace evidence is lost, or original patterns altered. If removal was necessary at the start, they should have been left off and packaged for the lab analysis as is. Several pages are given to the description and detail of the clothing and patterns. The expected detail of external and internal features and injury are included, the my review would indicate injuries consistent with the opinion in the reports that the subject died on his way to Dubois, as the amount of internal bleeding from the gunshot would have been fatal fairly quickly.

Photos include Polaroids and 35 mm prints of the body, clothing, bullet and wound holes (clothing and body), and damage to internal organs. All of which can be deciphered in conjunction with the narrative descriptions by the investigators and pathologist.

The inquest was held in Dubois about a month after the incident, and handwritten notes are included as to the witness list, testimony, and selected jury. A copy of the transcript, exactly as it would have been submitted to the Clerk of District Court, is in the file. A summary of the testimony is as follows:

Initially, the coroner convenes by procedure and is the 'moderator' and inquisitor in the process. He notes the basic circumstances and situation as to originating in Teton County and the relationship to Fremont. He then proceeds with the witnesses. He notes the proceedings are being recorded.

First is the pathologist, who basically goes through the details and findings of the autopsy and the cause of death. In response to questions he states survivability of about 30 minutes, probably the subject was knocked off his feet and unable to ambulate, but able to talk for a while. He notes no powder tattooing on the clothing. He notes the toxicology results and meaning for the jury.

Second is a woman from Jackson, Wyoming, who with her husband was working as a hunting outfitter (guide) in the area of the incident. She relates her contact with the brothers on the evening of the shooting when they approached her about renting horses. Both are described as "extremely intoxicated". She also identifies the surviving brother in the room, although did not know their individual names.

Third is another hunter that was camped in the immediate area, close enough to hear "hollering" and then two gunshots. He is able to define generally a time frame in the evening (8 p.m.), sequence of the hollering (15 to 20 minutes) and the gunshots (less than a minute apart) in his opinion. He notes he heard a vehicle leave by their campsite roughly a half hour to 45 minutes later. Deputies arrived to question him around 1:00 in the morning.

Fourth is another hunter from the same camp of the previous witness, who describes the same basic time frames and circumstances noted by his hunting partner.

Fifth is another hunter who was on his own and sleeping in his jeep at the time of the shots, within visible distance of the brother's pickup. He describes a similar time frame and notes the first shot woke him up. He also describes the gunshot interval as less than a minute, and offers that the pickup truck fired up and left in his opinion "a short span", maybe "about five minutes" after the second shot. Deputies reached him for interview around 2:00 in the morning.

Sixth is a National Park Ranger that had contact with the brothers earlier in that day around 5:00 p.m. while he was patrolling with another Ranger. They noted probable intoxication and erratic driving, and escorted the brothers to their camp area and told them to stay there. The deceased was the driver at that time and appeared the most intoxicated, with the other brother "in control of himself", so they had him drive. The brothers said they were going to try and find some horses to rent, at which the Rangers advised they stay in camp until sober. He noted two rifles in the pickup, which were checked and unloaded before they let them proceed (lever action was unloaded but a bolt action had one in the chamber). They had another patrolman in the area keep an eye out for the vehicle, which she did see, but noted it was being driven "in a confident manner" and she had no reason to stop it.

Seventh is the deputy coroner investigator, who witnessed the autopsy and took photos, which are detailed as exhibits to the jury. He describes the evidence collected, chain of custody, and lab reports of analysis received. He notes that the negative findings of gunshot residue from the parties involved is not as significant since rifles are involved rather than handguns. He details standard research at the time regarding evidence of discharge distances and residue.

Eighth is the lead investigator for the Teton County Sheriff's Office, who starts by detailing the sequence of notification and response. He details his interview with the brother of the deceased. According to the brother, the deceased had pulled a rifle out of the pickup when it discharged. He was not facing his brother at the time but away and facing the fire, but saw him when he turned at the shot, noting the barrel of the rifle was pointed away from him. He walked over to his brother to grab the gun away, and when he did, thought that the butt of the weapon hit the truck and discharged. The investigator describes the interview testimony as "extremely hazy" with a good deal of uncertainty. The witness notes his brother lay on the ground "for a while" and he walked back to the fire. The investigator states the witness thought it took some time before he realized his brother was shot, and when he did, threw him into the truck and took off for Dubois, which he thought was closer than Jackson. The investigator did not think the witness was intoxicated at the time of the interview, which was some time later after the incident. He notes he went to the scene the next day, and attended the autopsy. Teton County was in charge of impounding and examination of the involved vehicle, which had a considerable amount of blood most likely from the transport. He notes examination of the weapons which were in the custody of the city police. At that time, both the 30-30 lever action and 30-06 bolt action had rounds chambered. The investigator declined to discuss the nature of firing the weapons or possible scenarios involved as he was not a gun expert. He describes the general overview of the originating scene.

When asked by the coroner if there is anything else he would like to relate to the jury, the Teton investigator notes that city police related that the brother had stated he stopped at a gas station when coming into town, as he was almost out of fuel, and to get directions. The investigator contacted the workers at the station, who noted the brother came in, laid a $20 bill on the counter for gas. When the individual found out the nearest hospital was in Riverton, Lander, or Jackson, he stated his brother had been shot. The attendant called the physician to meet them and arranged for another worker to lead the vehicle to the doctor. The brother left the money on the counter, did not get gas, and left to follow the employee. At the doctor's office the worker described him as "visibly shaken and crying", stating "he should have never been messing with the guns", and, "it's all my fault." The investigator also noted the vehicle in question registered three quarters full, but had two tanks. He also adds further information that the involved weapon appeared to be the 30-06 and when he asked the brother why there was another round in the chamber, he responded that it must have been automatic due to his military and hunting training.

Ninth is a Teton County Sheriff's Deputy who was one of that office's first responders responsible for securing the scene and interviewing the nearby hunters. He describes the circumstances of the interviews and search of the originating scene, described as using a diagram of the area to detail what was found to the jury. He notes several areas described as the site of "scuffles" with certain evidence apparent in the ground that had been previously muddy and froze overnight. This included foot tracks, tire tracks, imprints of clothing weave in the ground, and assorted debris and trash that may or may not have been associated with the most recent occupants. There were cartridges and a bullet that were recovered and locations defined. Distances to the surrounding camps are given. He notes some evidence was recovered the next day also when a metal detector was used to find the bullet and casings. The jury asks the witness questions to orient things in relation to previous testimony. No blood was seen on the ground in the area, which was searched after being gridded for documentation.

Tenth, the jury recalls the previous hunter witness to have him note on the map and diagram the location of his jeep in relation to everything else, and the location of the involved vehicle and direction it left.

Eleventh to be called is the brother of the deceased. His lawyer introduces himself and notes that the witness is present in response to the coroner subpoena, but declines to testify. The coroner confirms that he is invoking his constitutional rights (which is entirely appropriate) for the record, then calls a 15 minute recess so the jury can review reports and documentation.

When reconvened, the coroner notes that the jury was sworn in over the body so they could examine it as required by law. This actually is more of a tradition from when the jurors and the coroner were the only death investigators, long ago, and is not actually statutorily required by current law, nor was it at this time. It does tend to impress the gravity of the situation to the jury, however, and is not prohibited. More a matter of choice on the part of the coroner. The jury then recalls several witnesses.

First, the Park Ranger is recalled to detail the position of weapons when he stopped the vehicle. He notes the lever action as being next to the driver, barrel to the floor. The bolt action 30-06 was in the passenger side, same position. Second the coroner investigator is recalled to bring out the overalls for detailed jury examination. He is asked about the firearms and ammunition, but declines to answer as he did not examine them. Third, the Teton investigator is recalled to further explain positioning on the scene map and which gun was reported by witness interviews to have been the involved firearm. He also is asked to explain some of the wording and conclusions of the lab reports on the firearms. He notes that the weapons testing could not ascertain that the bullet recovered from the scene was fired from the specific lever action rifle, although it was a size common to that caliber rather than the bolt action 30-06. He also notes that range testing on the 30-30 determined that powder residue ceased to be observed if the distance was greater than 1 ½ to 2 feet. Jurors then asked about the contents of the known vehicle, and confirmed the presence of blood in the vehicle but absence at the scene. He was asked, if the victim lay on the ground, why there was no blood at the scene. The investigator responded that it would only be speculation, but perhaps most of the blood was on the interior of the coveralls until position of the deceased in the truck enabled it to come out during transport. He was asked again about aspects of the interview with the brother, and to describe how the casings eject from the weapons, which the investigator did try several times but noted it was not a scientific test. He notes that they did test at the lab to see if the 30-06 would discharge when being struck, noted no issues with that or any other malfunction, but the investigator expands to say the lab qualified "that anything is possible" and they won't commit to saying it could not have happened. The investigator closes with "and neither will I."

The coroner then clears with the jury as to whether they feel they have enough to render a verdict, and they respond yes. He notes the witnesses will remain during deliberations in case they wish to recall. An unspecified time later, the coroner reads the verdict: "that [said person] came to his death at [location] on [date] by hemorrhage from a gunshot wound inflicted by [the brother] under suspicious circumstances." No manner of death is given by the jury.

To finish off the file, there are some assorted handwritten notes that do not add any significant information, most stuff being documented in the reports. Two newspaper clippings are here, one noting the original incident and pending inquest, the other noting the basics of testimony and conclusion of the inquest. In that one the coroner notes it now goes to the Teton County prosecutor to decide what to do next with the evidence. There is no record in the file as to what did happen on that. Working copies of the death certificate are in the file, and the final one also. It is signed by both the pathologist and coroner, cause being "right hemopneumonothorax [sic], massive intrapleural, intrapulmonary, and intraperitoneal hemorrhage" due to "gunshot wound right chest, lung, liver, right kidney". Manner is listed as undetermined. A note on the file folder indicates the original inquest transcript went to the Clerk of District Court in late April 1982, with a copy to the Teton County Coroner.

At this point it should be noted again that we are indeed fortunate to have all this documentation. At the time, the county coroner had no office provided, and he worked that function out of his home. That was still the case when I first started as a deputy in 1998. Thus at this time, files and reports could be in his home, or at the funeral home (where he worked), or at a fire station (where he volunteered), or at a coroner deputy's home, or at the coroner investigator's workplace at the local police department where he worked. This situation is probably the primary reason we are missing much of the documentation from the period. The coroner of the time actually stored skeletal remains from some cases in his basement, which might seem weird (and was to me), but there you go. Part of my job over the years was to collect a lot of this from various storage spots, like the county vehicle maintenance shop, and organize and consolidate the files so we could create an accurate database of what we have. Files go back to 1885 and currently number around 7,800 cases, so a lot of information is there, but so are a lot of holes. Now we have an office, storage, secure file room, and other amenities not available in the past, and policies to maintain them. Filing and documentation are relatively modern skill applications that need no justification, even if it is a boring subject, and it cannot be over-emphasized their importance for modern death investigators.

As to the manner of death, even with all the documentation, there is legitimate questions as to whether this is a homicide or accident. Natural obviously not, and suicide is highly unlikely with the wound track and description of evidence and event. This also illustrates the issue an investigator may run into with the meanings of manner of death. The questions on exact circumstance are obscured by the probable intoxication, trauma of the incident experience, and lack of a 'smoking gun'. Statements such as "it's all my fault" in a traumatic incident can mean anything from a basic confession to just an innocent off-hand guilt reaction to not having defused an incident or circumstance. We cannot definitively exclude an accidental event, and behaviors under such circumstances really have no typical response. A homicide is also possible through carelessness, as intent has nothing to do with it for the coroner as far as manner of death. The investigation appears very thorough with the use of most of the tools that would have been available at the time. Just as in some modern cases, with all the documentation, evidence, and analysis and testimony, sometimes it remains undetermined.

One final note on inquests, it is the coroner's job to make sure the jury understands it should come to a conclusion, not only on the cause of death, but also the manner as well. They are there and active in the immediate appraisal of the testimony and evidence, and if they also come up with undetermined, then we could perhaps feel better that there was no other choice. By the way that the jury phrased their cause of death as being suspicious, that might imply that they were unsure as well and leaning towards undetermined, but that is only supposition and it should have been spelled out in the moment if that was the case.

Case 29. #82031 (1982) Now we come to another unique set of circumstances where the coroner will end up with an undetermined case. This involves missing persons. There are some cases in the files where the coroner's office has a wealth of materials and information, due to our involvement in searches, investigations, or other aspects as an assisting agency to law enforcement, if they have reasonable suspicion of a death, but have no body. Technically, it is not a case for us until there is a body, as there is no verification of death, but at times there are strong indications even without the body, and death investigators have the skills that are often useful to other investigative agencies during the process. So we are brought in on a case as an advisory agency, and current policy is to document everything as if there was a body and case, so that subsequent progress has a background in the file. Some of these types of cases have long and extensive history, and are returned to periodically as a cold case investigation. This sort of documentation is also handy for comparisons if unidentified remains are found, or inquiries from outside the county are received on a body found that might match one of Fremont's missing persons.

The other circumstance is when a Court of jurisdiction declares a person dead, even without a body. This is called a presumptive death. When individuals have been missing and are believed dead, next-of-kin may petition the District Court for an Order of Presumptive Death. The Court will weigh the facts presented, and may issue such an order. The order will designate an effective date of death. This procedure is frequently used in cases where a body is never recovered, or when a person has been missing over a set number of years with no trace. Legal counsel on behalf of the family must provide all documents that support Court's declaration. Upon the ruling of the Court that an individual is declared dead, an order is issued, and a certified copy of that order must be presented to the coroner in order for a death certificate to be issued. When such an order is received by the office, it is directed to an investigator who performs a search to ensure that the decedent has not already been reported to the coroner, or that it is a case we have assisted on in the past. If not, the investigator prepares a case file. The death certificate is then completed with State Vital Records through a registrar. A date of death should appear on the court order, and if not, the date of the order serves as the date of death. The attorney or family should then be sent a letter advising them that the Certificate has been filed.

That is the circumstance in this case, that of a white female that was 34 years old at the time she went missing in 1975. Seven years have passed, and the mother of the deceased filed with District Court for the declaration.

There are no copies of the justifications presented to the Court, but we must assume they were adequate to the judge in the case. We have the court order on file, and the date of the order is used as the date of death with the age of 41 listed on the death certificate. The spouse is listed on the record also, with "(unknown if living)" noted after the name. Was he missing too? A search of the database shows a male with a very similar name, slight difference in the last name spelling but same first and middle initials that died in 1998 and would have been a similar age to the missing subject. However, this man is recorded as having married someone else two years prior to the female's disappearance, an unlikely circumstance in a small community where bigamy would have been obvious. Most likely this is a coincidental similarity of a common last name that has variable spellings. We will have to assume that the Court knew what it was doing. While no manner or cause is listed on the copy of the certificate in the file other than a reference to the court file number, in these cases they would be both entered as undetermined. There is just enough information in the case file to make it a curious case with unanswered questions.

Case 30. #82094 (1982) Here is an unusual case of an unidentified fetus that was found by work crews while unclogging a residential sewer line. A report of the clog was made to the city in late August, with the original work order memo by city operations in the file. The coroner report notes the complaint and location of the find, which the city crew placed in a box and took to the city shop to turn over to authorities. The particular sewer line is recorded as being accessed by and serving 10 separate residences in the area. The remains were photographed (photo prints are in the file) and then taken to the local pathologist for examination. He stated that decomposition was too advanced to determine a cause of death. Remains are described as about 10 inches long, and of unknown age or sex. A small hand drawn diagram of the city area is in the report, and a list of the residences and owners applicable to the sewer line. A supplemental page records the reporting party as one of the homes involved, and that all residents were interviewed by police. One resident noted there had been a party at his location the previous week, but was not aware of any persons who "would have been in a position or situation" to result in the incident. The included photos do not reveal anything in particular other than the remains are human and decomposed. A newspaper clipping documents only the initial investigation. A copy of a police index card file notes the case as a possible homicide with no details, and is stamped "closed" two months later. An actual city blueprint of the area involved mapping the sewer lines is also in the file.

Four pages of handwritten notes are present. In reviewing those, some additional detail is found. Hospital emergency rooms were evidently contacted for any cases of vaginal bleeding or delivery complications without birth. Someone determined an estimate of second trimester age, 18 to 24 weeks at most, but there is no attributed source for that information. The final document in the file is a subpoena to the investigator in his capacity as a police officer to appear before District Court as a witness in the matter of the State versus one of the residents noted as owner of one of the attached sewer lines. While there is no record of exactly what the proceedings were for other than the matter of the discovered remains, it is noted that the subject in question was the person who originally reported the blockage to the city.

On another note, remember that under current Wyoming statutes, stillbirths and miscarriages are not coroner cases, and a birth has to be viable and take a breath to be alive. If not technically alive, there is no death, thus not a coroner case. Medically and by current court standards, 21 weeks is considered to be the minimum viable gestation, even with advanced medical attention that has some less than that as surviving. Those cases are still pretty rare and no court currently has seen any need to change the standard, and I will not get into the political or philosophical aspects of that question. Those instances do not even get a standard death certificate, but a stillbirth registry signed by the physician. In this case, based on available information, this may not even have been technically a coroner case, although we do get such found remains occasionally because the coroner has the best resources to determine pre-birth age, such as autopsy. Once that is completed, disposition is dependent on the findings. A good forensic pathologist can often determine if the lungs ever inflated in a body less than full birth term, or establish a reasonable gestation time frame of development to the range of miscarriage, or even a reasonable cause of the issue or death. This situation was complicated by the decomposition, but it would have been interesting to see the results of a modern forensic exam with the tools available now. That might have defined the case even better. In any case, this one remains listed with both manner and case in the database as undetermined, since the parameters are borderline.

Case 31. #83055 (1983) This case from January of 1983 has serious documentation issues, as it only has a police department report, EMS narratives, and some miscellaneous notes – no coroner documentation whatsoever. The label on the file states the death of this 25 year old white male as "suicide/homicide".

The police report originates on the day of the call to a residence, but states the individual was in critical condition and air lifted to a hospital in Casper. There are no medical records or indications of the exact date and time of death at that location. When officers arrived, several other individuals were present, and the victim was found to have stable vitals but suffering from a gunshot wound in the forehead area between the eyes. The weapon was on the floor. Interviews with those present reported suicide ideations by the victim via telephone call. Friends responded to the location and found the front entry locked. One of the individuals went around to the rear and gained entry. When he let the others in, he had the gun in his hand, which he then put down and called police. That individual stated that when he gained entry, he reportedly found the rifle across the victim's torso and pointed towards the head as he was lying face up on the kitchen floor. No shots were heard by the responding friends, and all of them, including the victim, had been involved in a disturbance at a local bar earlier in the evening. Evidence logged includes a .22 cal. single shot rifle, spent casing found near the body, and several loose rounds in the area. All parties reported in a "highly emotional state" in police reports. An evidence sheet from the detective notes a baseball bat recovered that had blood on it with the note "process for gunpowder".

An attached police report notes that informants stated a female talking about having been there and being forced to witness the event, after which she left "in hopes he would die." The officer notes that due to dealings with this supposed witness in the past her statements "are subject to the highest scrutiny" and in consideration of her mental instability and "knack for lying with every breath", the validity of such scenario is in doubt. However, he notes, it does open the possibility of a homicide and that the female is quite capable of such an act. A note from another officer records a conversation with the ER physician who stated his surprise that there were no powder burns on the skin or near the wound, was surprised at the damage from a 22, and noted x-rays showed a bullet still lodged at the back of the head, which also surprised the physician for a 22. An attached EMS trip sheet documents basic findings and treatment at the scene, also notes an entry above the nose between the eyes, and no exit.

There is a copy of a handwritten letter from a male in jail to another female, evidently a biker who is scheduled to finish his sentence at the State Hospital in Evanston, WY (usually done for mental issues), describing the ton of money he was coming into and how he put out a "hit" on another female's "old man" and want to know if it is worth the price. Unfortunately, none of the names in this particular letter match any of those listed in the police reports for this shooting, so we do not know if this is related, or just miss-filed. Some telexes are also in the file from the Wyoming Division of Criminal Investigation regarding the letter writer as far as records in the system.

A couple of phone message notes document words on the crazy ex-girlfriend and previous suicide threats by the victim. The EMS personnel narratives of the event do not add anything useful to the sequence of events, and basically just record the arrival and treatment and transport of the victim.

First, to what we do know. We have an individual with reported history of suicide threats that is out at a bar with friends and gets into some sort of ruckus and leaves. Then later he phones one of those friends and says he is going to commit suicide. The friends arrive at his residence and one of them gets in the back and shows up at the front door with the rifle. This may sound suspicious, but the time frame and lack of report of a gunshot probably indicates he secured the weapon out of habit (many people, even family members or officers do that automatically without thinking at scenes, even though for investigation purposes they shouldn't). Then we have additional information that might point to a homicide that is either not directly connected in the reports, or considered dubious by the officers. The opinion of the ER physician about lack of powder burn or residue may be of concern, but is neither tested that we know of, and there is no autopsy report, if one was even done. The doctor's opinion of the 22 not exiting can be discarded, as I have seen numerous times when a 22 does not exit. It all depends on the angle, load, age, and other factors of the weapon and ammunition, as well as the skull density and physical attributes of the victim – and sometimes bullets just behave in an atypical manner. Second, we have no medical verification the person ever actually died of the wound or when, other than at some point the file was marked as a possible suicide/homicide.

Here is where the duties of law enforcement versus a coroner investigator can conflict if the individual is doing double-duty as both. While both agencies should treat any such case as a homicide initially, that is only to insure consistency of investigation and procedure regardless of outcome. Techniques are often the same for both coroner and law enforcement, but the perspective is vastly different for approach. The law enforcement investigator is geared towards criminality, and while that may be a factor in a death, the coroner investigator should be geared toward cause and manner of death. A subtle difference, but a critical one when it comes to perspective and objectivity. We are to be the independent set of eyes on a scene that avoids a rush to judgement, and avoids trying to make the evidence fit a particular outcome desired. Allow for all possibilities, but go only by the facts as known and avoid conspiracy theories. The coroner is not to be a subset or adjunct to the law enforcement view, but independent. There have often been times when my rulings have not been to the liking of law enforcement, but the facts are what they are, if a proper investigation is completed.

And while we can and do obtain and use law enforcement reports as part of a coroner investigation, that is only one factor in a judgement. Without the independent coroner perspective and summaries, even if done after the fact in a case where the individual died elsewhere, too much is unknown. Here even the police reports are incomplete as far as follow up, evidence testing, and connecting the dots as to relation or significance of various factors. Are we really less than 50-50 on the basis for a conclusion? I think this one should be undetermined mainly on the lack of information rather than on the information presented. Too much is unanswered.

Case 32. #85053 (1985) This case of a 30 year old Native American male presents an interesting challenge to investigators. The location is off a rural road in a high desert environment, and immediate scene is an abandoned automobile that was off the side of the road about 200 yards, resting on its top. The vehicle had been there for several years and used for 'target practice' and shot at, riddled with bullet holes of varying ages, with a majority showing rust, along with the general degradation and settling of the vehicle carcass. Two people in the area found a body in January in the semi-crushed passenger compartment, lying on the roof surface that was against the ground. The body is partially skeletonized and mummified, "badly decomposed", with the initial responding officers declining to identify as male or female. Those officers secured the scene and called for the coroner in addition to sheriff's office and Reservation investigators. This is a case of multiple jurisdictions due to the unknown nature of the extent of the scene or related locations.

The coroner report gives basic demographics of the deceased, based on eventual identification through dental records. The remains are more recent than the vehicle found in from the condition of the body and the known rough time frame that the vehicle has been there. Scene description is only basic, but there is a wealth of photographic documentation of the scene, body, and recovery process. Body description is basic and positioning is noted. Trauma is initially noted as "decomposition and animal mutilation". An autopsy is arranged on the remains, and most of the other information is noted as "unknown".

The sheriff's office incident report is included in the file, which details the circumstances of discovery and persons involved. A narrative is attached recording interviews with individuals who suspect the deceased may be a missing relative. The subject was last seen mid-August the previous year, which is consistent with the condition of the remains found as far as time frame and environment. At that time, seven people were in a pickup that got stuck in the area, and reportedly, six (all accounted for) walked into town for assistance and left the one with the truck. When they returned, he was gone. This story was related independently by another witness from that event. A note later in the report indicates the dental identification. The report of the second officer on the scene is basically the same as the first, and photos of the suspected identity are attached to the original report, with copies seen here.

A copy of a police booking record is included with individual identification information and indicating fingerprints are on file, but in this case, there is nothing to compare them to due to the condition of the remains. Full body x-rays were completed at the local hospital, with the radiologist reporting an estimate of 40 years in age, no metallic densities noted such as bullets or shrapnel other than several coins in the pants pocket. He also notes "no obvious trauma", but details a possible old healed fracture to the right fibula, missing left ribs #12, 11, 10, and 9; and several other artifacts that could possibly be old trauma or related to the decomposition process. Several handwritten notes, unsigned, do not add to the information in the official reports.

An autopsy report is included, this being the first of the undetermined cases completed by the forensic pathology services we currently use out of Loveland Colorado. Procedures and documentation are therefore consistent with modern standards, which represent a critical advance in the investigation process. The autopsy was completed the day after the body was found, in the presence of the coroner and the director of the Wyoming crime lab out of Cheyenne, WY. The pathologist details the condition, features, absence of trauma or defensive injuries, animal and insect activities and damage, possible soft tissue hemorrhage in the occipital area of the remaining scalp. Examination is unable to reveal a definitive cause or manner of death, although the soft tissue damage noted may suggest the manner as either accidental or by "foul play". He further details what changes are probably ante versus post mortem.

A newspaper article in the file reports the identification by dental comparison, notes that the parties that found the body were rabbit hunting in the area, and that the FBI was also part of the investigation, which would make sense as the land was reservation jurisdiction. The death certificate notes the date found as the date of death, and cause and manner as undetermined, although in "other significant conditions" there is "possible blow to the back of the head".

As previously noted, the photo documentation is extensive, with both prints and slides available for review. The originating scene and condition prior to recovery is seen with the body in position. Then the process included a recovery of the entire vehicle by crane to a flatbed trailer, after which it was covered with a tarp and transported to a location where it could be examined in detail. The scene is also documented after all removals, which is consistent with proper photography for investigations. With such decent photo records, we have an excellent supplement to any of the written records.

While the coroner report is still not as extensive as we would complete in modern day records, with all the other reports there is a decent documentation of the case. The dental records and written report of the identification comparison is not included, but the conclusion is noted officially. There is the analysis of a certified forensic pathologist for the first time in an undetermined case. As far as the original circumstances at the time of disappearance, there are a lot of variables of what may have happened. After all, seven people bouncing around in a pickup truck on rural roads in the area, could have been plenty of opportunity for accidental injury, and there is no notation as to the admitted presence or absence of intoxication at that time. If the story is true that all but the deceased wandered off, there are also numerous scenarios as to how and why he crawled into the abandoned vehicle. Once there, he would not have been seen easily even if searched for, and depending on the circumstances of the joy ride in the country, not even missed for some time. There could have been natural or medical issues unknown, environmental exposure, or an accidental head injury whose effects accumulated slowly. There could have been some incident of assault that contributed to the death. There could be any number of things that would leave no trace after a period of months. While a good deal can be eliminated to a reasonable degree, we still have too many avenues of possible manner and cause. This is finally a case where we see that all the best procedures of the day were employed, much as we would have done now, and the answer would still be undetermined for manner and cause. Sometimes it just is what it is, and the answers are elusive.

Case 33. #85012 (1985) This next instance is that of an 11 month old infant that was found unresponsive in April by the parents, who called for assistance. The initial responding police officer noted that the child was cold, discolored, and with initial rigor in the extremities. CPR was not initiated due to obvious signs of death.

The coroner report is once again not very detailed, but does note the scene exhibited a large amount of evidence of alcohol consumption. The parents report hearing the child move at 0500 and being found at 0800. They also note that the child was being treated with over the counter medications for chicken pox, which had already been seen in other children in the home. The report notes "evidence of chicken pox" in the trauma description. All present in the home are noted, and indicate four other adults in addition to the two parents and five other children. No recent medical attention or examinations of the deceased are noted, other than the parents saying there had been none.

The police report gives better narrative detail, including all investigative personnel and EMS responders. Over the counter medications in use reported to be children's Tylenol and calamine lotion, and no CPR was attempted by any of the adults in the home. The time frame of three hours is the same in this report as to what was stated by witnesses as last time noted alive to time of discovery. A form for 'investigative guidelines for suspected child abuse or neglect' is attached to the law enforcement report. It describes a chicken pox rash, notes the body was found in a crib, and also states the autopsy revealed the state of decomposition is at a level that exceeds the reported time frame by witnesses.

The autopsy is again by a local pathologist who follows the basic forensic procedures but is not certified as such. He notes the history of chicken pox, advanced decomposition and possible acute "bacterial tracheitis and asphyxia" but lists the final conclusion as "no anatomic cause of death found". The infant is described as well-nourished and absent of trauma. The interpretive comment details note the trachea was "virtually completely occluded" with additional bronchial involvement but he is hesitant to define that as a cause for sure because of the decomposition state. He specifically states the condition of the body is not consistent with the time frame of the witness statements. Toxicology was completed and showed the acetaminophen levels at mid-therapeutic range, with no other notable substances.

Here it is important to keep in mind that the Varicella vaccine for chicken pox was not introduced until 1995, ten years after this case. Even at that, the recommended age for the first shot is not until at 12 to 15 months, so even in modern times this infant would not yet have received it. Prior to the introduction of the vaccine, according to the CDC, yearly averages were 10,500 cases that required hospitalization with 100 to 150 deaths per year. With dissemination and application of the vaccine, after 2001 the death rate averaged less than 20 per year in the U.S. While most remember this illness as one of inconvenience, serious side effects can include dehydration, secondary bacterial infections of the skin and elsewhere, pneumonia, brain infections, sepsis and toxic shock syndrome, and death. Lack of a visit to a physician or the emergency room is not evidence of abuse – most families just worked their way through it as the pox worked its way through a family and children. Also, poor housekeeping or evidence of adult alcohol use is not definitive for neglect without corroborating evidence, and the child is described as in otherwise good condition. The fact that the adults did not notice the death within the time frame they thought is also not necessarily neglect. If there was some of the known bacterial complications from the virus, issues would have been masked by the general illness in an infant that cannot express specific difficulty, and that factor also clouds the time frame of decomposition. Fever and environmental factors in the home, such as temperature or blankets, which are not described in the reports, might accelerate decomposition and rigor, although still the stated three hour window is unlikely. Photos included in the file appear as the pathologist described. A rough estimate for time of death might however fit within the time frame from when an infant would normally have been put in the crib the evening before.

This is a case of where the pathologist did not do a bad job, but the experience and knowledge of a forensic specialist might have defined the death with more certainty, especially above the 50-50 level that is undetermined. In the absence of any other stated evidence, I suspect this was a natural death, with no evidence of homicide or accident, due to chicken pox and the complications known to exist with that illness. I disagree with calling this undetermined.

Case 34. #87073 (1987) This is the death of a 21 year old Native American male from a gunshot wound to the chest, reported in mid-February. This case occurred on the reservation and also was investigated by the FBI.

The coroner report scene description is simple, described as "living room of residence (messy)", but does note a 22 cal. Ruger single-6 pistol was reportedly lying across the room and picked up by a responding officer. Photos prior to movement and distances involved would have been real handy in this analysis. Distance of the weapon would have to be accounted for if beyond a reasonable space from the body for a suicide or accidental shooting. Without witness statements or interviews, location is unknown as to if at an appropriate distance, or moved prior to responder arrival as accounted for by relatives. This would be a critical bit of evidence to lock down in an investigation, as well as document in the reporting. The body description conflicts a bit as it describes the deceased as lying in the hallway between the bathroom, bedroom and living room. Included photos do not show the overall scene as they should, so proper orientation is not possible. Wound location is described as about 2 ½ inches above the left nipple in the chest. The trauma description is a bit better as it notes the bullet had passed through the coat (by the photos, a zipper-front dark medium weight garment) and t-shirt, and had also hit a zipper on the coat pocket. "Bullet hole in chest is not round." The weapon was collected by officers, and it is stated that there was no other blood in the scene other than the immediate clothing of the victim. Additional statements are recorded by those at the residence at the time, in which two women at the scene reported they were outside the home getting a vehicle ready to leave when they heard a shot. They went back inside and found the deceased, who had been the only one in the residence at that time. A small diagram shows a five chamber cylinder with a note "hammer setting on one shot fired." The witnesses note the deceased had been target shooting that morning and showed the deputy the target. A blood alcohol toxicology slip shows the level of the deceased at 0.16, or at twice the legal limit.

An x-ray report describes no unusual pathology or injury, but notes the location of a possible bullet in the right chest, also a possible old healed fracture of the left humerus. Autopsy is completed again by the local pathologist. He notes the individual died of a gunshot wound to the left chest, heart, and right lung; wound is left to right, slightly anterior to posterior and approximately 90° to the long axis of the body. Immediate cause of death is the cardiac injury. He states the wound is from an indeterminate range, and the bullet was recovered. As usual for this physician, there is considerable detail in the report as to injury, path, and other aspects of the examination as there should be.

Photos are included of the weapon name and serial number, but not the cartridges in the chambers or total weapon view. Photos of the outside coat impact area and t-shirt are not of sufficient detail to gauge range of fire, and it is unknown if they were tested for residue. The chest wound is without scale, but appears oval consistent with the angle described by the pathologist and evidence of the clothing. Impact with the metal zipper would have affected the shape of the bullet to some degree, but there are no photos of the recovered projectile.

Cause of death in this case is in no doubt, but the death certificate only notes "pending investigation" and the file has "possible suicide" written on the folder. Obtaining the final certificate from State vital records might show how this was eventually ruled, as the records are never left pending. The FBI reports would also provide better interviews most likely with those present at the event, and reveal if the weapon was ever tested for fingerprints. Personally, absent any evidence to the contrary, my opinion is that this could very well have been an accident due to careless gun handling while intoxicated. The angle of the injury would be extremely atypical for a suicide, and without any other evidence, homicide is possible but also less likely. While the living room is described as "messy", what little is seen does not indicate any conflict, struggle, or unusual disturbances. Even a messy room looks different between a plain poor housekeeping mess and one in which there was a disturbance. Just because there is not enough clear evidence in the file to define a specific manner, it is listed in the database as undetermined – but I suspect accidental death.

Case 35. #87048 (1987) Here we have a 34 year old white male who died as the result of a pedestrian/motor vehicle collision in early March. The coroner report is good and includes a wealth of information and narrative. The incident occurred around 10:45 in the evening on the main street in Riverton. Scene description is good, noting the lighting (street lights), clear and dry weather conditions, road surface and lane characteristics, body location and distance from the nearest intersection, body position, covering, and blood pool. The number of photos taken of the scene and body are listed. Body descriptions include basic characteristics, clothing detail, presence of EMS intervention items, general description of injuries and bleeding. Trauma description is detailed and include head trauma to the left side, bleeding from both ears, bruising to the left abdomen, and other abrasions. It is noted the body was transported to the local hospital for x-rays, which revealed fractures to the head and chest area. No autopsy is deemed necessary.

Incident narrative indicates that the deceased and his wife had parked their car in a nearby lot and were walking along the south side of the roadway, when for an "unknown reason" the deceased walked into the outside lane and bent over. The oncoming vehicle in that lane, identified by make, model, license number, and operator struck the individual and slide him approximately 19 feet. The driver immediately called police, who were actually nearby, and EMS also arrived shortly thereafter within a few minutes. Deceased was pronounced at the scene.

Cause of death is a massive head injury, and additional information details the clothing, property collected from the body, disposition time and location funeral home, and collection of toxicology samples which were sealed, secured, and documented as sent to the lab in Cheyenne, WY. A property sheet details the pocket contents and property signed for and released to the deceased's wife. Toxicology results show no presence of drugs; however the blood alcohol level of the deceased comes back as 0.22 – notably over twice the current legal limit. Diagrams note the location of trauma and injuries. An additional sheet detailing facts for pedestrian/auto deaths include a statement that "liquor was found in the victim's pickup that was parked nearby". Is also is noted that the driver of the vehicle that struck him was negative for intoxication and incurred no violation in vehicle operation. An additional statement by the driver narrates his movements and locations prior to the incident, stated that the time he saw an individual bent over in the road's outside lane on his passenger side and the impact were almost "instantaneous". He pulled over immediately and went back to the victim. He notes an officer was in visual distance of the scene and responded when he called to him. A separate time line is typed out of the investigation steps from incident to immediate completion of the initial investigation, which took approximately 2 ½ hours.

With the detailed coroner report is a State investigators traffic accident report, completed by the officer that was at the scene. The form is a typical law enforcement or highway patrol type that contains all the specifics one would expect to be documented. Time frame for the incident indicates the officer was nearly at the scene when notified, descriptions are consistent with the coroner report but a bit more detailed as to lighting and vehicle description. Damage to the vehicle is indicated, and consistent with impact centered and slightly to the passenger side. Tissue and biologics are noted at the impact site, headlights noted as on and at low beam. Skid marks are described on the roadway starting approximately 30 feet from the estimated point of impact of the pedestrian and slightly before the impact point, about a yard long and indicating vehicle was straight and in its proper lane of travel. Speed is estimated at about 30 mph, which is the posted limit. The officer's opinion on the report is that regarding the evidence and witness statements, the victim moved from the curb and into the path of the vehicle without warning. Recommendations are "no enforcement action." A detailed traffic diagram of the scene is attached. A later interview with the wife of the deceased notes that she stated they were driving down the street when the victim pulled over and got out and walked away. A note from another officer reports there had been "family problems".

Photo prints are included in the file, with scene detail and vehicle photos matching those described in the written reports. Injuries in the body photos are consistent also with the written reports, and with the scenario described for the event. A newspaper clipping reports the incident and notes no charges were being filed. A police department report from about a year before is included, with a booking photo and information stating the deceased was arrested at that time for property destruction at a local bar for breaking out car windows with an axe handle.

The death certificate reports the cause of death as "massive brain damage due to blunt force trauma to the head due to motor vehicle/pedestrian accident". The manner of death is listed as "undetermined". This is a case where one must be careful in what words are selected for the certification. Many people refer to such incidents as "accidents" as a general term, with no intentional relation to the meaning of accident as relating to manner of death. However, as listed, this can cause confusion, and it would be better to say "motor vehicle/pedestrian collision" in the cause line. That way there is no opening for confusion.

The reports are every bit as detailed as what we would do today in such an incident, and the documentation is great, especially when compared to what has been seen over the years up to this point. What is left out, however, is why and for what justification, this ended up 'undetermined'. Law enforcement indicates there was no way to consider this a homicide by the driver. There are no indications the driver did anything wrong, and the scene evidence is consistent with the narratives and statements. Obviously this is not natural as the descriptions also do not indicate a stumble or pedestrian veering into the vehicle path from a cardiac or other health issue. Suicide also seems unlikely. Only one note indicates there might have been family issues, but there is nothing in the narratives that indicates threats or suspicion of suicide. To be sure, suicide by vehicle is suspected to be more common on the highways than can be proven, and it is possible that an individual could willfully walk into oncoming traffic as a method that has been documented in other cases, but there is usually a more reasonable suspicion or documentation to prove it. Without such documentation, there is no reason to think of this incident as anything other than an accident.

I feel a key here is the intoxication level – which is at a point that could indicate irrational or careless behavior, as well as inattention to surroundings. With the description and evidence showing the individual stepped out into traffic and bent over, did he drop something? Or perhaps was there money or some other object that he saw and went to pick up, and was just intoxicated enough to be detached from his surroundings? On a well-lit street intersection, vehicle lights of the period may not have been as noticeable in a spur of the moment decision and inattentiveness. That could have been checked out with a bit more detail by looking at the impact point for just such objects or materials in the street. Or maybe it was and it is just not documented. One part of the report implies the wife and deceased were both out of the vehicle and walking along the street, and the wife's statement implies the deceased left initially on his own, with no justification given in the report/interview. That inconsistency could perhaps have been cleared up with a follow-up conversation after the trauma of the incident had subsided a bit.

The only obvious unstated doubt or conflict on manner would be between accident versus suicide, unless someone thought the wife pushed him into the traffic lane as a homicide. Again, the details do not indicate a push, rather that he was just bent over in the lane, so no basis for that is even hinted at, with public statements by officers to the newspaper indicating accident. The physical evidence and dynamics of a body reacting to a push would have been quite different than someone standing bent over when impacted. So that option seems highly unlikely based on the reports.

My philosophy is to be very cautious in ruling a suicide, as that is a hard thing for families to deal with, unless the evidence is at a high certainty. Families can wrap their head around the idea of a homicide, where another's actions result in a death, more than the irrational act of suicide. It is just difficult for a rational mind to understand or accept an irrational act, especially when there often are no 'reasons' or answers available. Thus unless there is no reasonable doubt based on the evidence to rule suicide, or we are at or below the 50-50 level of certainty, accident is better than undetermined in this or most cases. Investigators can drive themselves crazy after doing this a while with the myriad scenarios one can think of with any set of evidence, so try to avoid imprinting possible conclusions on any set of facts. Take it for what it is. The only person who knows for sure why he stepped out into traffic while intoxicated and bent down, is dead. Without any other indications in evidence, do not read something into it... This manner should have been accident.

Case 36. #87086 (1987) Several times a year the coroner's office will get a call from a medical facility regarding a death that may have suspicious origins of injury, or due to some of the statutory obligations for medical staff, such as reporting suspected child abuse. In those cases, there are unique circumstances and challenges for the investigator in that the evidence at an originating scene, or the scene and situation itself, may be long gone. Since statute states that the jurisdiction belongs to the coroner in whose area the originating scene location is, that is the first issue to resolve. Did the death result from an injury? Did the location of the injury fall within the jurisdiction?

Here we have a 64 year old Native American female that died of an internal cranial bleed that was the result of blunt force trauma to the head. While the location of the death was a local hospital, the originating scene may not have been in the county. In this case all we have in the file is the local police officer's investigation report, and again, this officer is also on file as a deputy coroner at the time, so he wears both hats at the same time as far as the investigation. In late March, a report is filed with the police department by hospital staff regarding a possible assault victim currently in their care. The subject finally died of the injuries about two weeks later at the same facility. While the law enforcement investigation initiates at the report of a possible assault, the coroner's investigation technically does not begin until the death. Coordination of both aspects obviously is needed in such a case.

Interviews with the hospital staff show that the ER documented that the deceased told them initially she "fell out of bed" and hit her head. After treatment the subject was transferred to an extended care facility in Thermopolis, WY (Hot Springs County), but returned after one day as that facility determined she was not "suitable for treatment" there. She remained then at the hospital in Riverton until her death. Hospital staff were unable to offer any other details about the originating scene or incident. At the death a report was also filed with the coroner's office. Hand written notes reference both the initial law enforcement report and the continuation after death, and note that an assault may have happened at a fast food restaurant in Thermopolis. If such a circumstance is verified, then the case should be referred to the Hot Springs coroner as their jurisdiction.

The record indicates the internal bleed resulted from blunt force trauma to the right rear of the head. This resulted in left side paralysis and other complications. The initial report by the subject stated that she was beat up, and in addition had fallen in the "drunk tank". The subject was noted as "somewhat unresponsive" at that time by hospital staff, and in addition the officer noted her as "somewhat disoriented and confused". She reported this event happened in Thermopolis during an altercation, and that local police arrested everyone and took them to jail. At that location, she stated someone pushed her down while incarcerated. She noted she had been living in Thermopolis, but had checked into a local Riverton motel a few weeks ago. A granddaughter was supposed to be living with her. The officer then contacted the noted motel, where the manager confirmed a suspicion of ethanol use, and noted there were often several people in the room. She confirmed the original need for an ambulance call was reported by a niece. The niece was contacted, and she reported the subject as a chronic alcoholic, and that she had been ill off and on recently. The niece reported she did not live there, but would periodically check on the subject, and on the day of the EMS call found her on the floor with her feet up on the bed. She also notes that she had seen her earlier in the day and her aunt appeared fine at that time. EMS logs fill in confirmation of this event locally.

The officer notes that the deceased had never been confined or arrested in Riverton, but there was a series of EMS calls on her behalf over the past two years. She had been seen at the hospital several days prior to this incident in question for other reasons and no injuries were seen or recorded. There was no record found of any incident at the noted fast food location, nor any arrest record relative to the incident described. A search of the county sheriff's records also are absent any contact with the deceased. Medical opinion when asked is that the injury could have occurred in a fall out of bed as one of numerous options. Based on the interviews and other background investigations, the officer concludes the time of injury to a roughly 5 hour period the day of the originating EMS call at the motel. He states "there is no supportive evidence that violence was involved" and closes the case.

This is a case where an autopsy might have been helpful to further define the time frame of injury and internal bleed, but unless there was some sort of pattern injury to indicate assault, an autopsy probably would not contribute to the source of that injury, only eliminate some possibilities. Obviously the tales of the deceased are decidedly inconsistent and unreliable without any confirmation, and some can be discounted by the absence of confirmation. No death certificate is included to show the final certification, and undetermined was initially listed in the database due to lack of information. On review, one could say we are at about 70% an accidental death, which is adequate for certification, being better than 50-50. Could there be an outside chance of some unknown assault? Sure, but death investigators have to deal with the fact that unless a particular event is reliably witnessed, there is always an element of guesswork in a conclusion on any case, even those with all the modern tools put into play. Probability, the process of elimination, experience, and sometimes even gut feeling, can all count with variable weight. Just try your best to be as factual and scientifically based as reasonably possible.

Case 37. #89070 (1989) For the last case considered from the 1980s, we have an 18 year old Native American female who was found deceased on an early July morning in an apartment living room. According to the coroner report, the TV, fan, and lights are on, as well as all the lights in the balance of rooms at the location. Standard double sliding glass doors off the living room have the curtains closed. The body is on her back, left arm flexed to the left, right arm flexed over the head, left leg folded under the body and right leg flexed against the glass of the double doors with the foot also partially under the body. A jacket is off and under the body. No apparent trauma or bleeding, eyes are open. Two people had gone to the apartment looking for the girl, saw the body through a window, and also entered through a window as the door was locked, and confirmed the death and subsequently called police. A rough diagram is included noting the body location in the apartment.

The law enforcement report detailed and identifies the reporting parties, responding officers, and notes the condition of rigor mortis. No signs of "foul play", no medications found, and the deceased's child (no age given) was asleep on the floor in the apartment hallway. Interviews with the two reporting parties state they had been with the deceased the evening before, noted drinking, but no depression or issues. The deceased was staying with the apartment renter, who was not present. The actual transcript of these interviews is attached to the report. According to the text, the parties first saw the child on the floor and grew concerned, so they removed a window screen and entered. When the body was found they described it as having "flies all over the face", so they knew she was not just passed out. An account is given of the contact the previous day and who else was present. An additional sheet gives the general conclusions of the autopsy and notes an interview with the father of the deceased, who stated he suspected someone smothered her with a pillow. Hand written notes state the deceased was a smoker, detailed her recent movements, noted no specific medical history or known issues, and described clothing found in the living room that reportedly did not belong to any of the occupants.

An autopsy was completed the next day at the Cheyenne crime lab by the forensic pathologist out of Loveland, CO. The report is in the expected forensic detail, and the only trauma noted is bruising to the anterior strap muscles of the neck and anterior shoulder muscles; abrasions to the posterior right shoulder, fingers of the right hand, and posterior right leg. Internal dissection of the neck shows open airways, intact hyoid, and no trauma with minimal hemorrhage to the areas noted as bruised externally. Mild CNS edema and pulmonary congestion is noted, but not considered to a significant degree. Mild generalized atherosclerosis is noted, which for an 18 year old certainly would not have bode well for the future. Radiology studies were all negative (report included), and all blood and urine toxicology was negative (reports included). The only finding in that area was CO level of 15%, a range which the pathologist suggests would be consistent with a heavy smoker, urban resident, or closed environment like a running motor vehicle – also not a significant issue in the cause of death. In the narrative, he notes that the above noted injuries indicate the deceased was involved in some sort of traumatic event of undetermined etiology, but this is not a cause of death. The cause may be natural due to sudden unexplained cardiac arrhythmia or arrest, but this would be speculative, as all physical and detail exams leave the cause and manner of death undetermined. He notes that the case may need to be re-opened in the future should any additional information be revealed in the investigation. A crime lab inventory lists all the clothing, samples taken, sexual assault kit obtained, and photos taken.

Due to some individuals being residents of the reservation, Bureau of Indian affairs investigators were contacted to follow up on parties of interest, especially in regards to a motor vehicle accident the day before the 18 year old was found dead. Interviews note the deceased was not in the vehicle and not involved in that particular accident. The other occupant of the apartment is reported to be in Salt Lake City, Utah. The Wind River Police Department traffic report and call log is also included with the BIA report.

A letter from the Deputy Coroner in the case is included as addressed to the police department, noting the undetermined nature and follow up questions from the pathologist, in particular in regards to the neck injuries and prior activities of the deceased 24 hours to being found. The letter also notes "a great deal of pressure to determine the cause", including from a U.S. Senator. As a side note, on many cases, especially if high profile or involving youth, there is often media and public pressure for information and conclusions... it is a continuous education process with both to educate and remind them that forensic investigations and procedures take time. Information release also must take into consideration the needs of the case, especially if adjudication is probable. Inappropriate release can harm a case or cause undue mental trauma and stress to the families involved.

A letter of contact to Salt Lake City law enforcement is in the file requesting information and interviews with those subjects in that jurisdiction that may have had contact with the deceased in the time frame leading up to the death, but there is no copy of any response.

Photographs in the file include 11 from the scene and confirm the reported positioning and lack of injury and biologics. Flies are visible on the face of the deceased, lividity appears consistent with position, but it is not reported as to whether or not it was fixed when the body was found. Autopsy photos are revealing only in the confirmation of the absence of anything of significance.

The only other document in the file is a request from a psychiatric institute out of New York requesting copies of the reports for a study on undetermined youth deaths, dated April of 1998, nine years after the death. A request for the study from the coroner is attached, but no copy of that study in the file. This would not be unusual as far as a request, as fatality information is often requested by institutions, agencies, or government to supplement what is found on file as a compilation of state vital records death information at the CDC. Current policy by statute is all such requests are to be in writing, and to file all those requests and resolutions in the appropriate case file. Now that would include media, public, agency or any others, however prior to the statute changes in 2011, all coroner information, including autopsy reports and case photos, were public if requested. Where information went was often not documented with the thoroughness found today, which is now an improvement in my opinion. Wyoming has some of the most restrictive confidentiality laws for coroners in the nation and specifically defines what may or may not be released, to who, and under what circumstances. Especially in today's prolific social media outlets there is no reason to have public broadcast of such items as autopsy photos.

The death certificate is certified as undetermined in both cause and manner, consistent with the conclusions of the pathologist. There is nothing in the file to contest that, follow up appears thorough, and unfortunately there just are those cases where there are no answers. I suspect that even today with what advances there are in investigations, this one would still be undetermined.

Section V:The Nearly There Nineties

The Nineties start to bring in an accelerating advancement of investigation techniques and tools, along with nationally more attempts at standardization of procedures. While this obviously will take longer to filter into the rural areas of Wyoming, we can start to see some of the changes in this decade. Inconsistency, however, remains the norm for undetermined cases.

Case 38. #91096 (1991) We start off the nineties with another situational case, one where the jurisdiction is transferred from the Adams County Coroner in Colorado, to the Fremont County Coroner in Wyoming. This was done at the request of the County Attorney in Fremont, due to the subject dying at a medical facility in Colorado possibly as the result of injuries received in an assault that occurred here. The perpetrator was currently in custody on charges of aggravated assault and the prosecutor was looking to see if manslaughter or homicide should be added to the offenses. Various letters and forms are in the file requesting and completing that change of jurisdiction from all the official parties involved.

A stack of assorted hand-written notes are included in the file, but no actual coroner report. This is poor documentation, as the best method would be to centralize all information and timeline of the originating history and subsequent follow up in a regular form/report to see the logic and resolution of the case. We do have the autopsy, however, which was performed by a Marine Corps Major and forensic pathologist at an armed services facility in Colorado. The subject is listed on the form as a U.S. Public Health Service beneficiary, and identified as a 42 year old Native American female. Numerous "well-healed" scars are noted, numbering more than 20 of various sizes and locations on and about the body, with several major ones to the face and head. The clinical summary states that the assault with multiple sharp force injuries occurred in May of 1991, and included a partial amputation of the nose with multiple superficial stab wounds to the chest and abdomen. She was transferred from a local hospital to the Army Medical Center in Colorado shortly after the attack, and was released early June in good condition. In late August she was re-admitted for elective surgical repair to the damage to the nose sustained at the time of the original injuries. As a result of the graft and reconstruction she developed multiple organism infection at the rib harvest site, which resulted in septic shock, renal and liver failure and consumptive coagulopathy. History of chronic alcohol abuse is mentioned. The pathologist's opinion states that the original injuries had healed at the time of the elective repairative surgery, and notes that the multiple scarings are healed enough that it cannot be determined what was a result of the assault or previous injury. He notes that the medical records and photos of the assault incident should be referred to for that documentation, and that while some scaring is consistent with defensive wounds, some is also consistent with an old suicide attempt. It is also stated that the condition of cirrhosis in the liver is to the degree it likely compromised the body's ability to deal with infection. The specific cause of death is stated as "septic shock resulting in multiple organ system failure after elective plastic surgery procedure". Contributory is "multiple healed sharp force injuries and resultant plastic surgical procedures and severe alcoholic micronodular cirrhosis". The manner of death is left as undetermined.

There are a few jurisdictions that include "complications of therapy" as a manner of death for certification, but they are rare and Wyoming is not one of them. In most cases this is not an acceptable form, and to me seems a bit like avoiding the hard questions. Overt negligence in medical procedures and therapy could be considered a homicide, and other instances accidental. In most cases however, you should look to the originating circumstance of an event or condition, of which the medical intervention is mostly reactive. A person that dies in the ER or operating room from unsuccessful mitigation of a cardiac event is a natural death. Unsuccessful treatment of injuries sustained in a vehicular collision may be an accident, or homicide, depending on circumstance. It is noted that if a death results *directly* from sustained injuries, the time interval is irrelevant. For example, if the septic shock in this case could be attributed from complications of the original assault trauma itself, the manner might be different and the prosecutor might be able to make a case. Generally speaking though, death from an *elective* medical procedure where the dangers and risks are known is also a natural death. In this case, the pathologist notes specifically that the injuries from the assault were well-healed, implying that they were not a direct cause on their own. He also specifies that the physical condition of the patient's liver, unrelated to the assault, was a main contributing factor in decreased recovery from known possible surgical complications of infection.

The injuries do sound terrible, and the assault vicious, but the coroner must avoid the perspective and desire of a prosecutor and law enforcement to make the facts fit a foregone conclusion that is wanted. But for the choice of the individual to have elective reconstructive surgery, all indications are that the injuries were survived and healed. I would rule this a natural death, although I am sure many might disagree.

Case 39. #92124 (1992) This is a case of an assist to Washakie County in the investigation of a decomposed body that was found in a rural area in that jurisdiction. Fremont arranged an autopsy and identification of this 67 year old white male through dental records in September 1992. A wallet was found in the property of the deceased, specifically the pocket of pants that were located in a sleeping bag that was in a tent on the back of a flatbed truck with the body. X-rays showed no evidence of trauma or artifacts like bullets. The vehicle was also registered to the identified deceased. Cause and manner are undetermined, and listed as such. Even with jurisdiction remaining with the Washakie County Coroner, this is exactly the type of case that should have all the normal reports and documentation expected, as most of the investigative work on the body was performed by Fremont investigators. While there are letters in the file giving the basics, formal reports are lacking. Whether your jurisdiction or not, full documentation standards should apply when assisting other coroners as they deserve the best efforts to justify an undetermined or any other ruling. That was not done here, but we are probably fortunate that the case was documented at all, as in this time frame, they usually were not.

Case 40. #93163 (1993) And now for a relative explosion of materials and records, contained in two 4 inch thick three-ring binders, all relative to this particular case. Unfortunately, we also run into the issue where the coroner still had no office, kept files at his home, and the lead coroner investigator kept duplicates at his office at the local police department. In reviewing and going through everything and pulling out duplicate copies, we can get it down to only one 4 inch binder – still a wealth of information. But guess what? There is no coroner report.

As a side note, these days when we receive medical records, the policy is to review them and summarize as a supplemental comment to the coroner report. That report should stand on its own as a concise record of the investigation without any need to go to the detailed documents unless verification is needed. The flow and relevant points of the investigation should follow a logical pattern to the end manner and cause, with the thought process in determining the final result apparent to any other agency or investigator. This also can be critical if called or used for testimony in a legal procedure, which may occur quite some time down the line after the investigation. In the nineties, we are not seeing this yet as far as reporting, but luckily for this review, at least the original source documentation is present.

In addition, for coroners in Wyoming, it must be remembered that all documentation belongs to the State, not the Office, and is required by statute and records retention rules established by the State Archives to be disposed of in a particular way, if at all. The current policy for this office was established by me in working with the Archives for an approved set of rules that conforms to the State regulations and needs of this office. Undetermined cases, for example, are treated as homicide cases and all files and documentation are retained forever, other than transitory duplications. The logic is that an undetermined case could turn into a homicide or an otherwise resolved case some time down the road as a cold investigation, so you never know what might be significant. Duplicates, however, by State regulations and our policies, can be disposed of, as long as the originals are kept. **More information is available on records rules in the appendix**. Also, all records of an agency or political subdivision are required by law to be turned over to the next administration or official.

Now the basis for this case is one of a 70 year old white male who died in late December at the local hospital. The cause of death listed is "aspiration bronchopneumonia" with other significant conditions listed as "severe malnutrition and possible neglect". The death certificate is marked "pending" for manner, but an amendment on letterhead from the coroner eight months later establishes the manner as undetermined.

While (again) no actual coroner report is in the file, there is a hand written time line of sorts to frame the records around. The individual was living with a son in a northern county when that house burned down and he moved in December of 1992 to Fremont County to live with another son and daughter-in-law. In January of 1993 home health care through the local hospital is initiated and recorded. In early July his care is reviewed by the Department of Family Services on the recommendation of the home health providers. In late July of 1993 he is admitted to the hospital for low weight and nutritional issues and several consults are obtained regarding his care. He is discharged to a nursing home based on care recommendations. After a period he returned to the relative's home, and DFS follow up is initiated in September. He is re-admitted in December to the hospital, where he dies, and an investigation is started by the coroner's office in conjunction with law enforcement.

Home health care records: typical logs and flow chart records for this type of service are presented; visit schedule for staff appears to be about once a week throughout the period. Comments include notes of frequent falls and being unsteady on his feet, frequent bouts of confusion starting in March, the family reports periodically combative, increasing incontinence over the period, and by May he is less and less oriented to time and place, also complaining more about the care by his family. Referred to follow up and appointments with physicians. Developing cataracts and poor hearing, blood sugars starting to be variable high to low, reported to wander at night. By summer months disorientation is increasing along with weight loss. Physician re-certifications note rehabilitation potential is poor due to chronic illness and head injury, which was a work related issue that had occurred 25 years prior and left him on disability. Visitation from home health is increased in frequency due to declining conditions. The date of the last visit on the home care discharge report is stated as late July when admitted to the hospital, noting progressive weight loss, frequent falls, neurologic and DFS consults, admission to the hospital with discharge to long term care facility.

After a hospital stay of four days, the subject is sent to a local nursing home, admitted there in early August. He is noted as a DNR by the legal guardian, the son he was originally living with up north, with the local son listed as agent and responsible party. Discharge from this facility is noted as mid-September. Discharge notes indicate that social services does not agree with the return to the local family home due to the need for 24-hour care, and that "ombudsman and adult protection will be notified", and discharge is against medical advice. Diagnosis is "failure to thrive, closed head lesion, & seizure disorder". During the stay, soft safety restraints were stated as necessary to prevent falls. Notes show the patient to be gaining weight with better nutrition, but progressively disoriented and combative, and of the opinion he is "treated like a dog" in the facility. The family notes they cannot afford to pay for the facility past the Medicare funded stay period. A bout of pneumonia is resolved during the stay and seizure activity had ceased due to medication. Neurologic consult indicates the remote closed head injury with memory loss, "progressive deterioration of dementia of the Alzheimer's type". The neurologist notes that care in this case by families can be provided, but it is "quite difficult".

Local hospital records are for an eight day period in December that culminated in the death. A six page discharge summary details the event and history. The subject was brought in to the emergency room unresponsive via ambulance. Family stated that he had been vomiting for several days, was checked when he got up from bed and had a blood sugar of 21 and shortly after collapsed. The ER found his temperature to be 86 degrees F., with severe dehydration. Fluid and temperature resuscitation were initiated. This physician was the personal care doctor and noted the history in the year since moving to this area. Weight over time had declined from about 150 lbs. to 100, consultations found "no organic reason" for malnutrition and she states there were "no problems with his ability to eat. (This is contradicted by the nursing home and home health care records that wrote that while he periodically ate well, he had trouble with swallowing and food portion size, and if not cut small enough would choke - weight gain under nursing care was noted in the nursing home, but declined during home health care) The permanent disability due to the head injury is noted, as are his vision and hearing issues, and the need for ambulation assistance. Blood glucose in the ER was at 94, blood chemistries abnormal. Most labs are detailed and stayed abnormal during hospitalization. X-ray summaries note the placement of a central line, with a second x-ray for placement after he pulled out the first one. Additionally, in ICU, x-rays of the lungs revealed pneumonia and interstitial edema stated as most likely due to "fluid overload". A CT scan showed diffuse cerebral cortical atrophy. The fluid overload was noted as a result of therapy and mitigated. After stabilization, the patient was admitted to a regular floor, and per physician orders, the corporate and county attorneys were contacted, as was the Department of Family Services. A "do not resuscitate" order was put in place per consult with the physician and family. Condition was "guarded" and nutrition and antibiotics continued. The attorneys, law enforcement investigators, social services, and all consulting physicians ordered DFS to arrange for guardianship, but the patient died the next day.

The summary notes bruising, scratches on the face and arms, and when communicative for a period, the patient accused the daughter-in-law as the source of injury. During the stay he ate well off and on between a period of refusal to eat and other times unresponsive. Condition turned critical the evening before the day he died, at which time the various involved agencies were contacted, and the coroner's office. Those agencies are noted as requesting an inquest into the death. The physician notes her opinion of the causes for admission as: malnutrition; severe starvation from intentional lack of feeding; scratches on the face and arm inflicted by the daughter-in-law; bruises from the face from a fall in the bathtub; hypothermia due to neglect; hypoglycemia assumed to be due to administration of hypoglycemics by the caregiver; aspiration pneumonia due to the care giver holding his mouth closed to prevent him from spitting his food. The physician notes that additional pneumonia could be hospital acquired.

The physician's final stated cause of death is multi-system failure, with underlying illnesses of adult onset diabetes, COPD, and head injury with delay, extremely hard of hearing and visual disability. Discharge diagnosis is listed as: multisystem failure; severe malnutrition; starvation; elder abuse; hypoglycemia; hypothermia; aspiration pneumonia; hospital acquired pneumonia; chronic obstructive pulmonary disease; head injury; vision impaired; and hearing impaired. It is obvious from the tone and wording of the summary that the physician has very strong feelings and is passionate about the case.

Additional records are in the file:

a. An additional internal medicine consult from May notes history is difficult to obtain due to the patient's inability to communicate effectively, and the son and daughter-in-law state they had only seen him once a year for about ten years prior to his move in with them, and cannot give a picture of the progression of problems. The previous head injury and falling issues are noted with possible Parkinson's-like tremors. Medication is prescribed to see if indeed it relieves the Parkinson's symptoms. A later follow up notes no change so the medication is discontinued.

b. A social service assessment from the December admission notes the conference held with the agencies and physicians mentioned in the discharge summary. The county attorney does not see any particular state laws that apply, but DFS states they will attempt to prevent the family from discharging the patient and returning him to their care. The possibility of placement outside the county is discussed.

c. In written letter from September, the internal medicine physician states that due to the closed head injury and progressive dementia, and in consult with nursing home staff and the neurologist, a custodial care environment is recommended for appropriate nursing and nutrition, with the patient only allowed out with family "on pass".

d. A neurologist consult from June states that the head injury was from an oil rig accident in 1967 in Alaska that resulted in a coma for two weeks before recovery. He notes mobility issues and physical signs of a past craniotomy, most likely from the accident. The patient is disoriented to place, time, and date, and hold his attention to about three minutes. An EEG shows defects and abnormalities consistent with a right hemisphere injury, also consistent with the past described injury.

e. A lab test result from the hospital in December shows <u>negative</u> values/none detected for the hypoglycemic medication (Micronase/Glyburide) that the physician above stated in her summary she suspected of being administered by the caregiver family. The date of the sample was during the hospital stay prior to death, but it was run the week after the death.

f. A counseling service psychological evaluation is presented from July. It notes the son and daughter-in-law's progressive concerns that the subject is increasingly unable to live in an independent setting. They note food gorging until he chokes, mood swings, poor sleep schedules, and wandering away from home. Assessment is difficult due to the hearing problem, and the subject's difficulty in dealing with complex instructions. The subject is noted as alert and cooperative, but not oriented to place and day, and "had no idea what this was all about". While confused, there were no indications of delusion or hallucination. He did get up spontaneously during the interview and appear about to fall. The psychologist estimates his intellectual level as marginal, and that "he will continue to present some difficult management problems and test people's patience". The family wanted to know about institutional placement, but in the doctor's opinion, the subject does not appear to qualify for either the State Hospital (psychiatric) or State Training School (mentally disabled or brain injury).

g. Department of Family Services reports on complaints of abuse – the first records show a complaint file was opened in July, ruled unsubstantiated in August, and case closed in October. The reports on this complaint note that the subject told DFS the daughter-in-law slapped him and is withholding food as punishment. On interviews the daughter-in-law stated that she had slapped him in self-defense and admitted withholding food after he threw it at her or on the floor. She noted the loss of weight due to medical issues, and stated she would prefer him to be in a nursing home, but the sons, including her husband, do not want that placement. She agreed to go to counseling for herself to help deal with the stress of care, and agreed to seek psychological evaluations to determine the setting he would most benefit by (these are in the file and noted above). An additional complaint report notes the removal from the nursing home against recommendations, and accusations of padlocking the home refrigerator, mental and emotional abuse, and the family using the subject's money income. Other notes indicate agency follow up, and completion of the requested evaluations. It notes that the patient went voluntarily when removed from the nursing home by the son. It notes that social services do not believe the subject is competent. The last records document the December hospital stay, meetings, conclusions, and have the letter from their agency stating to the son and daughter-in-law (dated two days before the patient died) that the department does not believe the relatives can provide adequate care and recommends only transfer and discharge to a facility where he can receive "proper attention". An interesting side notation is that evidently money received in settlement from the work injury was reportedly withdrawn by the son up north whose house burned down and that money was gone long before he came to Riverton; also none of the kids want him in the nursing home in Riverton as that is where their mother and his ex-wife also is staying. This documentation supports the daughter-in-law's contention that she would like him in permanent care setting, but the sons do not, and the one up north continues to control all the finances for the dad remotely from there. A final supplemental a month after the death notes the family had taken him to a doctor or public health a few weeks before the final admission to the hospital, that the autopsy revealed a long term fecal impaction that may have affected his ability to eat or retain nutrition. As they state, "so, the hospital apparently did not diagnose his condition properly". They also note the reluctance of the county attorney to prosecute for any offense.

h. Washakie County Sheriff's interview of the other son: the coroner investigator sent a request letter to the sheriff's office up north where the deceased lived prior to his move to Riverton. He requested that they interview the other son with the possibility of answering the following questions. When was the house fire? What was the origin? Is the son the legal guardian, and is that documented? Is there any information on where the oil field accident occurred and who treated him, and was there a settlement? Did the subject have regular medical care up north? Why was he taken out of the nursing home against medical advice? What was his source of income and who controlled it? Is there an estate and who is responsible for expenses? An interview in this regard was arranged by a sheriff detective in mid-January after the death in December. In summary, the son notes his house fire was a bit over a year ago, and his dad had lived with him off and on since the accident in Alaska 25 years prior. He describes the circumstances and injury, and reports he was disabled and unable to work since that time. He notes he himself was in another part of Alaska at the time working, and that he got concerned that his dad's girlfriend at that time (already divorced from his mom) was taking all his money. He got concerned at the people taking advantage of him and took him home, but his dad left and came south to Riverton and stayed by himself. As soon as his dad had saved up money he went back to Alaska, where he ended up assaulted and in the hospital for poor nutrition. After that he came back here for a bit, intermittently staying with his son, left to live on his own, fell and was in intensive care for a bit due to injuries, and after that stayed for years with is son pretty continuously until the house fire. The son did not like the personal physician (the one that wrote the discharge/death summary noted above) and did not think she did a good job with his dad's care. In reference to the nursing home care he notes his dad did not like being restrained, and the family as a whole met and decided to take him out. He states the personal physician "threatened" him with adult protective services. He notes that his sister-in-law was taking his dad to "all the specialists" but he told her that he did not feel that was needed, even if his dad had the money. Then he notes that he thought the physician should have hospitalized his dad sooner when he was seen in the weeks prior to the final hospitalization. He thinks his dad "wanted to die" and wasn't happy with the way things were. He is a bit confused on whether there was official guardian paperwork, but it is apparent there was a joint account for his dad's income, and he states after the move he sent most of the money to his brother and sister-in-law. He notes that the doctors after the original workplace accident gave his dad only about 4 or 5 years, but he certainly outlasted that. He states he and his wife took good care of him during the time he was up north, but it was not an easy job due to his dad's behavior. He notes that his dad was in a nursing home for a bit up north also, but that did not work out well either, and they pulled him out of both due to costs, and complaints from his dad on the care. He notes that his dad on his own was not able, or did not want to cook, so that always had to be done for him. Eating was always a mess and inconsistent, either gorging or nothing, and his behavior when out was "embarrassing". He continues to rail against the personal physician and her level of care. After the bulk settlement was gone years ago the income level is reported at about $900 per month between social security and Alaska workmen's compensation. There is no estate or property reported. He relays the names of physicians seen locally when his dad stayed with him and notes he was in the hospital there frequently for pneumonia. It is apparent in the interview that he is upset at the death, the doctor, and social services, and he states he would be willing to talk to any investigators at any time if needed.

i. Riverton Police Department: this report document the law enforcement response to the possible abuse complaint in the December hospitalization period. It notes the meeting with social services and hospital staff to discuss the condition of the patient. It notes the previous complaints were found to be unsubstantiated by DFS. There is a follow up interview with the daughter-in-law in late December. She relays testimony consistent with other information, notes that the son up north had told her to not use doctors as much, asserted the difficulties in caring for the patient at home, and produced a copy of the checks received to verify income for the subject. The detective's opinion is that she appeared to be intimidated by both the subject and his sons.

j. An EMS trip sheet and report from the December admission is included, but reveals no additional useful information.

An autopsy was performed the same day as the death. The pathologist notes the cause of death as bronchopneumonia due to aspiration of gastric contents with malnutrition as a contributing factor, general finding consistent with severe malnutrition and neglect. No manner of death is stated. Physical findings are extensive and include a height of 5' 5 1/2 " , weight 92 lbs., severe malnutrition and cachexia, negative for malignancy and wasting illness. The pneumonia is noted with fragments of meat and vegetable material in the lungs, coronary arterial atherosclerosis with occlusions ranging from 50 to 70 percent, no thrombosis. Old right cerebral contusion to the temporal lobe, severe colonic fecal impaction and multiple therapeutic interventions. No toxicology is completed due to the extent of hospitalization period. Full body x-rays are completed that note multiple fractures that are all old and healed in the arms and legs with old rib fractures. No recent fractures or dislocations are identified, and amazingly, no gross evidence of an old skull fracture is seen and no evidence of craniotomy is mentioned. This seems odd in the light of the description of the occupational injury, but that did happen 25 years prior to the death.

A sheet noting an inquest jury selection is in the file, but a check of the listings with the State Archives indicates no official inquest was ever called. There is a letter from the coroner investigator to the State Attorney General in January after the death reporting the investigation relating to possible abuse and neglect, and noting possible wrongful death and misuse of social security funds. Most State level pursuit on this sort of case would wait until the local County Attorney has made his own decisions in the matter, and the final document in the file is that decision, shown on a letter dated the next March.

The County Attorney notes that there was a meeting at the beginning of March to go over all the evidence gathered up to that point. He states that the problem in proving involuntary manslaughter or criminally negligent homicide is causation. Of the many contributing factors in the death, the State cannot disprove the actions by the deceased himself as a factor. Regardless of the fact his relatives "may have been less than desirable", the subject preferred to be at their home rather than in nursing homes. The State can prove he left the nursing homes against medical advice, but as far as we know, that was his choice and the State cannot prove that was neglect. The State can prove he died of starvation, but cannot prove that was due to being deprived of food when the evidence indicates he was not eating all that was offered. He notes that a person has the right to stop eating if death is desired. The State cannot prove medical neglect as he was taken to the doctor due to his caretaker's concern about his conditions. While "the circumstances surrounding the death are distressing, homicide cannot be proved beyond a reasonable doubt", and his office declines to file any charges.

So there we are. These above types of summaries today would be part of the supplemental coroner reports to show the context and procedure of the investigation leading to the conclusion. While we have no coroner report, it is still possible to gauge the opinions and emphasis of this particular investigator from the materials presented. The investigation was thorough and inclusive of available resources. The death certificate was not completed as to manner until August after the death, which indicates an ongoing investigation until all resources have been tapped, although there is no documentation as to why another five months delay in that occurred after the March meeting. Here are my thoughts on the matter.

One notable thing about the documents on this case is that there are numerous portions and statements highlighted on the text, and the indications are more to those items that are supportive only of a pursuit of the charges of neglect or homicide. Mitigating factors or statements are not emphasized. While this may not be indicative of anything in particular, this coroner investigator is again also a law enforcement investigator as his main employment. Knowing this person, there was always a tendency to use the law enforcement perspective in a death investigation rather than the objectivity that should really be the coroner viewpoint. There is additional material in the file that shows research being done on the law and how it might have applied in this case. While the objective coroner should be aware of statutes and how they work or apply to different situations, there is an undercurrent here of trying to make, or select, facts that fit criminality. That is the job of law enforcement and the attorneys, not of a true medical legal death investigator. Our job is to gather the facts and truly decide on manner and cause, regardless of what the consequences are within the judicial system. It should be independent and free of bias of perspective – the facts are what they are, and it is not our place to convict anyone of anything. I suspect that the months-long delay in certification resulted more from trying to convince someone of a prosecution, rather than continuing the investigation. While it may be unavoidable due to the investigator's profession, the overlap and confusion of purpose between the law enforcement and coroner perspectives can lead to inappropriate accusations, or seeing criminality where there is none. Of course, without a good coroner report to show the thought process and procedure, we have to admit to speculation. I suspect though, that the determination of 'undetermined' was more due to the fact that the investigator really wanted to call it a homicide. This is also seen in his questions to the Washakie Sheriff, which include questions that would be posed by a law enforcement investigator pursuing criminal charges, more than those of a concern to a manner and cause of death. Add to that the letter to the State Attorney General, prior to letting the local County Attorney finish his analysis, you have an investigator going against standard protocols with a reveal of probable obvious bias. Again, a confusion of perspective and tasks.

In review of this case, one must also keep in mind that at this time period, less was known about dementia or Alzheimer's, the difficulties of caring for such a patient in a home setting, and less social acceptability of family

139

efforts in this regard, and this includes medical practitioners. The legal, social, and personal opinions on death and dying, and the degree of the right of a person to decide his own fate in situations is still hotly contested and argued both publically and in court. In this case, some of the bias is apparent in the medical and physician opinion, particularly in the hospital death summary. The wording tells all: "intentional lack of feeding" (unproven), "scratches and bruises inflicted by the daughter-in-law" (unsubstantiated), intentional administration of hypoglycemics to cause low blood sugar (proven wrong by lab tests), "elder abuse" (opinion), and the accusation that the aspiration was caused by force-feeding, which in consideration of the medical records and history could have occurred due to the subject's own eating habits, and during the final hospitalization period, and is well documented. This stuff should not be in a diagnosis of cause of death, but expressed as an opinion. The doctor reveals her own bias vividly in the case. While those may be understandable feelings, all objectivity appears gone, which does not help an investigation, nor show any understanding of the difficult care situation faced by a family. Finally, it seems that all agencies at the end, in spite of the resolution of earlier abuse complaints as unsubstantiated, appear caught up in the emotionalism of the case.

We must also keep in mind that it is documented in several records that the family, while not happy with the nursing home settings, actively sought alternatives and placement other than at home. They tried to work the situation within their capabilities and capacity. It appears hypocritical for agencies to insist on, or recommend such placement, then leave a family hanging out to dry as far as any financial assistance in that regard. The State decided the individual was not eligible for the two publically funded institutions, the State Hospital or Training School. Medicare has its own built in limitations and requirements for on-going funding after certain time periods. There is no indication of any other assistance offered by agencies in that area, or that the agencies, other than shortly prior to death, might file for State guardianship, in which case they would have been financially responsible for care. Too little, too late.

While generally not my area of concern, I would agree with the County Attorney and his view. With the knowledge and perspective of what we know now about home care in these situations, it appears that the family did their best, and under the circumstances, can we really fault some of the missteps? In any case, we need to stay focused on the facts at hand and refer more to the pathologist's results. There is no physical evidence of trauma or neglect that would lead to a conclusion of homicide with reasonable certainty. Cachexia as a result of a person's willful failure to eat and drink at the end of life is usually considered a natural death. I prefer the term cachexia rather than starvation, as cachexia is a simple medical description and diagnosis, whereas 'starvation' has more emotional baggage and subjective interpretation. Aspiration can be accidental, but usually if pneumonia is the primary result and cause of death, and that act is part of a long-standing medical condition or mental disability, again it is usually ruled a natural death (and the death from pneumonia may also have been partially hospital acquired in this case, just like the "fluid overload"). In addition, there is well documented medical history of recurrent pneumonia of unspecified etiology over time in the records. If you strip away the more distasteful and unfortunate aspects of this case, and admit to the apparent willfulness and nature of the deceased's own behavior, in light of the pure facts, I would have ruled this case a natural death with a reasonable certainty.

Again, it cannot be over-emphasized, that the coroner and medical legal investigator's responsibility also includes shearing off inherent bias of perspective, to not only find proper objective resolution for the deceased, but also deflect possible inappropriate allegations against the living. To have accused the family of neglectful homicide in this case would have been, in my opinion, a gross miscarriage of justice.

Case 41. #94164 (1994) This case is regarding a 34 year old Male who had been missing in the desert for three to four weeks, and was worked in conjunction with Washakie County. All we have is some miscellaneous hand-written notes and telexes, and an indication the missing person was a resident of Hot Springs County. Both counties have a border with Fremont, and there are hints that the body was found possibly near the border of Washakie and Fremont. Without doing a search with the archives or vital records, we have no indications of determination of the actual final jurisdiction, and no coroner report of the investigation. This case is undetermined in the database due to incompetent documentation rather than anything else. This could also have been listed as an unknown.

Case 42. #95086 (1995) This 36 year old Native American male was seen floating in the Boysen Reservoir near the highway causeway that crosses the southern end of the body of water. This reservoir covers over 56 square miles and is contained by a dam at the north end. The southern end is fed by the Wind River, which has a large number of tributaries and feeder streams from the watershed of the entire valley and surrounding mountains – an area included within the boundaries for the most part of Fremont County and roughly a surface area of 9,000 square miles. Keep this in mind when considering the nature of this type of case. The body was seen floating on the 23rd of June by a citizen, who promptly notified authorities for a recovery. There is no coroner report, so we will consider the other documentation in the file.

The body is transported to Cheyenne for a forensic autopsy in conjunction with the State Crime Lab. It is quite decomposed, and full body x-rays are completed and reviewed. Clothing consists of worn jeans, underwear, socks and tennis shoes. The white shoes are written on with a marker, "L shoe" and "R shoe" respectively. Tucked in the left sock is a wallet with tribal ID, social security card, family photos, and no cash. The pathologist compares the IDs with the deceased, noting a possible chip on the inner aspect of the left upper midincisor and strong resemblance of general features, giving a tentative identification pending either fingerprint of dental confirmation. The procedure is documented in detail as would be expected, and no evidence of foul play or trauma is seen. Because of the degree of decomposition, the cause of death is undetermined but noted as consistent with drowning. An anomaly of a horseshoe shaped kidney is noted. Toxicology is negative for drugs, but blood ethanol registers 0.377 – this would be quite high even if discounting the small portion that would be accounted for by the decomposition. A dental chart is completed, and property retained by the crime lab as evidence. The skin is removed from the fingers that are the most intact and readable for post-mortem printing.

Records from the reservation police are obtained – we seem to have the entire file including the originals – which contain booking photos and fingerprint card. The State lab does a comparison and reports "the prints are of common origin". There is no official record of a dental comparison, which would not be needed with the positive result on fingerprints, but that option would have been available is the prints failed. Dental work is seen on the autopsy report and chart, and most Native Americans would have gotten the work done through Indian Health Services, who would have records. Booking records show a long history of offenses and incarceration for intoxication related incidents on the part of the deceased.

The death certificate lists a cause of death as "asphyxia consistent with drowning – could not be determined where or how this occurred". The manner is checked as "could not be determined". The date of death is listed as the date found. Photos are included in the file and are consistent with the pathology description and typical for a body that had drowned and been submerged for some time.

While there is no coroner report, some additional information is obtained by enclosed newspaper articles. The first describes the event of finding the body. A later article describes the identification of the deceased, and states that was determined through dental comparison. So indeed that method was used, and was probably faster to accomplish then waiting on the fingerprint comparison by the lab. Nothing wrong with pursuing multiple possible options, and with both, the ID is golden. The coroner notes that because the autopsy showed no evidence of violence, the items for lab analysis moves down their priority list for time frame of completion. The article also notes the individual had been missing for more than a week. That detail should have been part of a coroner report, but luckily we had the newspaper source to add it. An obituary copy is notable as it gives the information that the deceased lived out of state but returned to this area in 1986 – and the law enforcement records show continuous encounters with alcohol related incidents since that time. The final article notes an interview with the coroner who states that due to the high water at the time period, the individual could have gone into the river upstream at most any point, even miles away from the location found. He implies that there was an effort to track the deceased's last movements, but they are ill-defined, and unless a witness to an event is found, the circumstances will remain unknown. He is quoted as saying, "We hope nobody put him in the river, there's no evidence of that, but they could have." While we have no way of knowing the questions or context of such statement in a media interview, that certainly did not help put the family's minds to rest. There are no physical indications from the evidence of anything suspicious, and while such things cannot be completely eliminated due to the condition of the body, I would think that is not the sort of public statement one should make unless there is a basis for it.

The additional information from the media is appropriate to the case, though, in terms of understanding the event. The body in reviewing the autopsy and photos is obviously in a condition where it has resurfaced a period after the originating event, and thus noticed by the public. On drowning, the body usually sinks to below surface, so this one may have gone in anywhere upstream, possibly quite a distance away if the flow was fast and high as would be typical for the time frame and snowmelt runoff.

Depending on many variables that affect when the deceased will resurface, we can only get an estimate of the time frame. Water temperature at that time of year would most likely be in the 40s or 50s, which would give a range of ten to twenty days before it popped up by most studies. That would seem around the given time of disappearance reported. Interaction with debris, the bottom, and other factors alter the movement time frame from just the current in the river. Branched tributaries expand the area where it could have happened. The population center of Riverton is roughly 20 miles from the body location, Lander about 45 miles, so both are well within the water travel distance that could be covered in the time frame he was missing. For the time of year and being highly intoxicated, hypothermia and drowning would have been fairly quick, but that does not define any further the circumstances that led to his being in the water. Pushed, fell, or simply walked in, will be an unknown forever unless someone admits to a witnessed event. Accident, homicide, or even a natural event that cause him to go in, will never be known. Undetermined is a valid and legitimate conclusion in the case.

Case 43. #95173 (1995) This 56 year old Native American female was brought to the local emergency room in October via EMS after being found unresponsive. When seen by a niece about 6 hours prior the event, nothing unusual was noted. The ER record notes hypoglycemia, hypothermia, hypovolemia, severe metabolic acidosis, probable drug ingestion, possible sepsis. The admission record states a history of seizures, past overdoses, Systemic Lupus Erythematosus (SLE). Empty bottles of Soma and Tylenol 3 were reported at home. History of depression is noted by record. The patient was stabilized in the ER and admitted, gaining consciousness but remaining disoriented, prognosis "guarded". The discharge/death summary notes the patient as "no code", with the condition declining until death occurred within 24 hours. The final diagnosis was the severe metabolic acidosis with acetaminophen drug toxicity (level of 3.85 on toxicology). The acetaminophen level seen is probably a bit lower than what it was actually due to the therapeutic administration of fluids in the ER and other factors related to therapies and time frame. The cause was multifactorial, and included renal failure, hepatic failure most likely secondary to the overdose, and probable sepsis. An autopsy was requested.

There is no coroner's report, but once again the coroner investigator filed a police report that indicated an autopsy was arranged and medical records requested. Again, this confusion of jurisdiction and proper paperwork could actually have had legal repercussions if pressed. The officer has no jurisdiction to order an autopsy, and no legal right to request medical records without a subpoena or warrant. As a coroner death investigator he can do those things, but to note them on the police report could be a legal boggle when the roles are not kept separate. A copy of the medical records is in the file, and the toxicology notes a high positive for opiates in addition to the acetaminophen, but no quantitative. The balance of records of the hospital course support and match the diagnosis listed. A note written on the file folder indicates the physician doing the autopsy, but says "no report" in red, so evidently that was lost or never received. No copy of the final certification is included either, so this is listed as undetermined due once again to lack of documentation.

In the end, that is most likely justified without more information. Just because a person has a history of overdose episodes, often that is due to psychological attention-getting behavioral issues, bad habits when using opiates or other medications, poor personal medical behavior – not necessarily indicative of intentional suicide. Especially without detailed toxicology on quantitative levels, suicide would be a guess, and in light of her other physical and long term issues, probably not up to the 50-50

146

certainty level. It could very well be that the physical effects of her long term life style reached a tipping point leading to multi-organ collapse, which could be considered a natural death, or accidental if there was opiates in conjunction with too much acetaminophen. Undetermined it is.

Case 44. #97200 (1997) The next case was actually a death in Big Horn County to the north of Fremont County, which is near the Montana border. This 37 year old Native American male died at a hospital in April in that county, and the Fremont coroner, as well as the FBI, were brought in due to possible connections with this area as far as originating scene and possible source of a head injury. An autopsy was completed by a pathology service in Billings, Montana, and we will let the pathologist summarize: "A certain morphologic or toxicologic cause of death in this case is not seen. On the other hand, it seems clear that [the deceased] did not die from a head injury. He did suffer from severe alcoholic liver disease, which by itself, has been known to result in sudden death; and in addition, he also had increased levels of ethanol (0.39), chlordiazepoxide and THC present. These may have been sufficient to cause death if he were viewed as a very sick man because of liver failure. Other possibilities include mechanical asphyxia from a drug coma. I believe the underlying liver disease was important enough to be listed as the cause of death and that the drugs and/or positioning problems may have contributed to the death. The manner of death is undetermined."

In a nutshell, the pathologist eliminates assault trauma, but leaves it open as to being accidental or natural, thus undetermined is appropriate. Once the issue of homicide is eliminated, the FBI would have backed off, as they are only interested in major crimes in the area. If it had been determined as a natural death, the jurisdiction would be the Big Horn County coroner rather than Fremont, as jurisdiction only goes to another county if the 'originating incident' in a non-natural death occurred at another location. Since we have the possibility of a natural versus accidental overdose, we would have to know where the ingestion of substance occurred for an accident change of jurisdiction. Odds are, to have indulged in Fremont and then made it all the way to Big Horn before running into medical difficulties is unlikely, so it is unlikely that this is Fremont's case. However, we just do not have enough information to determine for sure the circumstances. As for a "coroner report", all we have in the file is some hand written notes on a scrap of paper and some others written on a restaurant handout. Pretty sad documentation, but fortunately the pathologist explained it well.

Case 45. #99021 (1999) Here we have a case from late January involving a 16 year old Native American victim of a gunshot wound that occurred on the reservation. The investigation involved the FBI, tribal police, and coroner's office. The coroner report is here and fairly detailed, and includes photos of the scene. The subject was found on his back in the dining room-kitchen area, and a .22 caliber rifle was lying on the kitchen table, no clip, but with one spent round in the chamber. One live round and another empty shell were found on the living room floor. The body description is detailed, noting an entrance wound to the right temple area, with the characteristics of a contact firing. No other features of significance are described on the body or clothing. No exit wound is noted.

According to the narrative, the FBI interviewed four other youths who were present at the incident, and according to those witnesses, there had been a "party" going on at the residence. The deceased walked out of the bedroom with a rifle and fired a couple of times into the ceiling, then he stated, "You want crazy? I'll show you crazy-", put the muzzle to his head and pulled the trigger. The rifle had obviously been moved prior to the investigator's arrival, but nothing in the narrative indicates who moved it. That information may have been in the FBI reports defining whether it was a witness or law enforcement responder, but they are not included in the file. Scene photos are consistent with the description, and include the wound, whole body, shells and bullets, and holes noted in the ceiling from the reported firings. The descriptions and photos are not adequate enough to determine the relationship to position fired from and the body or general scene. An autopsy is planned with the forensic pathologist in Colorado.

Generally, documentation from this point in time starts to improve on cases, as there is a new coroner. The former lead investigator has retired from law enforcement and was elected to replace the former coroner who retired after being in office for 38 years. While there still is no official office space and he too is working out of his home, forms and policies are improving, and documentation retention is much better. The investigator doing this case is now chief deputy, and while there is some experience with the job, there also are some issues. I myself have also been hired on part-time to the department at this point, so there will be a more inclusive familiarity with the cases and the people who worked them.

The first issue of note is that on the investigator's report, he indicates the death as a suicide. This investigator also completes the death certificate five days after the incident, and four days after the autopsy, noting the cause as "cerebral lacerations and contusions due to a contact gunshot wound to the right frontal/parietal region". He certifies the manner as a suicide. While the cause is worded as the probable preliminary result from the pathologist, the manner is the investigator's opinion, and erroneous in time frame. Final autopsy results and toxicology take weeks, and would not have been received at the time he filled out the certificate. In addition, law enforcement would not have completed their own investigation as to the circumstances. It is a grievous error to rule on a manner before all the evidence and information have been processed, which was the case here.

Four weeks later the autopsy report is received by the coroner. The toxicology shows the blood alcohol on the deceased to be 0.175 and the sample positive for cannabinoids (at this time the labs did not define and quantify the cannabinoids in the same detail they do today). In his narrative the pathologist notes that the investigation has apparently ruled out foul play. There are no supplemental notes in the coroner report to indicate the basis of this determination, but it would not be unusual to have the pathologist converse with the FBI in this regard during the period after the physical procedure before his final report. He notes further "Interpretation of this action is open to discussion. The action may be interpreted as suicide. It may also be the act of an intoxicated and agitated adolescent trying to impress, intimidate, or shock his friends. He may well have not completely thought about what he was doing, or perhaps only intended to fire off a round close to his head. It is my understanding when talking [with the investigator] immediately following the autopsy that he considered the act a suicide. I more favor a ruling of accident for the reasons outlined above. A ruling of "undetermined" (accident vs. suicide) may well be the best approach in classifying the death". Photos are included in the file from the autopsy. Notable in the report is that the deceased had 16 unfired rounds in his pants pocket; the bullet is recovered from the head; and the wound track proceeds from left to right, anterior to posterior at an angle backwards of approximately 40 degrees, and from inferior to superior at an angle of approximately 25 to 30 degrees. The hands were bagged and gunshot residue kits collected by the crime lab, along with other evidence, and the report on any results is not included with the other crime lab reports in the file.

After all the results are in, the coroner amends the death certificate with vital records, changing the manner of death from suicide to undetermined. Now, a few comments on this case, as I am personally familiar with it and the investigating parties involved. First, it is up to a coroner to decide policy on certifications and who completes them, and in my office the two full-time deputies are authorized to certify their own cases, but we discuss the case and their conclusions first, as the coroner is ultimately responsible and accountable for such things. Knowing the personalities involved here, we have a deputy who was known for being opinionated and somewhat arrogant about his abilities (he called himself the "Lander coroner"), and he obviously based his certification on his own opinion rather than the facts that came later. The pathologist is being diplomatic in his wording, and my opinion is the coroner went with undetermined to keep the peace with his investigator, or his inherent law enforcement tendency to look for criminality. Keep in mind that the FBI had no issues of a suspicious death, or any reason to doubt the testimony of the witnesses and the scenario of the event presented. Also keep in mind the levels of certainty that are defined for us to work under. We must be 50-50 or less in deciding certainty of manner of death for undetermined to be valid in most cases. There are no indications in the investigation of suicidal intent, and the event as described, as well as the opinion of the pathologist, leans towards an accidental death. To jump to a certification of suicide before all the facts are in can be a devastating conclusion for a family and is irresponsible. To leave it as undetermined still leaves no emotional closure as unjustified doubt will remain in the minds of the relatives, as well as possibly causing issues and unjustified accusations for those who were present. Based on what I know of this case and the individuals involved, I have a reasonable certainty that agrees with the pathologist's favoring an accidental death. This should not have been certified as undetermined.

An additional example is appropriate. Based on the recommendations from the National Association of Medical Examiners (NAME), willful engagement in risky behavior that results in death, is generally ruled an accident if the circumstances are defined by the investigation. A good example would be 'Russian Roulette', which is most often ruled accidental, although some jurisdictions disagree.

The procedure in place today for this office, especially on this type of case is first, do not imply or certify, or assume a manner of death before all the facts are in. Second, we discuss all questionable cases with the law enforcement investigators after their investigation before certifying. Those meetings are noted as supplemental summaries so that at least the basics of their information and results are available to justify the coroner conclusion. Note that this is not to get law enforcement's agreement or conclusion, but to make sure all the facts and evidence are considered – the final ruling is still up to this office. Complex cases are discussed openly among the staff and myself, with each presenting the justifications for a conclusion. If there is reluctance or disagreement, the coroner has the ultimate decision to make. Perhaps in a complicated case, an inquest will be arranged and the decision left to an independent jury. Final determination is statutorily the responsibility of the coroner, or that jury. Then, and only then, based on the evidence and facts known, can a manner be decided within a reasonable certainty. The facts are what they are, and the case is what it is, and that, and nothing else, should determine the manner of death.

Section VI: The 21st Century Knock on the Door

In the next series and period of years, due to the change of administration, the policies and thoroughness of investigation procedures start to be more consistent and well-documented. Partly this is due to the coroner's law enforcement background, as medical-legal investigators use many of the same principles for case investigation, although the focus should be different towards manner and cause. There will be still some obvious bias at times due to that same law enforcement background, but at least the methodology is improving. Files start to be more complete, thicker, and less guesswork will be involved in a review. This also reflects the national trend towards standardization through groups like the National Institute of Justice and National Association of Medical Examiners. Different states will still work through different systems, as Wyoming remains a coroner system, rather than a medical examiner or the mixed coroner/ME systems used elsewhere. Coroners here are still an elected official, so the various counties in Wyoming are still inconsistent as to the type of experience that obtains the office of the coroner.

For those who work under a medical examiner system, the coroner system may seem antiquated, but they both have their advantages and disadvantages, and it really depends on the person running the department. Some State ME systems I am familiar with are still subject to budget limitations and staffing issues, as well as subject to the administrative foibles of the head ME. Some cut corners as far as doing a complete exam on autopsy based on circumstance, which leaves cases open to error if you guess wrong on probable manner of death. We all have seen cases where as the evidence comes in, you may end up 180° from where you thought you were when you started. Thus the value of treating everything in a consistent way as a homicide, until proven differently. Sometimes you can move to an obvious natural death fairly quickly, but if you assume something at first and find out by evidence it was a homicide later, you may not be able to make up for it as evidence and scenes will be gone or changed by that time. The same for a forensic autopsy – you can't go back in most cases and pick up later if you did not do a full exam the first time. Thus the contract pathologists we use adhere to the standard full exam on every case, regardless of initial indications.

The disadvantage of having an elected coroner in Wyoming is obvious – you are subject to the whims of the electorate. While certification and training is required once elected, any person with any background can get elected, so what you start with is highly variable. Historically in Fremont

County there have been a variety of backgrounds and some performed well, others not as well. For a long period, the only people who ran in most counties were funeral directors (still common in smaller population regions), and that experience only helps in certain aspects, not necessarily including being a good investigator. These days the larger population areas have people in office for the most part with either medical or law enforcement background prior to serving, so at least there is a good basic skill set to build on. Some areas still have funeral directors, but most of those have been in office for some time and have gotten the hang of it as needed through supplemental training, and perform adequately for the limited needs of their county. Still, there are large variations in both the ME and coroner systems in how investigations are approached, the cooperation and integration with law enforcement, and administration and documentation under the laws of the jurisdiction.

During the period of these next cases, several things are coming to fruition in Fremont County. The County Commission agrees to provide a small office space for the coroner, which helps on retaining documentation, although past files are still scattered in other buildings. County maintenance provides a room for property storage. A new jail is built, and the coroner gets the old jail kitchen in the court house and converts it to an autopsy suite and exam room, as well as a cooler for body storage. All deputies are still 'occasional employees', much like volunteer firemen, who have their own regular jobs, but training is more pervasive and standardized. An administrative assistant is approved for hire, which also helps on documentation. Eventually the chief deputy position becomes the first full time investigator other than the coroner.

This pretty much remains the situation until right before I took office, when a new justice center is built, and the coroner's office gets a portion of the old sheriff's office for use. This enables me to pull in all files to one secure location, along with a secure property room, space for supplies and materials, adequate office space for myself and now two full time deputies rather than using the multiple 'occasional' staff, who may or may not have been available due to their regular jobs. We even have an old circuit court room for inquests if needed. With other changes in policies, procedures and implementation, the office is finally generally up to the medical legal investigative standard it should be, the result of a long growth process with many contributors of the past.

A long road, and one that continues, as change is progress. If you do not change with the times, you don't stand still, you essentially go backwards as everything else leaves you behind.

Case 46. #200134 (2000) This 32 year old white female was found unresponsive in mid-October in bed and in her home. She was last seen alive by neighbors as she was mowing her lawn late the day before being found. The coroner's report is pretty basic in scene and body description, notes no evidence of trauma; medical history indicates "Serotonin Syndrome" as a diagnosis with medications at the scene indicating treatment for illness such as depression and sleep disorders. A book with writing on the inside cover is collected at the scene. I was actually at this scene and assigned documentation of the location as a supplemental, which I completed in detail, including a diagram. Nothing out of the ordinary or indicating any disturbance was noted.

An autopsy was arranged with a local pathologist. While this particular doctor was not forensically certified, he was through and detailed in his exams in a forensic procedure, rather than just the medical pathology. My only caution for this physician's reports after working with him over the years is though he was thorough, he tended to equivocate in his conclusions, being somewhat reluctant to commit to a particular manner of death in the more complex cases. Toxicology now is to the point where if the presumptive tests are positive, the samples are sometimes sent to an outside lab to be quantified. In this case there was a lethal level of meperidine (147 mg/L), high oxycodone (0.51 mg/L) and acetaminophen (125 mg/L). Physical finding include bilateral lung aspiration and edema, brain edema consistent with hypoxia, and a lacerated tongue consistent with seizure activity. These finding are consistent also with the effects of the overdose of the specific medications. The pathologist's conclusion states that due to uncertain history, he reports the death as undetermined. While not specifically stated by the pathologist, absent any other significant findings, the cause is an overdose of the meperidine, which is at 8 to 18 times the fatal level seen in studied cases, and over 800 times what is usually considered therapeutic levels.

EMS records indicate a call 15 days before the death, where the subject was transported to the hospital for seizures and hospitalized for four days. The diagnosis at that time was the Serotonin syndrome crisis, most likely from the use of Prozac in a therapy regimen that had started three weeks prior for depression. After the admission she stabilized and was found negative for all other tested conditions and screenings. Confusion and personality changes were noted initially that also stabilized with treatment.

The book recovered at the scene is about understanding suicide, and it is noted that over the years, there have been numerous popular publications about or "how to" suicide that regularly turned up at suicide scenes. That, however, may only be coincidental and cannot be considered definitively related, unless, like in some cases, the methods used are the ones discussed in the publication. Sometimes people are just curious and we need to avoid unsubstantiated opinions. The note inside the cover written by the deceased reveals no particular intention.

Normally in a case like this, I would note the script for the prescription and estimate the number of pills needed to obtain the levels of the fatal drug, but that information is not here or in the medical record. While not knowing the script, the average oral dose results in a blood level of 0.17 mg/L – which would be over 800 pills. That medication does come in injectable and liquid form, but there is no indication of that at the scene. No recognizable pills were seen in the stomach at autopsy, which would have been the case if a large number of pills were consumed prior to death. The possibility remains that the drug in injectable form could have been obtained illegally. In most cases of drug/pill suicide, if the number of pills is so high that it indicates intent, and evidence of recent ingestion is seen, you have a reasonable certainty of suicide. No one takes handfuls of pills by mistake. Also note that intentional or volitional self-termination is usually considered suicide, regardless of mental capacity or conditions.

There are some questions here that are unresolved, such as the relation to the previously discussed conditions and seizure history. The exact source of the meperidine level is not apparent, outrageously high, with an outside possibility of accident or homicide. Undetermined is probably a safe bet if you do not feel a reasonable certainty of the manner, but without any indications of forced induction of the drug, suicide could also have been a reasonable conclusion.

Case 47. #201036 (2001) This 37 year old Native American male was transported in full cardiac arrest to the local emergency room in early March where he was pronounced. He showed obvious signs of assault and internal abdominal bleeding, and according to the girlfriend he lived with, had been involved in an altercation the day before. He had been seen in the ER after the assault, was treated and released. The subject at that time had stated that during the assault he had also been kicked in the abdomen and back. The next day he developed difficulty breathing and then went into cardiac arrest which resulted in the terminal episode. Reservation police indicated that they were not called about any altercation on the previous day. Photo documentation at the ER was obtained and an autopsy scheduled.

The forensic autopsy documented multiple contusions and abrasions, noted no cranial hemorrhage, but did find a hepatic laceration on the inferior right lobe, which resulted in a very large amount of abdominal bleeding. In addition there was one right rib fracture on the back. Other physical findings included liver disease and severe coronary artery disease. The pathologist ruled that he died from the massive intraabdominal hemorrhage due to the laceration of the liver following blunt force injuries. The injury is estimated to have occurred greater than 12 hours, bust less than four or five days prior to death, resulting in a slow bleed. The other injuries seen were not considered terminal. He notes the manner of death as undetermined due to an ongoing investigation. Toxicology was negative for drugs and alcohol.

EMS records for the day before death report that the subject stated he had two seizures and fell, had a history of seizures but had not taken his Dilantin for a month. He also stated he had been beaten up four days ago and complained of abdominal pain. ER medical records for that visit note stable vitals, a blood alcohol of 0.256, CBC and metabolic panels in retrospect might show the symptoms of an internal bleed, but that is hindsight only, as they were not so far off as to be life threatening. A CT was completed of the head which showed encephalomalacia (loss of mass) consistent with remote injury, early atrophy considered more advanced that one would expect for his age, no evidence of acute injury. Being stable, he was released.

The second EMS record reports on the transport on the day of death. The subject was in full cardiac arrest when they arrived, and a majority of the report deals with that aspect, although it is noted he was transported the previous evening as a possible assault victim. ER records indicate his blood alcohol was negative at that time with CBC and blood chemistry values worse when compared to the previous visit. Creatine Kinase, for example, is four times the value of high normal. They were unable to reverse the arrest and pronounced the death.

There are two handwritten notepad pages from the coroner in addition to the deputy investigators report, but no supplemental information as to follow up, other than noting the FBI was notified as a possible homicide. The death certificate was completed as 'pending' the day after the autopsy by the investigator, and amended by the coroner to 'undetermined' over ten months later. There is no logic or narrative of the justification as to why this was not ruled a homicide. The death causing injuries are obviously not self-inflicted. What we know of the time frame of the assault is questionable from the reports, but whether the day before, or four days prior, either one fits within the time frame established by the pathologist. It also would not be unusual for a pathologist to leave a manner as undetermined pending the investigation, but the coroner is not locked into that manner and can change it based on the total evidence later. There are no indications that his previous medical conditions caused or contributed to the death. Whether law enforcement ever established exactly when the assault occurred, or by who, is unknown, but also irrelevant to the manner of death. I did not participate in this case and do not know any of the details of the delay in certification, but regardless of intent or time frame, if the injuries caused the death, this should have been a homicide.

Case 48. #201199 (2001) Here is a case where the coroner was notified of an impending death, and while technically not his jurisdiction prior to the actual death, this is a good idea if this sort of assistance is needed, as we are the ones to coordinate resources after the fact. Exactly when notification occurred is unknown due to the coroner's habit of scribbling on any available scrap of paper and not completing a formal and detailed report and time line. Some of the case can be reconstructed from the notes and emails, and luckily he assigned background research to one of the occasional deputies that had a habit of thorough documentation. I was aware of this case and it was discussed, but only indirectly participated in the investigation. Death occurred late November with notification to the coroner roughly two weeks prior.

This case involves a 68 year old white female who had a provisional diagnosis of Creutzfeldt-Jakob Disease (CJD), commonly referred to by the public as "Mad Cow Disease". That is only one of the variants of the prion classified illnesses, but the public tends of react and call all variants that name regardless of etiology. Historically the patient had been seen regularly for her chronic COPD, atrial fibrillation, hypertension and atherosclerotic cardiovascular disease; also there was a history of a previous myocardial infarction 10 year prior to the death. Other than those conditions, records showed a capable, reasonably active and responsive patient. Starting roughly three months prior to the death, there is noted a remarkable degeneration in her mental capabilities and condition, with an additional diagnosis of dementia added. EEGs completed in early November by a neurologist suggest CJD as a possibility. A lab test for 'neuron specific enolase' around the same time gave a result of 348 ng/mL, with the report noting that results greater than a value of 35 are indicative of CJD. Medical staff contacted the coroner in light of the impending death to see if an autopsy could be arranged after death to confirm the provisional diagnosis. While technically there is no jurisdiction here as an attended and anticipated death, there is nothing wrong with assisting on non-jurisdiction cases if within our capacity.

Not a lot was known at the time about prions, which are twisted proteins that are not technically alive, other than they were not contagious in most circumstances unless the nervous system containing them was breached. They were known to not be affected by common cleaning and sterilization techniques, radiation, autoclaves, or acid baths, and basically force one to consider the body as a very hazardous material. While more is known about them now, they still are a bit of a mystery and include chronic wasting disease in wildlife, and mad cow and other diseases in domestic animals. CJD is a rare and human form variant.

The deputy reports include a time line review of all available medical records showing the progression of the illness from the personal physician, local hospitals, and nursing home facilities. The detailed summary notes the rapid decline in mental status and ability from communicative and ambulatory to a basic vegetative state over a six week period. This led to the neurologic consult and testing and provisional diagnosis ten days prior to death. Her basic report notes the time line of her research, which included the records, and a consult with the coroner/pathologist in Casper, who provided basic disease information as well as possible alternative diagnosis. It is noted that an autopsy is at this time the only way to confirm by actual examination of the brain tissue.

The local hospital pathologist declined to do an autopsy due to the risk and inability to decontaminate the facility afterwards. The forensic pathologists from Colorado, Wyoming State Crime lab, Utah State Medical Examiner, and Colorado Department of Pathology refused for the same reasons. The Mayo Clinic in Minnesota was willing if the coroner's office would book a private plane to fly the body directly to the facility, which for budget considerations, was not feasible. An autopsy to confirm the illness was therefore not possible. The Wyoming Department of Health epidemiologist was contacted, as this is a reportable disease, to make sure they were aware of it. They noted they were working on protocols to deal with CJD, and at this time morticians were not allowed to embalm such cases due to its potentially infectious nature. It also turns out that the CDC has recommended protocols for biologic and tissue sample retrieval and handling, but, of course, to do that you have to find a pathologist willing to breach the nervous system. After death, the body was sent to a Casper, WY funeral home for cremation. [This is particularly interesting in that as of today, research has shown that prion diseases may even survive cremation, so the recommended method of disposition is direct burial in a sealed casket.]

The researching deputy also noted that according to literature at the time, this was most likely a case of classic sporadic CJD. Gene related inherited CJD is not indicated, as there would be other familial history of dementia, which is not seen here. Likewise, this is not acquired 'Mad Cow' CJD, as that presents different neurologic symptoms and does not register the same on an EEG. Even if not physically confirmed by examination of the brain tissue, there is a definite reasonable certainty of what is going on here.

And guess what? By statute this is a coroner case. The law specifically notes that the coroner has jurisdiction if a public health hazard is presented, which trumps the aspects of being an attended and anticipated death. This part of the statute comes in to play in any communicable disease, or events such as a pandemics or Hazmat situations. In conjunction with other statutes, the coroner is to work in conjunction with state medical officers in dealing with these kinds of deaths. That makes perfect sense, as there is special medical authority and powers given to the Department of Health in those situations, and the coroner is best able to investigate, track, and see to the disposition of such instances.

The deputy did a stellar job of this case and her documentation. The random notes from the coroner, and the emails in the file, do not add anything of significance to her reports, but would have been simpler to review and go through if an actual summary report was presented. The death certificate was originally filed as 'pending' and then amended about a month later with a cause of "probable CJD" and a manner of undetermined. I totally disagree with 'undetermined' in this case. The CJD is diagnosed within medical certainty, and none of her other conditions were terminal at the time by record. Even if not physically confirmed by tissue examination, in saying "probable CJD", using "probable" on a medical diagnosis does not require a manner of undetermined. In many cases of natural death, especially those with no autopsy, we are ruling based on a reasonable certainty from medical records and history, added to what is observed at the scene, on the body, or from investigation. No one expects 100% certainty in certification, by accepted national standards, just a reasonable one. This disease may be weird and the case unusual, but this is a natural death.

Case 49. #201215 (2001) This 44 year old male died at the medical center in Casper, Natrona County, with jurisdiction transferred to this county by that coroner due to the originating incident occurring here on the last day of December for the year. He died the evening of the same day. The original EMS report indicates his "wife" reportedly found him in an "altered state of consciousness" and awake but unresponsive after falling out of bed. He was transported to a local facility and then transferred to the medical center in Casper. The Natrona County Coroner's office obtained records and did the investigation on the Casper hospitalization. The individual the EMS reported as the wife turns out to be a girlfriend, not married to the deceased.

The local hospital history notes indicate the patient was an oil rig worker that had recently gotten back from the field. The partner noted no unusual problems up to this point, other than that he fell asleep during sex the night before, which she thought a bit unusual. Around 4 am she thought he fell out of bed, was incontinent, unable to stand, and incoherent, so she called 911. Admission notes indicate initial suspicions were of meningitis; labs results showed a blood glucose of 425, pH of 7.0, blood alcohol of 0.0182, negative for acetaminophen, and salicylates at 108 (therapeutic is 150 to 300). He was unconscious by the time of arrival at the hospital and stayed that way throughout the course of his hospitalization. The patient was stabilized and prepared for transfer to a higher level of care.

The Casper hospital narrative indicates that antifreeze may have been mixed with another liquid and that the deceased also ingested a "white chemical powder", which apparently was collected and accompanied the patient to Casper. The source of the story is not indicated. By the time he is in Casper the story related is that he lost consciousness during intercourse. Testing for meningitis was negative and he was found to be in severe metabolic acidosis. He was prepared for dialysis but went into arrest within five minutes of that procedure being started. All interventions were unsuccessful. Due to the questionable circumstances, the coroner was contacted.

Lab tests at Casper showed an ethylene glycol level at 8.6 mg/dL (greater than 2 is considered toxic, greater than 20 is lethal). Troponin was at 14.1 (normal is less than 0.4) indicating organ and cardiac damage. The white powder was tested at the state crime lab and found to be ammonium nitrate, a "non-controlled substance", used in industry, as fertilizer or in explosives and freezing mixtures. The Natrona coroner deputy did take photos of the deceased, but they are unrevealing due to the time frame and medical intervention.

The subject's personal medical care was handled through the VA, and those records were also obtained. They show the last visit about a month before the incident for a psychiatric evaluation. Conditions reported include chronic alcohol abuse but stated as sober for over a year. The presentation is diagnosed as "provisional schizotypal personality disorder" possibly due to long term ethanol abuse, and notes previous psychiatric encounters with other agencies. No current dysfunction however, no major medical issues or medications. Balance of record over time indicates periods of sobriety of one to two years interrupted by DUI relapse and retreatment for the alcohol addiction. No indications in the record of any suicidal tendencies or ideations.

A copy of the local police department interview of the girlfriend relates the activities and time line of the day prior to the incident, and does not contribute any further information other than normal activities and behavior. A coroner deputy has a one page supplemental report in the file documenting his activities in obtaining various records and reports. Two handwritten scratch-pad notes from the coroner add nothing new, and no formal report from him is in the file. A letter from the relatives of the deceased indicates they are suspicious of the girlfriend and her activities, but offer no evidence or substantiation of anything. An email from the local coroner to Natrona indicates a request for the local pathologist to run an ethylene glycol level on admission blood, with a result of "110", and also noting the release of the body to the funeral home in Casper. A copy of that lab report however is not in the file, so we do not know the quantification parameter on the ethylene glycol. An amendment to State Vital Records two months later changes the death certificate from pending to a cause of "profound metabolic acidosis due to ethylene glycol intoxication, level 108 mg/dL" and a manner of undetermined.

Without an actual coroner report, once again we are clueless as to the sequence and logic of the investigation, or the specifics of how the conclusion was obtained. Of note, without all the lab parameters, we cannot confirm the initial local hospital level in comparison to the one in Casper, or with the certification amount. Different labs will express results in different parameters, such as mg/mL versus g/dL or mg/dL, and one has to be cautious in the conversions to compare different results. It is entirely possible that the Lander level of ethylene glycol at "110" compares to the Casper level of "8.6" by decimal point movement per metric conversion, but we cannot be sure. Metabolism and fluid therapy can quickly alter the levels over the course of treatment, so we know that the toxic level seen in Casper probably indicates a higher initial level. Why the certificate level is given as "108", which does not match any of the records in the file, I have no idea.

Regardless, the source of the toxicity is at least partially established. There is an average of five thousand deaths per year in the U.S. from ethylene glycol poisonings, often adult males. Due to the sweet taste of the fluid, it also results in numerous pet deaths from kidney failure. It also would not be generally noticed if mixed with another fluid drink, depending on concentration, either intentionally or unintentionally. The symptoms described in the medical records and resulting issues and cause of death are consistent with ethylene glycol poisoning. There may be another factor, however. Ammonium nitrate is sometimes confused with amyl nitrate, alkyl nitrate, or other nitrate/nitrite variations that had some reputation and use as enhancing sexual activity. If this error was made, there may have been contributory toxicity from that substance, but there are no indications in the record that the investigators were aware of that possibility or that the blood was ever tested for the substance reported as the found powder. In any case, the cause of death is well documented in the medical records and the toxic effects of the primary substance found are well known.

As for the manner of death, while the individual's psychiatric record documents some unusual thinking and behavior, those records specifically do not indicate suicidal ideations or tendencies. There is no record elsewhere that would lead to that conclusion, so suicide is probably not of high consideration. There is a definite possibility of accidental ingestion and death, either through unknown circumstance, or intentional misinformed usage that it may be a substitute for ethanol. (People do the same thing intentionally to get "drunk" with methanol, which is also toxic and destructive to the system.) There is an outside chance, totally without any evidence to support it, that the ethylene glycol was slipped in as a "mickey" into his drink. That, regardless of intent, could make the death a homicide. About the only thing we know for sure is that this is not a natural death. Without any other evidence to the contrary to eliminate guess work, we might struggle to get above the 50-50 level towards any particular manner, so undetermined is probably the best bet.

Case 50. #202090 (2002) Now we have another case involving antifreeze, one of a 37 year old white male who was found in mid-May in a rural area below a scenic overlook. The altitude is around 6, 900 feet in elevation with cliffs, steep slopes and rugged draw areas below the overlook, which is accessed via a dirt road from the nearby highway. An abandoned car was found about 2 ½ miles away from the immediate scene and was impounded by the sheriff's office. A search for the owner finds it registered to a man from Pennsylvania who was reported missing by the family. Search & Rescue personnel initiated a search of the area, thus finding the body, as well as an open jug of antifreeze on the hillside just above the body.

The body was decomposed with notable insect activity, lying on his back in a boulder field, fully clothed but wearing only a light jacket. The crime lab was requested by the sheriff's office to assist in the investigation, so the body was not recovered until the day after being found. Temperature at the time ranged around the mid-fifties during the day, high thirties at night, and the area was dry with no recent precipitation. Photo documentation was completed, along with GPS of notable features and evidence, and I made rough diagrams of the scene to reference the different points. In particular, we walked the descent from the overlook to the body, the route being somewhat limited by the terrain, and noted no other particular significant evidence. The remains were contained and transported for forensic autopsy.

At autopsy a dental exam and x-rays were obtained for possible ID, which were compared to those sent out by the prospective family a few days later – ruled inconclusive by a team of odontologists from an Air Force Base in Cheyenne, due to the lack of any comparable dental work. DNA comparison of the deceased to the possible family members was then initiated, with a time frame of several months to complete at an independent lab. This eventually provided confirmation of the presumptive ID in August by the crime lab report, about three months later.

The coroner's report is in the file and has a sequence of events, but ends when the biologics were sent to the crime lab for DNA comparison. My own supplemental report details the scene and body description, as well as the sequence of recovery, plus assorted maps and diagrams. Sheriff's Office reports included are the impound report, vehicle registration information, credit card usage report that shows a last registration approximately three weeks before the date found, at a motel in Riverton, which is about 25 miles north of the scene. Activity registered in the same general town for about three days prior to the last usage, with activity across Wyoming the prior few weeks.

On autopsy, the pathologist determined the body condition to be consistent with death generally around the time of the last credit card usage. The cause of death is listed as consistent with hypothermia, but he reports that in a conversation with the forensic toxicologist it was noted that while the tox results were negative for both ethylene and propylene glycols (the main ingredients of antifreeze), gas chromatograph tracing was consistent with the breakdown products of either of these substances. Crystalline renal deposits and erosive esophagitis are also consistent with the consumption of the antifreeze. No other trauma or injury was seen, or evidence of foul play. He states that while the cause is listed as hypothermia, a combined toxicity from the antifreeze is also probably "in play" in the case. A manner of accident, undetermined (accident versus suicide), or suicide, would depend on correlation with the investigative history.

The Sheriff's office investigation included a processing of all evidence at the crime lab in Cheyenne, and interviews with all local businesses and motels that had contact with the deceased per the credit card records. Contact with the parents revealed a history of "manic depressive disorder", and the credit card statement was obtained from them. History of drug or alcohol usage is unknown. Nothing of additional significance was obtained from the interviews in the area other than verifying the last locations and usage of the credit card per as indicated on the statement.

The death certificate was completed and filed in August once the ID was verified by the DNA testing. The cause was listed as hypothermia with antifreeze toxicity listed as a contributing factor. Manner is listed as undetermined. The case for the most part is well documented and detailed, and while there are indications this may have been a suicide, that determination over an accidental death would depend on the comfort level of the certifier. Cases are often not 100% certainty, and where the decision falls more often depends on the perspective and interpretation of the sum of the evidence by the investigator, rather than having a nice neat package to work with. In this case, the coroner was not comfortable with either in more than a 50-50 proposition, so undetermined it remained.

Case 51. #202160 (2002) The next case is that of a 50 year old white female, whose occupation is a nurse, that was found dead in her bed at home in August. The scene description in the coroner's report states there was no signs of struggle or disturbance; "see pictures" was written as a note.

At this point it is worth taking the time to discuss reports and technology and how they interrelate. We are finally getting to a time period where, more often than not, documentation and reporting has improved, and many of the tools of modern medical-legal death investigation are more commonly utilized. Processes are becoming more standardized and procedures are coming in line with national recommendations. The one thing the investigator must keep in mind, however, is the progression of technology, and how change has accelerated in the last few decades.

While it had been around a while, photography really started its heyday in the Civil War of the 1860's in public application. It took decades for the technology to improve enough to where it started to become common in investigations. Larger departments might have a 'police photographer', but more often, private or newspaper photographers supplemented their income by contracting themselves out to departments when needed, as the skill and equipment needed to take and process film was financially out of reach of most agencies. This situation in some areas continued into the 1970's, until cheaper 35mm cameras became available and processing could be done through local vendors. The numbers of photos at a scene were still limited by developing expense and number of shots per roll of film. Polaroids had a relatively brief popularity due to their immediate viewability versus waiting to get the film developed, but for detail 35 mm remained the standard. In the decade of the 1990's and early 2000's the first digital cameras came out, and they used a 3 ½" computer disk as storage – depending on setting, they could take around 50 to 100 photos per disk rather than being limited to frames on a roll of film. As memory technology improved in the last ten years, we can now not worry about frame number capacity and just fire away with our digital cameras, take hundreds of photos if needed, and just change a memory card for more. Photos are then downloaded to a computer rather than developed, and only printed when necessary. Advantages, yes, but also several new concerns arise that previously did not have to be dealt with.

The oldest photo we have in the Fremont County Coroner files is from 1938. It is an old print, a bit brittle, but still good after sitting in a file for almost 80 years. The same circumstance exists for all the other prints on photographic paper in all the decades since that time, depending on the quality of print and paper. The period of Polaroids was a disaster from an archival viewpoint – within a few years the color fades, changes, the prints stick together or peel depending on storage, and generally will be lost unless scanned and copied in the next few years. 35 mm slide or film negatives also become brittle, but still can be used to print from if necessary decades after they were taken. The same cannot be said for all the digital media we currently use unless specific steps are taken to preserve the data. Some download the digital photos to compact disks or DVDs to file, but few realize that the life span of these commercially available disks for readability is only about 5 to 10 years in cheaper products. The disk layers start losing integrity and data with age and become just a random piece of plastic. If you need to review a case ten years from now, even if the disk is readable, will you have the technology to read it? Take the first digital cameras for example. Every computer at the time had the standard disk drive to read a 3 ½" "floppy" disk ten to fifteen years ago. Now no computer has such drives, and you have to search to find a peripheral drive like that to plug into current systems to hopefully read them (we have one on hand). Even if you find such hardware, five years from now will it plug into your new system? Even the connections technology changes frequently. Archives are not only having to store media and information, but also maintain the hardware for old technology to read it. And unless you have stored your photos on a specially designed and long-life media or drive, there is a good chance it disappears in a decade. Even to this day, all the fancy modern technology, for all its advantages and convenience, cannot beat an old photographic print on good paper for storage life. So what does that mean for the modern investigator?

In your written reports, use "see photos" to support and further define your scene and body descriptions, not to replace the written narrative. Photos do not show everything, and can sometimes be hard to put into context without a good and detailed written narrative. And so far in civilization, our paper products, even with their own limitations, will far outlast most digital media. Do the archivist and cold case investigators a favor, as you never know to what purpose your investigative work today, will be used for down the time line. Use the best permanent storage you can. The Wyoming Archives can readily advise on current best practices.

Anyway, back to the current case. According to the description, the deceased was lying on her right side in a sleeping position, with vomit around her mouth and on the pillow. She was last noted alive by her husband when they went to bed around midnight, and found unresponsive early the next morning. EMS was called and the deceased pronounced at their arrival. Medical history included a history of bipolar affective disorder and fibromyalgia. A pill count of medications is included which indicates over use of the medications Lorazepam and Hydrocodone. Toxicology results show a lethal dose of hydrocodone and a high toxic level on the Lorazepam (it is noted that 14 pills of Hydrocodone regularly were taken in one day with the script being for 6 per day). An autopsy decides "profound respiratory depression and sedation" due as a result of the noted toxicology, possible aspiration, with no other significant findings. Manner is certified as undetermined.

I would disagree here on the manner. Just because a person has a history of a mental illness or disability, do not assume suicidal intentions. The number of pills taken to reach the fatal level, while more than prescribed, is well within what is often seen in those with chronic pain conditions who have either developed tolerance or over self-medicated in error. The Hydrocodone level is just barely over low fatal by studies, and the benzodiazepines would have contributed. This is nowhere near a case where the number of pills consumed leaves no doubt as to intent. While it is entirely possible that an experienced medical professional such as a nurse, might know exactly what to do to obscure suicide, there is no indications in the record of any other supporting information for that manner. Such a professional would also know that borderline fatal dosage would also have a good chance of not having the intended effect, if that is what it was. My preference in cases where we do not have reasonable certainty of suicide to a high degree, is to rule it an accident. I think we could certainly be more than 50-50 sure here that accident was the case, even if we do not get to an 80 to 90% certainty. Also, leaving it undetermined leaves doubt in the minds of the family as to what happened, and our job is to make the hard decisions on their behalf rather than the safe one. I would have gone with accident rather than undetermined.

Case 52. #202265 (2002) The next case is one we will have to skip at this time, as it is an active cold case. Generally it involved a shooting among siblings that had issues on whether it was to be considered accidental, a suicide, or a homicide. In such a case, a manner of undetermined is well justified for certification, and one of the reasons to do so, as later investigations on cold cases can sometimes resolve it, even decades after the fact. The certificate can always be amended.

This case was reopened after I took office as coroner in 2015. After consultation with the County Attorney's Office to clarify that the coroner was responsible only for evidence "on or with" the body by State Statute, we consolidated and cleared out the property room by turning over all appropriate evidence to the law enforcement agency of jurisdiction. This 'stock' of old property was again the result of the previous coroner's tendency to confuse the role of his former law enforcement background with role of the coroner in investigations. We had way too much stuff that we should have never collected ourselves. Original documents indicated that this was Sheriff's Office jurisdiction, but on research, it turned out to be the FBI's. Special Agents took custody of the case file, all evidence from property, which included a rifle from the event scene, and reopened it as a cold case. While the status in the end may stay as 'undetermined', that is what should have happened with the evidence at the time to insure a proper investigation. Only law enforcement has the resources and jurisdiction to process and follow up on such interviews and evidence.

Case 53. #203117 (2003) This is a case of a 44 year old Native American male that died at the medical center in Casper, WY and then was referred by the Natrona County Coroner to the Fremont Coroner, due to the originating incident occurring in this county. There is no coroner report in the file, so we will reconstruct the case from what is available. The original call occurred in the beginning of June, with the subject dying in Casper two days later.

EMS records indicate they were called late morning when individual was 'found' unresponsive lying in the front seat of a car at a residence. Witnesses state he had been there since the day before and they assumed he was just sleeping. Patient was unresponsive, vomiting, and had fixed and dilated pupils of different sizes. Cardiac rhythm was abnormal but they did get him to the local emergency room. The ER notes he may have been down two days, and had evidence of a left subdural hemorrhage. He was stabilized and then transferred to the medical center.

The medical center physician notes rumors of a possible assault, and that the status was "pretty dismal" from the degree of hematoma and infarct to the brain. Due to the possible time frame of the injury and accumulating results, intervention would not improve the outcome, which was considered terminal eventually. He was kept on comfort care until he died, and the coroner notified due to the suspicious circumstances. The case was FBI jurisdiction, and their office also notified. An autopsy was arranged with the Colorado forensic pathologists.

The autopsy showed no major injuries other than the head injuries associated with the brain injury, although there were minor blunt force injuries to the chest, buttocks, and limbs. Admitting toxicology showed a BA of 0.05 and no drugs present. No impact to the back of the head, no skull fractures, and internal acute subdural hemorrhages were left sided and necrotic, estimated to have occurred at less than a two to three day period. These injuries are listed as the cause of brain death. The pathologist noted that while a majority of alcoholic injuries of this type are to the back of the head, no injury was found in that region. There was a healing injury to the right side of the head that may be related, but not with any certainty. Since it cannot be ascertained whether the fatal injuries were from an assault or accidental fall, the manner of death by his opinion was undetermined.

It is unknown the outcome of the FBI investigation into the matter, although they would have reports on file if asked. Unless their end came up with a witnessed event that could be proven to be related within the time frame, or substantial testimony of circumstances, it is unlikely that this went very far. In cases like this, even if they came up with a plausible scenario to pursue, the coroner must not base the manner of death on law enforcement perceptions. He only has to justify the manner based on the physical evidence, and let any subsequent legal pursuit fall as it may. The pathologist is very specific in his inability to attribute the injury to accidental or homicidal acts, so undetermined here is appropriate, regardless of any subsequent judicial action. It may make law enforcement's job more difficult, but that is their task, not ours.

Case 54. #203160 (2003) This 39 year old white female who died in August three days after transfer to the medical center in Casper also is similar to the previous case in some ways. There is a coroner report that documents the contact from the Natrona County Coroner's office and arrangements for autopsy, but little else. While these are 'after the fact' investigations, it still is handy to use the report for documenting the follow up with other agencies and summaries of the medical information obtained. As it is, there are extensive medical records from EMS, the personal physician, and local hospital, but none from the Casper hospital, all of which were reviewed since there was no summary.

EMS reports it was dispatched to a possible horse accident injury, and found the patient on the ground on arrival. They note a horse nearby in a different corral and no riding equipment around, and according to the bystander she said "the horse hit her" but there were no witnesses. She was dressed however, in chaps, belt and boots. To be fair, it would not be unusual in such situations for individuals to remove the stock from the immediate area to a different corral for safety, but there is no record this was done or the question asked. EMS transported to the local hospital from the rural area where she was stabilized and prepared for transport to Casper for care. Notable is the toxicology on admission, which was negative for drugs of abuse, but showed a BA of 0.268. Also significant is a check on her Dilantin level, which was within therapeutic limits.

The only reference to the medical center information is that the physician there questioned the "details of the injury". While there is no investigative report from the sheriff, there is an offense log that shows a history of numerous DUIs, intoxicated pedestrian offenses, driving while suspended, 'failure to appear' warrants, and incidents of assault – most of which she was the purported victim, but a couple where she was the accused perpetrator.

Medical records show an extended history of seizures which are diagnosed as "alcohol related", chronic and treated with Dilantin & several injuries related to past DUI crashes. Personal physician records indicate a highly volatile personal life with both past husbands and current paramours.

Autopsy diagnosis for cause of death lists an abrasion on the right occipital region, numerous contusions to the left breast and extremities. The main cause is closed head trauma, with subdural hematoma (right greater than left) inferior right temporal and superior left frontal lobe contusions; mild subarachnoid hemorrhage, and bleeding into the base of the brain. As for manner of death, the opinion of the pathologist notes that while the injury occurred to the back of the head, the absence of skull fractures 'militates' against being kicked by a horse. "More likely, the decedent suffered an impact to the back of the head while intoxicated. The possibility of a ruptured aneurysm precipitating a fall resulting in additional injuries cannot be excluded. The manner of death is deemed undetermined, though an accident is favored." Undetermined ends up as the ruling by the coroner.

A natural event (ruptured aneurysm) that precipitates a chain that results in death, could be ruled natural if no intervening event is "more fatal" and the natural condition not survivable. There are numerous scenarios here for accidental death. There is an insinuated suspicion of homicide in the record with no basis reported in the documentation available. While the sum of the multiple possibilities favors an accident, I agree with the pathologist and the coroner on the ruling of undetermined. Unless outside investigation reveals anything different, that is probably the best we can do.

Case 55. #203159 (2003) Here we have a 37-day old male infant that was found unresponsive in August, around 11:30 in the morning. The EMS report states that when they arrived a "combative" crowd of about 20 people were present, and a female came running out of the home with the infant and gave it to responders, saying the family would meet them at the hospital. The EMT noted the infant was warm to touch, "showed lividity and blanching to the facial area... no breath, no pulse... asystole... signs of rigor in the arms, in the neck, the legs and in the jaw... there was a scant amount of white matter in the mouth, but I was unable to open the mouth all the way due to rigor... lividity also noted in the chest and abdominal area and no lividity noted on the back," No resuscitation efforts were attempted due to the estimated down time, but the infant was transported anyway to the local hospital, where it was pronounced and not even admitted due to being DOA.

Technically, in those circumstances, if the subject was so obviously dead, it should have remained at the scene and the coroner and law enforcement notified. Medical control for EMS or the responders themselves are not (and should not be) responsible for transporting dead individuals. I have seen, however, that in some situations, especially with infants or smaller children, the transport will be made anyway due to the concerns of the family, emotions of the EMS responders, or, as in this case, the decision was made to remove out of a possible dangerous or combative crowd. In any case, once such a decision has been made, then we simply have to deal with it and still do an investigation as best we can.

The coroner report notes the basic situation and information, notes the originating scene was not viewed, and has no other descriptions of the body. It does in this case, have extensive supplemental reports added. The first note a week later gives the initial conclusion of the local pathologist that it was "shaken baby syndrome" (autopsy was performed the same day the baby was found), pending completion of labs and microscopy. The next day the FBI is contacted, as it was their jurisdiction, and procedures initiated to obtain medical records and history on the infant. The "unsafe scene" is noted. Conversations with the treating pediatrician notes that the infant had been admitted earlier in the month for congestion and possible viral infection, at which time a heart defect was detected. The physician also noted discolorations on the buttocks, left wrist and ankle, but x-rays found no trauma, and a consulting doctor felt the marks were birthmarks. Public Health visits to the home after the birth noted no unusual or adverse conditions, but did record they had advised the parents not to sleep with the infant. There is no record of any law enforcement examination of the scene or interviews with those involved, but it is noted that the infant was found "face down".

Another supplemental is a deputy review of medical records. The infant
was born at 36 weeks, listed as "premature" and delivered via C-section as
the pregnancy started as twins, with one miscarried earlier. Age of the
mother is 16. Birth notes record markings described as "Mongolian spots"
in the areas noted on the buttocks and elsewhere. In the weeks after the
birth, the infant is treated for recurrent congestion, dehydration, and
hypoxia. Nursing notes indicate the mother is reluctant to ever put the
infant down, and that the baby is continuously irritable and fussy. It
occasionally it noted to be "posturing" in a questionable seizure episode. In
the period just prior to the death, medical records note improvement,
healthy appearance, and statements from the parents that they have
purchased a bassinet for the sleep environment. The review includes a
summary of the basics of shaken baby syndrome.

The local pathologist (not forensic) autopsy report states that the
"underlying cause of death is consistent with blunt force trauma applied to
a broad area over the right side of the head", the manner of death as
undetermined, and sufficient grounds for a child abuse investigation.
Specifically the cause of death is listed as cerebral edema, due to
microscopic subarachnoid and scattered intracerebral micro hemorrhages,
due to deforming, non-patterned, blunt force trauma to the right side of the
head. No evidence is seen of any recurrent or established pattern of
injuries. A further note is that a "Secundum-type atrial septal defect is
confirmed, most probably of mild physiological significance". Toxicology
is negative for all tested substances.

In March of 2004 the next year, all records, reports, and photos are sent to
a forensic pathologist in Colorado for a review and consult. His results that
he is "comfortable" is stating are: first, the infant was prone long enough
prior to discovery to have developed fixed lividity. Second, some of the
evidence noted in the autopsy may be SIDS related and to say they are
evidence of pre-mortem hypoxia is theoretical. Third, there does not
appear to be an impact site on the scalp. Fourth, he does not find the
microscopy findings in the subarachnoid space or in the brain that
impressive. He sees no definite bleeding, but agrees with the cerebral
edema. Fifth, pulmonary exam results have been associated with "near
smothering" episodes in one study, but can also be seen in resolving
pneumonitis. Several of the findings on the photos are suspicious for postmortem artifacts. He notes smothering is a possibility but hard to prove.
The death could be SIDS if the story supported it. He sees no conclusive
evidence for blunt force injuries to the head causing death. He suggests

examination of the brain tissue by a forensic neuropathologist might be helpful. [This option could not be pursued as the local pathologist did not fix the brain prior to cutting it.]

In January 2005, the coroner certified the death from pending to undetermined, and used the first pathologist's specific causes noted above. The coroner report does not have any explanation as to some of the delays, or any of the logic or train of thought that indicates the process or justification to use the first autopsy results instead of moderating the cause with the consult results. While I did not actively participate in or work this case, there was always in the office an undertone of not wanting to let go of the possibility of criminality in the case. This again reflects the coroner's law enforcement background, but my opinion is the facts are what they are, or are not, and while I agree this is an undetermined case, the delays in certification and listing of cause are not right, in my opinion. Cause should have been modified by the forensic pathologist review, and at the very least, not implied criminality. As coroners, we are also in the business of just presenting the facts and not trying to implicate the possible innocent parties unnecessarily. This case also shows the deficiencies in using a basic pathologist for convenience over a certified and well trained forensic pathologist. This case might have been clearer if the forensic had a crack at it at the beginning rather than as a reviewer, and certainly would not have taken as long to certify.

Case 56. #204062 (2004) As seen in the last case, infant cases can be the hardest to investigate and determine what was going on, and tough for deciding the manner and cause of death. The circumstances and situations can be obscured even in the best of times when there is an appropriate coroner response. This next case presents an overwhelming range of complications to deal with.

At the beginning of May, a phone call is received from a mortuary in Colorado, which is documented and detailed on a follow up fax sent by the facility. The mortician in Colorado received a phone call from a mother, stating her daughter had a stillborn in her home, and was seeking advice on what to do. The mortician told them it was a coroner reportable death and that he would be happy to assist them. He then notified the local coroner there, who advised him to take possession of the body and call the Fremont County Coroner in Wyoming. According to the mortician, in conversation with the family, the daughter *"had been seeing a guy. She got pregnant. They broke up. She had been a flagger in road construction, but was recently unemployed. The pregnancy was going well, so with her lack of income and insurance, she did not seek prenatal care. She had not felt the baby kicking recently, but wasn't overly concerned based on literature she had read on pregnancy. ...at her home in Lander, WY, she felt a fair amount of cramping and decided to take a bath to ease the cramping. She does not have a telephone, so she could not call for help. By then it was too late, and the baby was born in the bathtub. I did not inquire about the baby's whereabouts between birth and when I received the call. I hope this information will be helpful."*

The coroner's report simply includes a synopsis of this, and no other information, either to supplement the follow up, or thought process involved. Luckily, there is other documentation and this case was discussed in depth in the office at the time, due to the unusual nature of the circumstances. A check with the local police department for records on the day of the birth reveals they produced a log and were called earlier that same day to the residence for a "family fight" between the birth mother and her ex-boyfriend over the ex's drinking habit. They were separated and the officers suggested if it was an issue, she would have to get a trespass order if she does not want him back. No mention is made of any physical conflict, just verbal.

An autopsy is arranged with the forensic pathologist in Loveland Colorado, and the mortician delivers the remains to that service. The pathologic diagnosis results include: 1. Term (38 week male fetus) with maceration and decompositional changes; 2. No definitive trauma; 3. No congenital anomalies noted; 4. Torn umbilical stump with no vital reaction; 5. No placenta recovered; 6. Neogen Panel [a birth/newborn screen for abnormalities]; 7. Toxicology: Liver ethanol, none detected; Liver drug quantitation: Methamphetamine = 1,400 ng/g, Amphetamine = 220 ng/g. The written opinion is as follows: "This estimated gestational age 38-week male fetus, suffered the result of intrauterine fetal demise of undetermined etiology. Without examination of the placenta, the mechanism of death cannot be determined. There was no definitive trauma, congenital anomaly, or disease process to explain the case in this death. Maternal amphetamine/methamphetamine use may have been a contributing factor. The manner of death is undetermined."

Emails are included in the file with follow up questions to the pathologist from the county attorney, relayed by the coroner: First, how was the determination made this was intrauterine demise? – "no evidence of eating or breathing, skin slippage noted (although this could also be a postmortem artifact)". Second, would the drug levels present be fatal in an infant? – "there are no reliable lethal levels in fetuses, in theory, it would only mean recent maternal use... these drugs could have caused placental abruption which would lead to death". Third, what information would an examination of the placenta provided? – "cord abnormalities, infection of the membranes, bleeding behind the membranes, placental infarction, etc." Lastly, based on the examination should this have been a live birth? – "no evidence to say unless someone heard it cry". [Note: in most circumstances the pathologist would have noted inflated lungs and evidence of breathing in that case.] A final follow up question again asked if it had been a live birth, would those drug levels had been fatal? The pathologist notes that while any drug levels would be bad, there are no studies at the time that establish fatal levels in infants.

For comparison, current studies show fatal liver levels of methamphetamine in adults recorded as high as 4,800 ng/g, but death has been noted at much lower levels also. Meth can be extremely variable in how it affects the body or causes death in regards to quantities in the system, with no real hard lines of fatal toxicity.

While in most death cases the Fremont Coroner can justify an investigation by statute as the originating incident occurred here, it must be noted that an outside of the state coroner is not legally obliged to follow that unless their own state statutes specify that action. They are subject to their own state laws, and over time, we have had an inconsistent response from other states as far as following up incidents that occur here and are transferred out of state. Here the coroner in Colorado was probably just glad to get it off his desk. He could have just completed the case on his own in basically the same way, as we have often cooperated with background investigations from other states.

Another issue in this case is that stillbirths are not by statute coroner cases to begin with. An infant is not considered a live birth under the law if stillborn, and with no life, there is technically no death, thus not a case. Remember we have to go by the law as written in statutes, not by any personal opinion or belief on what is considered alive or not. While we do some cases like this in order to establish forensically whether it was a live birth or not, once stillbirth or fetal death is determined, it is not our concern to pursue the legalities, whether we like it or not – we have no legal justification or jurisdiction. On occasion, in the absence of medical certifiers, we will certify the stillbirth record at the request of vital records, but that is rare, and only because if a physician will not, or cannot, the coroner is the only other person authorized under the law to sign off on it. This case was certified as a fetal demise that could not be determined. The opinion of the county attorney at the time is that the only violation of the law that could be proved, was a misdemeanor charge against the mother for transporting human remains without a permit, as she obviously by admission took it from Wyoming to Colorado to turn in to a mortuary. Regardless of yours or my personal opinion in the matter, that is where it ends under the law.

As a side note, Wyoming law specifies, and case law has determined fairly clearly that a person can only be charged with a homicide if the infant was born alive. There is an additional penalty for a perpetrator in the death of a pregnant female if the jury can establish that the defendant knew at the time that the victim was pregnant. There is also various laws concerning abortion, but those statutes and the ones on homicide all concern an act committed by another person, and no regulations address the failure of a mother to get prenatal care, or if the commissions of the mother herself cause fetal death. All this is consistently based on the legal definition of life and viability. The wishes and opinions of segments of society, or a particular coroner, are irrelevant in these cases, as we are sworn to adhere to the law as it exists, not as we wish it would be.

Case 57. #204128 (2004) This 66 year old Native American male suffered a fall at the location of a refreshment vendor who served out of one of those small portable shed type buildings set up in an asphalt parking lot. The individual was transported via EMS to the local hospital where he died on the same day.

The coroner responded to the hospital, while I investigated the originating scene. Photos and a detailed diagram of the location were completed, and included inspection and documentation of the stairway and landing up to the vendor window. There were no unusual variances or hazards noted, no remarkable influences of weather other than it was 85 degrees, and no reported or witnessed unusual events or altercations. The individual was evidently standing up on the landing at the vendor window, which was a measured height of 22 inches in elevation. He suddenly collapsed backward off that elevation, striking his head on the pavement. Later examination prior to securing for autopsy showed no open trauma to the head, or other injuries except those things associated with medical intervention at the hospital. Law enforcement responders to the scene reported that the wife of the deceased stated that the subject had been drinking alcohol earlier in the day.

The EMS report notes that the victim fell "about four feet". Considering that the individual was 5'9" tall, and I measured the stairway and landing he was on at about 1' 10" high, that is an interesting statement. That's why we do the documentation and note the reference meaning. A standing fall would be from the person's own height (5'9"), or he fell from the landing height (1'10"), or his head hit the ground from a total height of 7'7" (his height plus the elevation of the landing), or they are talking about the linear distance from where he stood backward to where he hit measured parallel to the ground. If the latter, that was greater than 4 feet, so it is unknown what they are talking about. EMS did note that there was an immediate and steady decline in condition from the moment they arrived to getting him to the hospital.

The hospital record states he "stepped backwards" off the platform and fell, but does not note the source or basis of that comment. No particular medical history is known by the family. He is already neurologically absent of reflexes. A CT of the head shows a massive depressed fracture to the upper occipital and posterior parietal regions, very large subdural and extensive subarachnoid hemorrhages with significant shift and basilar herniation. Blood alcohol on admission was 0.109. A consult with a neurologist at the medical center in Casper noted the injuries as fatal for which there is no good treatment. The patient is put as a DNR and admitted for comfort care until the point at which he died. Records from his personal physician note treatment periodically for alcohol withdrawal, chronic back pain from a fall 30 years ago, but no other particular noted medical issues, and no regular medications prescribed.

An autopsy was performed by the local pathologist, non-forensic. The results confirmed the closed head injuries and brain hemorrhages with contre-coup contusions. Additional findings showed atherosclerotic cardiovascular disease with decreased circulation and congestive heart disease, alcoholic hepatitis, and emphysema. Based on the evidence of myocardial ischemia and heart disease, the pathologist's opinion is that the fall was induced by a syncopal episode. He thus states the death as natural. A further consultation was held between the coroner, the pathologist, and another pathologist who was a coroner in another county, and they came up with a ruling of undetermined.

Here we must keep in mind that neither pathologist is a certified forensic pathologist, and there is a difference in how things are approached, as well as a variation in comfort level understood when determining manner of death. I have noted over the years that regular pathologists often only feel good about a higher level of certainty than the standards of the National Association of Medical Examiners, and often will say undetermined unless they can define the manner with closer to 100% certainty. NAME recognizes a standard previously noted, and that undetermined should only be used when at 50-50 or less certainty. They have another useful tool, called the "but for" rule. Here it can be stated that the cardiac ischemia or syncopal episode "but for" the head injury, was survivable. Plus the neurologist and record indicates the fall trauma was fatal in and of itself, regardless of circumstance. The amount of brain hemorrhage and injury clearly indicates the body stayed alive until death occurred from that injury, not due to a heart attack or syncope. In other words, if the syncopal episode had happened while he was sitting in a chair, probably no death occurs. So whether he fainted due to the heat, dehydration from drinking alcohol, miss-stepped the stairs, or otherwise, the specific precipitating event is irrelevant in this case. This is not a natural death, nor undetermined. There is a reasonable certainty that this is an accidental death from fall trauma. I disagree with the certification.

Case 58. #205001 (2005) In early January EMS is called to a local physician's office, and on arrival, find a 33 year old Native American female in respiratory arrest with CPR being administered. During transport, full cardiac arrest occurred. Initial report is that the patient had a severe and immediate anaphylactic reaction to a steroid medication being used on a nasal polyp. According to the physician, the patient had received this medication previously with no allergic reaction ever noted. The patient was stabilized in the emergency room and admitted to the ICU, never regained consciousness, and died the next day. The coroner report documents just the basic information as known on the day of death, and an autopsy is ordered and performed two days later with the Colorado forensic pathologist.

Medical records do not appear in the file. There is a request for the hospital records and a note recording that the nursing director of the facility refused to provide the records as she stated that since the death occurred longer than 24 hours after admission, this was not a coroner's case. This shows a remarkable ignorance of the law. Many hospitals have a policy that if a patient dies in their care in less than a 24 hour time frame since admission, they call the coroner due to a possible lack of familiarity with the circumstances or history, and the treating physician is not comfortable with signing off on the death. That however, is institutional policy and not the law. Any case that falls under the coroner statutes as a case is our jurisdiction regardless of time frame of hospitalization (statutes do not define any such time frame). Often, if it is a clear natural death and the physician is comfortable signing off on it, the coroner can terminate jurisdiction to the physician, but that is the coroner and physician's decision, not a nursing director's. In this case, the coroner had two basic options – contact the county attorney and have him inform the nursing director of the law and force compliance, or call and inquest and subpoena the records himself. Refusal in the case of an inquest would be contempt of court. Statutes clearly state that a case of accident, apparent drug or chemical overdose or toxicity, or if the cause is unknown, is the jurisdiction of the coroner. At the time of the death, even though an anaphylactic reaction can sometimes be considered a natural death, in this case that is not known if that was the specific cause, and in some cases it could be considered accidental. Either way, both State and Federal law exempts coroners and medical examiners from all restriction of medical records access, which makes sense, since a thorough investigation is the whole point, and you cannot determine the relevance of a record without examining it.

There is no note as to what the coroner did in this case, other than we know there was no inquest, but there are no records present in the file from either the hospital, or the physician treating at the time of the incident. Both are necessary in this case to be thorough, and the patient history information may or may not have helped keep this from being undetermined, but at this point we will never know.

The drug is identified in the autopsy report as Kenalog (triamcinolone, a corticosteroid), which is not known for such severe side effects, although anaphylaxis is listed as a very rare side effect. The autopsy report lists causes of death as central nervous system edema, massive pulmonary congestion and edema, and renal acute tubular necrosis, leading to acute anoxic injury with brain death following a reported anaphylactic reaction to Kenalog injection. Toxicology is negative on admission blood. No other significant physical findings are found. Consultation with the pathologist determines that the manner is best left as undetermined.

As noted previously, depending on circumstances, anaphylactic death can be considered either a natural, or an accidental death, and in this case we are clearly at a 50-50 position, so no argument from me to contradict the forensic pathologist. It would have been possibly helpful to have in-depth medical history information, however, to see if there was anything there in the past that would have given us a clue as to why this occurred.

Case 59. #205028 (2005) As noted at the beginning of this study, skeletal remains offer some interesting issues and challenges. Once the number of cases that are not of medical-legal significance are cleared out (historic or prehistoric) by anthropological determination, most of the remaining do not end up as undetermined due to being associated with investigations that have a specific suspected manner of death. The forensics that can determine firearm or sharp force injuries on skeletal remains can give you a homicide, or the physics of trauma to determine an accidental fall versus animal predation, or other investigative successes, all end in a determination that leaves relatively few that remain as undetermined. The next case, however, in spite of extensive and detailed work on the investigation is one of those frustrating results.

In February, two adults that are rabbit hunting in a rural area of dense brush and trees, discover a human skull, along with other remains. They report it to State Park employees, since they were within those boundaries, and those personnel go to the scene and confirm that they are human remains. Park officers then report the find to the sheriff's office, who in turn notifies the coroner's office. All agencies respond and do an initial basic survey of the scene. The remains are scattered over a considerably large area in seven separate locations, and visible evidence includes clothing and other property that indicates this is a contemporary time frame and medical-legal case. Due to the extent of the area involved, the scene is secured as best possible and planning done to obtain more personnel to investigate and recover the next day. The sheriff's office initiates collection and investigation of all missing persons reports on file, and initial interviews.

Five different agencies are involved, including volunteer Search & Rescue personnel to coordinate line and grid searches of the region. Specific areas with known remains or possible evidence are cordoned off with scene tape, and command trailers and collection areas are setup. A contract archaeologist/anthropologist is obtained to go through the remains as they are recovered, identify as human or not, and arrange in anatomical position to track what has been found. Law enforcement is in charge of property and evidence recovery including that from what appears to be a 'camp site'. Luckily for this time of year, the weather is reasonable (37 degrees with no recent precipitation) and there is no snow cover on the ground.

All locations and individual remains are marked first with evidence flags, and documented as to location. Base zero points are established by GPS, and distances charted and diagramed for the main locations. Once completed, the remains are then recovered and taken to the central collection point where they are identified and laid out if determined as human. While the seven scattered main areas are worked by coroner staff, the balance of the area is canvassed by search and rescue personnel. Once the main areas are cleared of obvious visible remains, then personnel do a detailed ground search by hand to move or remove weeds, reeds and brush, and in this manner recover additional small bones, ribs and teeth. Several areas, such as beneath the skull location, are screened to find additional fragments, and in some cases, obvious hair. Due to the frozen nature of most of the ground, some dirt was collected to a depth of several inches in critical areas for thawing and later examination.

Law enforcement turns up a promising lead on a 42 year old male that had been missing since April of 2002, almost three years ago, from a local nearby town. While some of the property recovered indicated a possible connection, nothing definitive was correlated at this point. Newspapers from the camp site had a most recent date of January 2002. A bible recovered had a presentation date of 1973, and was traced to a family in the southwestern U.S., that when contacted, had no idea how the book had ended up in Wyoming, and had no missing family members. This ended up being just an interesting side note and not related to the case. While a good lead on the identity was in hand, the case remained open to any local or national missing persons cases until identification could be established. Public release of the find was made to the media to increase the chance of leads.

A dental exam and charting was completed of the skull and mandible, but unfortunately there were no dental records for the main suspected person, however this was useful in eliminating other individuals as a possible source for the remains. Several sets of dental x-rays for other missing persons were received by our office from other states and agencies, and were specifically ruled out.

Once the contract archaeologist/anthropologist completed an inventory of the skeletal remains, they were then packaged and transported to the University of Wyoming Anthropology Department in Laramie, where a forensic examination was completed. The conclusions of that exam were as follows: "Sex-male; race-Caucasian; age-45 to 55 years estimated; stature-approximately 5'8 ½ inches; pathology/trauma-some loss of teeth during life is evidenced, but no other pathological conditions noted. No sign of perimortem trauma was found on the skull or any other part of the skeleton. Time since death-the nearly complete skeletonization of these remains (in a dry cool climate like Wyoming suggest that this individual was deposited for a period of years rather than months or weeks. Of course micro-environmental conditions can accelerate or retard these processes. The fact that reasonably well preserved [clothing] exists does not necessarily mean a recent death. Items of clothing like this can last for a decade or more in this arid region of the West." Several skeletal features are noted on the skull that are stated as unique to an individual that might prove as certain as fingerprints for identification, should life x-rays of the skull be located. Unfortunately, as in the dental records, no x-rays of the prime suspected individual's skull, or anything else, for that matter, could be found in any records. This did however, add to the evidence used to exclude other individuals as possible ID.

The main suspect was found to have been incarcerated over time locally, but all records of that incarceration were lost, as well as any medical records which were past the retention period for most institutions. The suspect's family was not able to provide any useful photographs. A Xerox copy of a sheriff's office booking photo was located finally in a small town police department record.

Having had training in the skill, I personally then completed a clay forensic reconstruction of the individual on the skull, based on known procedures and principles, and completed the task in June. Aging and weight and other parameters are based on the findings from the forensic anthropologist. Once done, the reconstruction is then staged and photographed. Meetings are then set up with the family, and the photos shown to other individuals that had close contact with the suspect during life. Area law enforcement, community individuals, and most family members considered the reconstruction to be an adequate likeness to the person in question. The mother of the person, however, refused to believe it unless there was a DNA comparison. Such is the effect of all the 'CSI' shows that were popular at the time – the balance of presumptive evidence gathered was not good enough for her.

A DNA sample was obtained from the suspect's mother, and that was sent along with the hair recovered from beneath the skull, and other specified bones, to the State Crime Lab in Cheyenne. In November they reported they were unable to obtain any DNA from the hair, and would send out the bones to an outside contractor, as they did not have that capacity for analysis.

In March of 2006, over a year after the original find, the lab sent their final report on the DNA comparison. They noted that they could only give a definite exclusion of the suspect, not a definite inclusion. Their wording specifically is "the unidentified donor of the vertebrae cannot be excluded as being the biological son of the [cheek swab donor]. Unofficially the lab said that off the record, it is considered a positive ID, but since there is only one parent for comparison, that is how they word it. Realistically, even in DNA, just like in determining manner, we are basing conclusions on reasonable percentages in consideration of the evidence. Things are rarely 100% certain, just producing a reasonable conclusion.

That same month, based on the evidence at the scene, the facial reconstruction, and DNA analysis, it is announced that there is a positive ID, and the remains released to the family and funeral home. The local media is also informed of the conclusions. Due to the lack of any specific conclusive evidence, the cause, and thus the manner of death are both ruled as undetermined, and certified as such. There is reasonable speculation from evidence at the scene that in conjunction with alcohol use and the time of year he went missing, that hypothermia could have been a factor. Natural or other manners cannot be excluded, however. Although the remains were scattered most likely by predator and animal activity which was evidenced by the anthropology exam, and homicide or accidental injury that only involves soft tissue is rare, undetermined is a reasonable conclusion in this case.

The file as a whole fills a large binder, and includes the sheriff's office logs, reports, and interviews; extensive coroner reports including detailed description, diagrams and photos, case narrative and time line, logic and justification for identification and certification, and a Power Point program summary of key aspects; Forensic anthropology reports, charts, photos and documentation; dental charting and photos; crime lab submissions, reports, and chain of custody; emails , letters, and responses on possible missing persons matches; complete inventory and photos from the scene anthropologist; complete documentation and photos of the forensic reconstruction process including a second Power Point summary; and finally copies of all press releases and newspaper coverage.

In this case, as far as the undetermined cases go, there is for the first time, a complete documentation in the file, to the point where anyone at a later date could go back and review the investigation process and clearly see the progression, steps, logic and justifications for conclusions. Today, even twelve years later, I do not see anything else that was missed or not considered in resolving the case. To be sure, a good part of the effort was involved in satisfying the coroner's first responsibility, that of identification of the deceased. But the same detailed effort of all agencies also went into determining manner and cause of death by an extensive process of elimination through analysis of the evidence. Even at that, sometimes you legitimately still end up with undetermined, and that is often just the way it is. It is our job though to make sure that those cases are as few as humanly possible with accurate and well documented forensics.

Case 60. #205122 (2005) This case has some similarities to the previous case #57 in that it involves a stillbirth that would by statute not normally be a coroner case for investigation. Here, however, the 24 year old mother came into the emergency room with "abdominal pain" and subsequently delivered the infant in the obstetrics department. Of concern to the medical staff was that the mother's toxicology was positive for cannabis and methamphetamine, so the coroner was notified. If requested by medical staff, we certainly can consult on a case due to the specific resources we can bring to bear, as sometimes a case has to have an initial look to determine if there is jurisdiction or not. Also, there is a general statutory authorization of jurisdiction for any deaths where a public health hazard is presented, or in apparent drug or chemical overdose or toxicity. At this period of time, there were rampant issues with meth abuse in the county, including 15 meth related deaths for the year for our office alone. This was the highest rate in the county seen for that drug, either from before 2005, or since, so doing an investigation from the aspect of a public health hazard is justified when requested by the medical community. Another instance would be in the case of something like flu or other pandemic, where the Department of Health needs assistance in tracking and researching natural deaths that would not ordinarily be coroner cases.

The coroner report is pretty basic, as there is not much to describe that is unique about a delivery or emergency room scene unless something bizarre happens. The same simplicity applies for the initial description of the body as a "fetus wrapped in a blanket". Obviously in a case like this, all detailed examination is deferred to the pathologist. We are still left, however, with just the basics, the autopsy report and medical record of the birth, with no justification or explanation of the thought process to conclusion. There is a handwritten note documenting the collection of the placenta from the hospital, and another that states that according to the aunt of the mother, she had witnessed the use of drugs over the summer (the delivery was in August). She also noted her niece had been "out" all weekend prior to the incident.

Medical records and notes from the obstetrician state that "movement" had been felt up to the day before delivery, and that there had been no prenatal care, also noted a recent diagnosis of active Hepatitis C in the mother with no follow up appointment kept. Brief ultrasound noted no cardiac motion even though the heart of the fetus was clearly seen. The obstetrician notes the need for an autopsy. Gestational age is estimated at 36 weeks, or close to term.

Autopsy notes early autolysis, no congenital anomalies, negative Neogen panel, and HIV screen negative. Toxicology on the liver tissue showed an alcohol content of 0.085, methamphetamine and amphetamine at less than 200 ng/mL each, and the presence of hydroxyzine (antihistamine), acetaldehyde (from synthetics or cigarette smoke), and theobromine (primary alkaloid in chocolate). The pathologist opinion says "...succumbed to intrauterine fetal demise. Maternal methamphetamine use may have been contributory. The presence of meconium within the fetal membranes suggests additional episodes of intrauterine stress prior to the terminal event. The anatomic findings suggest the death occurred approximately one day prior to delivery. The manner of death is undetermined." No other injuries, infarcts or other issues are noted in the detailed record.

Again, just like the other fetal meth case, there are no scientific studies available at the time to determine what affect the drug use may have had, other than the logic that it certainly did not help the situation. And likewise, under the law, a stillbirth precludes most avenues for any legal considerations. Cases like this, even though technically undetermined in manner and cause, and from some viewpoints not coroner jurisdiction except under the public health aspect, should still be investigated and documented with the same detail and attention given to 'regular' cases, if asked. The information obtained and documented can be vital in tracking and research done by the Department of Health in the public interest.

Case 61. #205128 (2005) This 37 year old white male was found unresponsive in his bed by his wife in mid-November late in the evening. EMS arrived around 2200 hrs, and noted the wife stated she had last talked to him around 1600 hrs. EMS also noted on their report that rigor had set in and lividity was present, and that the wife had turned him prior to their arrival. He was pronounced dead at that time and no resuscitation was attempted. Sheriff and coroner investigators were called to the scene.

I responded to this case with the sheriff investigators, and noted the lividity and rigor position was not consistent with how the deceased was found, the same as noted later in the EMS report. The wife also described her actions to me. Another item noted was a blackish purge from the mouth, but no notable major trauma or injuries were seen. The home was very cluttered and trashy but did not seem unusually disturbed. Due to the age and unknown circumstances, an autopsy was planned. I also did the transport to the autopsy with the forensic pathologist in Colorado. Initial medical history provided by the family noted recent complaints of chest pain, hard productive coughing, asthma, smoking, and recent back surgery.

Autopsy results showed acute multilobar pneumonia as the main issue, and toxicology showed hydrocodone at about five times the therapeutic dosage but at half the minimum adult lethal dosage; also there was 12 times the therapeutic level of cyclobenzaprine, which was mid-range for a toxic level. The body was also cachexic and had cardiac issues developing most likely from the chronic hypertension. The opinion of the pathologist was that the main cause was the pneumonia, with mixed drug toxicity contributing, "the manner of death is therefore undetermined".

Medical records show the reports on the recent back surgery, which was completed without any complications. The records of the personal physician noted controlled hypertension and treatment for chronic anxiety and depression, as well as no complications from the healing laminectomy. Records from his counseling service were obtained that noted a long history of alcohol abuse, drug usage, most currently sober and referred to the service as a condition for violating probation by alcohol use. The service notes the depression issue and specifically states no indications of suicidal tendencies. Pharmacy records are obtained from all local providers, which indicate on review a high opiate usage and a bit of "doctor shopping" for pain medications.

The death was certified as indicated by the pathologist and noted as undetermined. While there was a clear indication that the pneumonia was severe enough to at some point be fatal, the consensus was that the drug mix was contributory to a degree that obscured what was the fatal event initiating the respiratory arrest. As it turned out, the immediate family on his side from out of state had not had any particular contact with the deceased for four years prior to his death, and once they found out about it, suspected the wife of killing him off. They were not happy with the investigation and came to the area and stayed for several months trying to convince the sheriff's office that it was a homicide. Both the S.O. detectives, the Sheriff, and our office were unable to convince them that there was no forensic basis to pursue that suspicion, and eventually they left the area. I believe undetermined was an acceptable call in this case due to the reasons noted above, but it must be remembered that the uncertainty in that ruling will often complicate dealing with relatives later.

Case 62. #206017 (2006) Here again is a case that has similarities to cases #57 and #61 reviewed above. In this case we have a 31 year old female who by report did not know she was pregnant at 28 week gestation (determined by the pathologist) and delivered at home in bed. The EMS report notes the call as originally for "abdominal pain", but while in route they were advised they now had a breathing infant. Once there, they noted the child appeared very premature, was blue, but did take at least one breath in their presence. Mother and child were transported to the hospital with ventilations and compression in process on the infant until given to the ER staff. The placenta was also collected at the scene.

The emergency room summary from the same day in February reports that there is no clear history that the child was breathing other than "irregular gasping respirations, however nothing life sustainable". Their diagnosis is "very premature newborn infant, likely still born. Resuscitation was unsuccessful." This is an interesting summary in that still born means not breathing, and "irregular and gasping" is still breathing regardless of sustainability. Perhaps they did not believe the EMS report due to the gestation period, but it is not only possible, the lungs were seen as slightly inflated at autopsy. The coroner's report is again unremarkable, brief, and inadequate in detail, but does state the birth was "live" as far as he was concerned based on other responders. Supplemental reports from the transporting deputies are included in the file (one of which was me).

The autopsy lists the primary cause of death as "pre-term precipitous delivery with vaginal entrapment of head of fetus", no obvious congenital anomalies. The placenta did show minor evidence of inflammation, but that was not was seen in the fetus, nor was there any other trauma.. Toxicology showed no alcohol, but did have 472 ng/mL of methamphetamine and 80 ng/mL of amphetamine. The manner is again listed as undetermined. That also is what is certified on the death certificate, and the cause worded as the pathologist indicated as the main reason above, meth listed as contributing.

In the file is an extensive criminal history and arrest record on the mother, evidently obtained from the sheriff's office. There is also a copy of the Wyoming statute regarding endangering children in relation to controlled substances. While it is understandable the level of frustration in the department over the rash of probable meth related fetal and infant deaths, this reveals the perception from law enforcement viewpoint rather than what a coroner should have. Researching past criminal records, or trying to fit a death within the application of criminal law is not the coroner's job. That is for the county attorney or other prosecutors to determine and pursue and may indicate a loss of objectivity on the part of the investigator. The office of the coroner is there precisely to provide independent and objective investigation of manner and cause of death. If you endanger the public perception of the office's objectivity, that can compromise the validity of what we do. We are not the death investigation arm of law enforcement. In this case anyway, the county attorney, even with a live birth, is in the same situation as the previous two reviewed cases. In the first two, there is no rationale under the law to charge anything for a stillbirth, since there was no life. In this case, there is life, but at this time still no scientific research or data that could be used to prove a fatal effect of the methamphetamine on a fetus over any of the other possibilities. For good reasons, the county attorney refused to bring charges on what would have been an unwinnable case. The facts and evidence of an investigation are what they are, and should not be influenced by where we would like them to lead. I personally hate undetermined results as I feel in the back of my mind that I did not do my job or missed something, even if I know better. But such is the nature of death and investigations – sometimes there is simply no clear answer. One positive that did arise out of the series of unfortunate events is that the coroner's office in conjunction with the Department of Health did an extensive awareness campaign on the dangers of methamphetamine and pregnancy. We have not seen such a clump of these types of deaths since, so hopefully that contributed.

Case 63. #206089 (2006) This case concerns a mother who went into a local hospital in labor, was discovered to be presenting breech, so was prepared for a C-section. Before that could be completed, she delivered an estimated 31 week gestation premature male infant. That infant was stabilized and prepped for transfer to an out of state children's hospital, and the mother was admitted to the local hospital. Roughly two hours later she delivered a stillborn female infant, and by record, neither the mother, nor hospital staff, were aware that there originally had been twins. Toxicology was negative for the mother, who also was new to the area and had no local prenatal care – whether there was any obtained at her previous out-of-state residence was in question. In this case the coroner facilitated an autopsy on the stillborn at the request of both the family and hospital staff. A statement of record of the incident by the mother was completed in writing after she had returned to out of state to be with the surviving child.

Autopsy by the forensic pathologist on the stillborn showed evidence of birth trauma, no evidence of pulmonary expansion, and no other issues found. Analysis of both placentas indicated there may have been abruption in the case of the stillbirth. There was not gross or microscopic indication to suggest the demise occurred greater than 12 to 24 hours prior the delivery of the twin, but it could not be excluded that death may occurred a few hours prior to the first birth. In the words of the pathologist "had this been a live birth, the manner of death would best be considered undetermined."

The medical records document the situation and event in detail, including the lack of knowledge that anyone knew there were twins. The family obviously was thinking in terms that the medical staff had done something in error, but while we can facilitate an exam through our resources, that aspect or its resolution does not change the fact that a stillborn in most circumstances, is not a coroner case. An odd fact is that the coroner signed off the regular death certificate, rather than a stillborn short form: age, 16 minutes; cause of death, delayed delivery; and manner of death, undetermined. While I remember this case being talked about, I have no idea why this was done. There is nothing in the coroner report, or the medical record, indicating this was anything other than a stillbirth. A stillbirth certification should have been completed by the delivery physician, not the coroner.

It is certainly acceptable to facilitate assistance in some cases that are not our jurisdiction, however, it should be specifically recorded as to what is being done and why, and where responsibilities start, and end. This was not a coroner case, and a coroner would be justified to leave it to the medical community to work out the follow up or exams, if it looks like something that would unnecessarily draw the office into a bad legal situation. Regardless of personal beliefs of feelings, a person must strive to stay objective, and leave it to other more appropriate processes. Sometimes when you have no jurisdiction, you should just say no.

Case 64. #207060 (2007) Some cases will have an extended time frame for investigation and still end up undetermined in spite of an investigators best efforts. This investigation in this particular case started in March of 2007, and certification was not completed until a year and a half later in August of 2008. Up to that point, it was listed with Vital Records as "pending", which is basically a holding pattern. Realize that the State, the family, and any associated insurance or estate claims are also on hold until the certification is finalized, often to the dismay of involved parties and the bureaucracy. Dealing with that just goes with the territory, as certifications are not completed until the process is finished, however long it takes, even if frustrating to those involved. We serve the truth, not wishes. A key to coping with these realities is to keep all parties informed on status – they will remain frustrated, but it tones down some of the contention and conflict.

This case is large and complex enough that the file is in a large binder, with additional records referenced and stored separately. At the time I even created an index for organization as there were always multiple threads going on at the same time for investigation direction. Multitasking is often the name of the game and on a complex case, and the investigator will get lost if not orderly, as these cases continue in and amongst all the other tasks and cases that come up on a daily basis.

In incident seemed to start normally enough... a part time deputy coroner was called to the med-surge floor of a local hospital for the death of a 64 year old white female who had been admitted a short time before in late March through the emergency room. The deputy's report is pretty uninformative, noting a recent surgical history of work done on her colostomy earlier that month, with suspected peritonitis. He noted distention of the abdomen and a "foul odor". The body was recovered and secured to the morgue, and an autopsy was planned for the next day. The ER physician suspected complications of a perforated bowel, and the family suspected medical malpractice as a cause. Logically, an autopsy would be needed to define whether this was a natural death, or one that was accidental or related to any medical procedures.

The autopsy, however, gave a few surprises. According to the forensic pathologist, the woman died of acute hydromorphone and diphenhydramine (Benadryl) toxicity. The hydromorphone level was within the lethal range "even given the decedent's presumed tolerances to opiates for pain relief." The diphenhydramine, "while usually relatively non-toxic ...may have contributed to the loss of consciousness and respiratory depression in the concentrations found here."

The deceased was being treated for chronic low back pain with a subcutaneous infusion pump, which had been most recently serviced by her pain specialist physician about a month prior to the death, loaded with enough in the reservoir for a 90 day infusion. If the pump was working properly, it could not result in the post-mortem dosage found. The decedent was also prescribed hydromorphone elixir. The small amount left at autopsy in the device reservoir suggested the possibility that the drug was withdrawn and administered intravenously. The pump was carefully removed and contained at autopsy as evidence to be analyzed by the manufacturer for malfunction. Relative to the family's suspicions, no evidence was found at autopsy of a perforation or peritonitis, however the pathologist did allow that extensive abdominal adhesions may have hidden an obscure site. Additional findings included hypertensive and atherosclerotic cardiovascular disease, cirrhosis of the liver, and numerous decubitus and pressure sores from her immobility from transverse myelitis. The cause is listed as the drug toxicity with the manner pending the investigation. Keep in mind this is a final summary, and the final written report was issued in August five months later. The tox came back in about a week after the autopsy to the pathologist, which stirred the pot as far as the investigation through many phone conversations prior to the actual written report.

You can see the issues here, especially since the autopsy pretty much rules out a natural death. There are several ways this case could end up an accident, but depending on if and who and how medication was removed from the device and possibly re-administered, maybe a homicide or suicide. So off we go.

All possible medical records and pharmacy records are requested. The medical device itself is handled under the principles of chain of custody as evidence. In a case like this, over the course of time while working on records, the various physicians are put in contact with the pathologist to discuss all possible aspects of the case. For example, the pain specialist and he go over the mechanics, procedures, and workings of the device, as well as options and possibilities. Records start coming in, and it is noted in the ER record from the March admission, that several places list a patient allergy to morphine, and in one place there is a doctor's note "pt given a dose of morphine in the ER". So now we have another complication, that is, is an allergic reaction involved, was the medication actually given, and how does a morphine allergy relate to the use of hydromorphone? Research is done with the records and hospital staff and determines by the pharmacy logs that no morphine was withdrawn from stock and the physician note is in error – initial order had been rescinded but not logged properly. The pathologist and physician consults will research the issue of hydromorphone use relative to a morphine allergy. In this case the morphine allergy did not translate to an allergy to the synthetic analogs.

My research on the FDA website indicates there may have been a recall on the medical device from 2006, and a software recall in 2004. More detailed research on the device by serial and model number is initiated. The device is secure mailed back to the pathologist for detailed measuring of drugs left in consultation with the pain specialist. Records request to all pharmacies locate med lists, eliminate 'doctor shopping', and refill schedule and history on the elixir and other medications. The pharmacist is also brought in on consult in regards to the case, and the consensus is that the next step is to get the device tested by the manufacturer relating to function. We are now into July, and the manufacturer is contacted for starting that process. DEA paperwork and documentation delays the movement of the device and its controlled substance contents between the lab, and return to us for shipment to the manufacturer, as evidently there are precise forms and authorizations to be sending the drug in the device around the country. The issue apparently is that DEA rules would not allow the return by the lab of a medication containing device to a non-law enforcement coroner, and the pathologist did not have (or usually need) the registration to receive a controlled substance in that manner. So he had to file for the registration and forms, then he could get it, and then send it to us, to send to the manufacturer. This helps document the chain of custody aspect, but complicates the time frames. We contacted the local DEA to try and expedite the process by explaining the case and what we need, and that finally helped. At this point, local law enforcement has been also informed of the preliminaries to just keep them in the loop in case the whole thing blows up as a criminal case.

The device manufacturer provides procedures and protocols for their testing processes. Family members are contacted and kept up on the investigation progress periodically. In January of 2008 we finally receive the device back from the lab, note chain of custody intact, reseal and ship to the manufacturer per their instructions. Extensive medical records organized, reviewed, and summarized. In May, the initial report from the manufacturer is received, which notes several key elements: first, the device and programming are all functioning normally. Second, the servicing physician is instructed to use the provided refill kit from the manufacturer, which provides a non-coring needle and template to prevent device scarring. Proper and consistent usage of the equipment would have to be confirmed by the servicing physician (this was done by both interview and records). The manufacturer will further examine the device for tampering, and then will package to retain the integrity of the workings and return to us as evidence. Analysis report received about a week later noted multiple coring needle marks and scarring on the reservoir wall, which would not have been seen if the device was properly accessed with approved methods. This report includes detailed photos of the findings.

The death is certified in August as the cause of drug toxicity as the pathologist noted, and manner as undetermined. A formal request was provided to the local law enforcement agency of jurisdiction to initiate an investigation to assist due to suspicious circumstances being verified, but they could find no clear basis for any further investigation, and the case was closed in October of 2008.

While the original coroner report is pretty paltry, there are six supplemental reports summarizing the findings and sequence of the investigation. There is chain of custody documentation for the evidence, autopsy and consult documentation, device manufacturer testing procedures and protocols, as well as their initial and final reports, and all documented conversations with them. There is a large amount of medical records; correspondence, emails, and phone records; research notes on the device and the FDA history – the original recall was for a defective catheter, not the physical device, and both that and the software issues were resolved prior to the installation and application to this patient.

Investigation is often a process of elimination. So what did we eliminate? There were no direct natural causes in the death, nor any allergic reaction. The medical background and conditions may have contributed to the susceptibility to overdose, but for the overdose, they were survivable and continuing. The medical device was functioning normally with no defects in hardware or software, and the software was programmable and accessible only by the treating pain specialist . All prescription drug amounts were accounted for as far as regularity on refills. The hydromorphone elixir had a good portion left and in and of itself could not have resulted in the blood levels seen. All accountable resources, consults, and agency involvements were taken advantage of in relation to the case.

Then there are the more subtle aspects of the investigation. The deceased's quality of life was poor, with chronic pain issues and lack of mobility. By all accounts and interviews, she was not the most pleasant person to be around. Her family members through encounters could be described as "odd" and somewhat difficult to deal with, both in personality and behavior, but this can be a reaction to circumstance and the length of the investigation, and should not be over interpreted as suspicious. While law enforcement could not come up with any clear indications of suspicion either, they did have reservations about the family dynamics. So what are we left with?

We have a medical device that shows obvious tampering, with a probable result in an overdose of medication. While we know this occurred sometime after the last physician visit about a month prior to the death, and probably a very short period before the death, there is no direct evidence indicating who did the tampering. The port was accessible by anyone. If the deceased did it herself, it could have been an intentional suicide or accidental overdose. If someone else did it while she was incapacitated or unconscious, it could be considered a homicide regardless of intent. Manner is undetermined. Sometimes no matter the length of the investigation or the effort involved, that still is what you end up with.

Case 65. #207109 (2007) In July a 46 year old male is found in his home by a friend doing a welfare check. The doors to the home were unlocked and open, and the deceased is found sitting upright on a couch with a cell phone in his left hand, clothed only in his underwear, which were pulled down to his ankles. Initial observations note set lividity and breaking rigor, with discoloration and marks on his neck that are possibly suspicious. Based on phone answering machine messages on his land line and mail in the outside box, the window of date of death appears to be two to three days prior to being found. There is evidence in a basement cubby of frequent drug related activity and "crash pad" furnishings. Tracking evidence of medical info at the scene leads to a personal physician, who noted a recent work related knee injury and surgery for which he was still receiving physical therapy, and possible prescription drug abuse. Once next of kin are located, they also note assorted drug issues in initial interviews. An autopsy is arranged for two days later with the forensic pathologist.

Coroner deputies proceed to go through phone messages and conduct interviews, and some of the messages reveal definitive trafficking in prescription drugs, and interviews with friends show a rather incoherent set of comings and goings to the residence in recent days, some within the time period that it is estimated the subject was dead. All serves to appear to increase the likelihood this might be a suspicious death. A sister of the deceased indicates the subject had "accidentally overdosed" at least six times in the past, and this also shows up in medical records. Other interviews note that the last any of his friends will admit to seeing him alive was two days prior, and that he was heavily "stoned" at the time. Receipts are found that coincide with materials and food at the scene, also from two day prior. Some indicate change was received, but no money of any kind was found at the scene or in the located wallet. Neighbors noted a lot of traffic to the basement part of the home.

The body is in advanced decomposition by the time it gets to autopsy. No evidence of trauma or foul play is found, and the neck also is free of evidence of traumatic injury. Liver toxicology reveals a fatal combination of morphine, alprazolam (Xanax) and cyclobenzaprine (Flexeril), a muscle relaxant. The pathologist notes the cause as multi-drug toxicity and considers the results to be sufficient to an accidental death.

Deputies prepare a summary of information, interviews, and a timeline, and turn over all information to a police detective. A diagram of the scene is also made, and medical and pharmacy records collected. Work force injury records are obtained as well as counselling records, which do not indicate any history of suicidal ideations, but reveals an active conspiracy theorist and concerns about government "taps and brain chip implants", and as the therapist puts it, "poor reality testing". While a large number of prescription medications were recovered from the residence, there are no scripts or bottles of opiates found, other than an empty bottle of hydrocodone – certainly no morphine. A bottle of Flexeril is included, but only loose pills for Xanax. Indications are that the home may have been "cleaned out" of desirable controlled substances, illegal drugs, and cash. It should be noted, however, that while that is a concern for law enforcement, it is only peripherally related to the cause of death and not something the coroner investigation would follow up. With the lack of any indications of trauma or foul play on the deceased, or unusual disturbance at the scene, his friends may have been cold and crude, but not particularly implicated in the death.

There are several serious questions here. First, why did the coroner deputies pursue an investigation in aspects that would be law enforcement responsibility? As it turns out, the lead responding officer at the initial scene refused to notify a detective – he did not think it necessary. The coroner at the time, then fell back on his law enforcement career and started the deputies in pursuit of law enforcement duties. While in some jurisdictions, medical-legal investigators will be a part of a law enforcement agency, that is not the case for coroners in Wyoming. This was totally inappropriate. If officers refuse to do their aspects of an investigation, the coroner is not a law enforcement officer and cannot presume that authority. In any case, anything in that area would be inadmissible for that reason unless directly related to the coroner investigation of manner and cause. While there is a certain overlap, and different jurisdictions decide in different ways on how that interaction occurs, there are logical lines to be observed and standards expected. For example, the coroner may inspect a cell phone to search for information on next of kin, but should not presume to document drug transactions and interview those involved. The phone should be handed to law enforcement for that, and officers consulted later to see what they found and if it was relevant to the manner of death. One of the coroner deputies involved was also a bit of a 'loose cannon', and took the coroner's encouragement and ran with it. This was also poor oversight, as that puts non-law enforcement personnel in possible hazardous positions they are in no way qualified to deal with. After the fact later, a detective did come in on the case to review and follow up on his own the leads acquired, after receiving copies of the coroner reports. We each have our own responsibilities and authority. How that is handled is up to the agencies involved in the jurisdiction, but a lot of this was out of line by any standard.

Second, as it turned out, the deceased was allowing a local prostitute to use the basement cubby for "business" and the whole group was involved in dealing in prescription and illegal drugs. Police interviews finally found out that the prostitute was providing oral sex as rent payment to the deceased when he got ill and went unconscious. At that point she gathered up all the money-making drugs and available cash as a "fee for services", and left the resident in his drug-induced stupor. While a whole lot of legalities are involved here, none were relative to manner and cause on her part, other than being a witness and co-participant at the probable time of drug ingestion.

Third, why was this ruled undetermined? The coroner forgot the standards that we deal with reasonable percentages and an undetermined is 50-50 or less. While one cannot be 100% sure that the friends did not in some way contribute to the death, there was no forensic proof found, and certainly no reasonable indications of the standard of homicide. The deceased had a documented history of occasional accidental overdose by records. The opinion of the forensic pathologist was accident. The other interviews with friends indicate a willing use and consumption to get high as usual, and no suicidal intent indicated by them, or his therapist. Ruling an accident, however, did not sit well with the coroner, so he ruled undetermined to leave the case open for law enforcement, where an accident would not assist their case. Again, this is inappropriate. The forensics are what they are, and we do not rule for the convenience of law enforcement or attorneys... we serve the truth. There is a very high reasonable percentage this is an accident, and an accident is what it should have been certified as on the death certificate.

Case 66. #207154 (2007) In September EMS is called around eight in the morning to respond for a one month old infant. It is found with the mother, no pulse, no respirations, pupils fixed and dilated, lividity to the back. According to the mother, the infant appeared fine when fed around 4 a.m. The baby was full term and no complications with delivery, as reported by the mother. Death was pronounced and both law enforcement and the coroner's office notified. The responding deputy coroner interviewed the mother and had her describe the sleeping position, which was on a couch. The infant was towards one end, parallel to the back of the couch and partially facing the back cushion. A fleece blanket was folded and under the infant. The mother stated she was lying with her head at the baby's feet on the balance of the couch, rather than next to the infant. On examination the deputy noted no specific marks, discolorations, trauma or injury on the infant. An autopsy is arranged with the forensic pathologist.

The autopsy finds no anatomic cause of death and the infant is morphologically normal for its age. Cultures, toxicology, and metabolic screens are negative. The pathologist notes that the possibility of asphyxia due to wedging, or blockage of airways by the sleeping surface and bedding cannot be ruled out – "asphyxia may occur without any observable autopsy findings," as he put it. No congenital anomalies are noted, and his opinion is both the manner and cause are undetermined. Medical records confirm normal delivery and a healthy infant. Law enforcement notes consistency in the narrative and nothing unusual in follow up interviews, and the mother was clear of both drugs and alcohol.

The situation leaves really only two options – accidental asphyxia due to the sleeping environment, or a natural death due to something beyond our ability to discern. With no reasonable certainty or additional evidence to put it beyond a 50-50 tossup, an undetermined ruling is legitimate in this case. This would be one of those where some investigators might feel an accidental death is justified based on what is known, and if their opinion is secure at even a 55 or 60 – 40 certainty, there would be nothing wrong with that certification. We can often be faced with cases where we are just barely above the 50-50 certainty one way or another, and that call is really up to the comfort level of the investigator, and legitimate if made.

Case 67. #208008 (2008) This mid-January case is a good example of the difficulties that may be encountered in the Mountain West where we often have a good number of people from out of the area engaging in recreational activities, especially in the winter seasons. This 43 year old female was cross-country skiing in a remote area of the Wind River Mountains with a partner when for no apparent reason she suddenly collapsed. Her partner managed to get contact out and both EMS and Search & Rescue personnel responded. Due to the area and access in the snow covered mountains, however, it took a good hour for responders to arrive at that location. Her male partner had been doing CPR for that entire time, but responders could not revive her, and the coroner was notified.

In many cases of tourists from out of State, especially 'flat-landers' from the Midwest or coastal areas, the altitude change in coming to the mountains can be physically hard on cardiac systems, especially if there is any pre-existing conditions. Non-acclimated persons will account for at least one or two natural deaths a year when the stress of altitude and exertion causes cardiac arrest, and the issues are usually pretty clear from the symptoms leading up to the fatal event. In this case, however, the subject was a Wyoming resident from Casper, which is roughly only about 175 miles from the location they were skiing, although a good 3,000 feet in elevation difference. She was a military veteran, whose VA records showed her to be in excellent health and physically fit, athletic, and a frequent skier and runner. She did not fit the profile of a person one would expect this sort of cardiac incident. They had been in the area for two days, and interviews with the partner did not reveal any unusual activities or symptoms leading up to the fatal event. The body was recovered and transported to the morgue pending an autopsy. Coroner reports are very thorough and detailed as to circumstances, scene, and background.

The forensic autopsy showed toxicology to be negative, no traumatic injuries, no coronary artery disease or myocarditis, no evidence of pneumonia, asthma, or pulmonary hypertension. The pathologist stated "the circumstances are consistent with an electromechanical cardiac event", and probably a manner of natural death, however, the cause is undetermined. In other words, there were none of the usual signs and finding associated with an altitude triggered event, nor any underlying conditions found. The only positive is that a lot was eliminated by the autopsy.

In these cases the investigator has a choice. It would be acceptable in certification to rule, based on the witnessed circumstances, that it was a natural death due to a probable fatal cardiac arrhythmia, which is accurate, but does not really tell you anything. Or, the investigator could consider the cause undetermined, which therefore makes the manner undetermined. Here the investigator chose the latter. Either way would be correct, and it is more a matter of what the investigator was comfortable with. Some circumstances leave you with a reasonable certainty that it is a natural death, but no clear picture of a cause, or a choice among several possibilities. If unable to define between possible natural causes, or unable to find a specific cause, those are valid rulings of undetermined manner.

Case 68. #208081 (2008) Mixed-drug toxicity is another of the areas that are difficult to discern a manner of death and can take a considerable amount of time and after the event research. This was a 26 year old male who was pronounced in the local emergency room in late May as a possible suicide. Coroner deputies responded to the ER, and the coroner report gives a detailed description of the body. There was no notable trauma or injuries other than what would be expected from medical intervention. According to the family, the individual was at his parent's home and after dinner went up to his parent's bedroom to take a nap – his mother was already there and asleep. When she woke up she found her son face down in the bed and unresponsive. The family started CPR, which was continued by EMS on their arrival and as they transported him to the hospital in full code. The ER was unable to revive this suspected overdose. The ER physician notes he considers it a suicide.

The initial family history given was that the deceased was on a lot of medication, had been diagnosed with depression, and also had a considerable pain condition as a result of a vehicle accident three weeks prior. The family also noted that there had been no indications of anything unusual the last few days; his behavior was normal and involved with family activities. In the evening of the event he appeared to be "acting straight and feeling great". There were no reported recent issues with his taking his medications properly, and that care had been monitored closely by the family. The family also preferred no autopsy as they wanted organ donation completed, and it was jointly agreed that toxicology could provide the information needed to determine cause and manner. Arrangements were made to retrieve his medications from the originating scene. The case was designated as pending investigation for toxicology and medical records.

Medications retrieved for the subject also included two bottles of pills prescribed to a female that had been a drug overdose suicide two months before this case, who was known by the deceased. After about a month, all tox results were back and medical records received, including those from the mental health provider. Medical records note a diagnosis of a slight heart murmur 12 years ago, with additional history of hypertension and substance abuse. Psychiatric history includes a diagnosis of bipolar disorder, anxiety, panic disorder, depression, and agoraphobia for several years. There was a history of suicide ideation with the most recent attempt by vehicle three weeks prior to the death. That resulted in a basal skull fracture and internal injuries. There was detailed medical follow up on those injuries with no signs of physical complications. Both the physician and therapist notes, and family testimony, indicate that the medications had stabilized the psychiatric issues. There is no report in the immediate time frame or days leading up to the death of any indication of mental issues or distress of the nature indicated by the history. Inventories of medications do not indicate any unusual amounts missing. Identification of the medications are consistent with the labeling. The two bottles that were found that were not his were only non-controlled substance analgesics.

The toxicology showed no indications of substances of abuse. Present were benzodiazepines (anti-anxiety) at low therapeutic range; amitriptylines (anti-depressant) slightly over the high end of therapeutic range; imipramines (anti-depressant) at mid therapeutic range. Levels of all three individually are well below what is reported as toxic levels in references, and far below any level that would indicate intentional overdose by ingestion. By research, it appears highly unlikely that the combination of these levels would interact in a fatal manner, just based on the levels of drugs. There are, however, possibilities listed as adverse reactions that include arrhythmias and other cardiac effects for the individual scripts. An additional drug, Metoprolol, that the deceased was taking, has known interactions with the anti-depressants, but this is generally a retention factor and not indicated by the levels seen on toxicology. In addition, the deceased had been taking all prescriptions for some time with no notations of adverse effects in the records.

Toxicology does not support the suspicion or the ER physician's opinion of intentional overdose. It appears unlikely that a conclusion of accidental mixed drug toxicity can be justified. Circumstances leading up to the death do not indicate any immediate physical distress indicating cardiac involvement, although not all arrhythmias, such as those associated with side effects, will manifest in a dramatic fashion. In the absence of any autopsy, any long term physical effects of the prior vehicular incident cannot be ruled out, although he had been closely medically monitored for that in the period after the injury. Having been found face down might lead one to suspect asphyxia or contained space effects, but again, that would be an unusual circumstance in a young adult, especially without any ethanol or opiate influence.

This is a case where as investigators, we got caught by the physician's presumption and the family's wishes, although to be fair, most cases similar to this come up with tox levels that are clear indications to either a suicide or accidental death. An autopsy might only have eliminated some of the other possibilities, without defining a true cause, but by the time the records and toxicology were received and studied, that option had passed. And while there is a psychiatric history as well as a recent previous attempt at suicide, that in and of itself cannot be a basis for a manner without other supporting evidence. There are a lot of people walking around that previously attempted suicide but lead stable lives once properly medicated, and indications are that it was working here. So unfortunately there are too many unknowns and we are left with undetermined for the manner and cause of death.

Case 69. #208133, #208134, #208135 (2008) This concerns a 1 year old, 2 year old, and 3 year old that died in a fire at their trailer home. This will be a case where the cause of death is readily determined at autopsy, but the manner of death becomes the sticking point. Fire deaths generally are most often accidental, but it is important to remember that any volitional act that results in another's death, regardless of intent, can be considered a homicide for manner. Arson deaths, for example, under NAME standards, can be ruled homicides, whether the arsonist intended to kill someone or not. The same would be true for any direct negligent fire by another individual, but keep in mind that the investigative circumstances are critical in the final judgement. We have had cases where an adult leaves an ignition source active, a fire results, and a death occurs in spite of all heroic attempts of the responsible adults and responders to save the trapped individuals or children. In those circumstances, most, including myself, would rule them accidental deaths. Here we have something else, however.

On an early August morning a fire is reported by neighbors in a local trailer court. Responders from assorted law enforcement arrive shortly, and local fire also responds quickly, but the trailer involved is soon totally engulfed. If you know anything about trailer fires, they go up quickly, and even before that the smoke and fumes produced are highly toxic to anyone caught inside. Two single mothers reside in the trailer, along with seven children. Investigations determine that one mother and her four children were asleep in a center bedroom of the trailer by her narrative. The other mother's three children were asleep in the far end of the trailer opposite the living room where the fire started. The adult that was present is awakened by smoke and fire, and with the exit hall already obstructed, tosses her four kids out the window and the crawls out behind them. She realizes that the other three are still at the rear of the trailer and attempts to go through the door to retrieve them, but is unable to pass the smoke and flames and is badly burned in the attempt. Law enforcement, fire, and EMS responders, as soon as they realize the situation, break through the wall of the rear of the trailer and manage to retrieve one child but are also soon forced back by the flames. That child was transported and died at the hospital. The remaining two would later be recovered by coroner staff after the scene was determined safe by the fire responders.

In such situations, the lead investigators are the State Fire Marshal's staff, working with law enforcement and coroner investigators. These cases obviously take considerable time to complete the investigation, usually a period of a month or more. Scenes are documented, diagrammed, and reported in detail, with each agency concentrating on their appropriate aspects. The coroner on the immediate area of the bodies, law enforcement on interviews to determine witnesses, circumstances, and sequence of events or connected issues, and the fire marshal on the nature, cause, and sequence of the fire itself. The various agencies remain in frequent touch to update each other of the progress and findings, coordinate investigations, and everyone has their own focus and legal responsibilities. The entire trailer is secured by law enforcement as a possible crime scene until determined otherwise. The scene is also documented in detail prior to removal of anything, including the bodies.

Once the remains were recovered, the involved room where the deceased were located was screen sifted, both to make sure all remains possible were recovered, and to look for any other additional evidence. The remains were secured individually, and along with the other child that died at the hospital, transported to forensic autopsy. The pathologist determines that all three were alive at the time of the fire, and died from the inhalation of toxic by-products of the fire and smoke. The child at the hospital also had burns over 30 to 40% of her body, while the other two were partially consumed post mortem. All such deaths, at least in this county, are autopsied. Several decades ago, three children were found in a trailer fire and it was determined that at least one was dead before the fire started. In that case, as it turned out, they were killed by their parents, who had started the fire and locked the trailer doors with them inside to hide at least one homicide. They both went to prison for three homicides. Aside from the standards that should prevail for anyone investigating such deaths, this county is somewhat sensitive to these fire circumstances.

The details of each agency's investigation are extensive and will not be related in this review, as the conclusions are what are important for our purposes here. Hundreds, if not over a thousand photos from the combined agencies document the scene, including media photos that were taken of the event while it occurred. Interviews of all neighbors, responders, and parties involved are completed. Detailed diagrams are done, and reconstruction of the sequence of the fire as it started, grew and spread, are completed by the fire marshal investigators. As it turns out, the fire started in the living room area beneath a dining table. Below the floor surface in that area in the fire debris is found the remains of a propane torch and crack pipe. The totality of the investigation determines that the narrative of the one mother in the trailer who escaped with her kids, is entirely consistent with the investigation and sequence. There was no evidence of alcohol or drug use on her part. Statements by the other mother, who originally told investigators she woke up on the living room couch and tried to put out the fire, were not valid. It was determined she was most likely not even in the trailer at the time. The probable cause, but one that could not be proven, is that the propane burner might have been left on after another person or persons left the living room and trailer, and thus unattended, started the fire while the mother in the center bedroom and the children were asleep. In any case, it was human caused at a minimum, after all other possible sources were eliminated.

While it cannot be proven who was present and left what ignition source, the fire was human caused, and depending on circumstances, the deaths of the three children could be homicides. On the other hand, to be fair, it could also be an accident, depending on circumstances. So while we have a detailed known sequence of events once ignition started, and a defined cause of death, the unknowns prior to the fire demand the manner be left as undetermined, being unable to defeat the 50-50 nature of that pre-fire period. Not satisfactory, but it is what we are left with, even after months of investigation and follow up.

Section VII: Arriving Better Late than Never 2010's

Case 70. #210034 (2010) At this point, we are finally at the time where, for the most part, reports are complete, detailed and extensive where needed; documentation and additional resources are being taken advantage of; forensic autopsies and principles of medical-legal investigation are being followed. It is becoming obvious that the coroner's office has for the most part, caught up with where it should be, both in record-keeping, and investigative procedures.

In this next case, a 49 year old Native American female was found bed in the early morning hours of late March when her husband woke up and found her unresponsive. There was no evidence of anything unusual or suspicious at the scene, and although the family members had a large number of prescription medications for various conditions, the deceased was noted as healthy without any particular issues. Since there was no clear indication of manner and cause, an autopsy was ordered with the forensic pathologist.

The autopsy found no physical issues other than pulmonary edema. Lung congestion in and of itself can be part of the dying process and discounted if no underlying issues are found in microscopic exam, other testing, or examinations. Toxicology was negative except for a blood alcohol of 0.170, which being only about twice the legal limit, would not be considered a fatal factor. In the pathologist's opinion, there was no anatomical or toxicological cause of death found, and the manner would be undetermined. Medical records only showed basic health maintenance visits with no unusual history. Nothing in the history, scene investigation, positioning, or interviews and activities leading up to the death offered any clues.

Sometimes even with the most complete investigation, reporting, documentation, and autopsy, there simply are no answers, as unsatisfying or frustrating as that may be. In this case, there are not even any reasonable pointers to give a direction for anything further to look at. Cause and manner remain undetermined.

Case 71. #210084 (2010) This 54 year old white female was found unresponsive on her living room couch in early morning in mid-June. The home was a mess and extremely cluttered, but nothing unusual or indicative of a disturbance was noted. Since many people are not particularly good housekeepers, or organized in how they live, the investigator must be able to discern the difference between a disturbance indicating suspicious activity, and a simple mess. Even a home that is habitually a disaster can show a disturbance in how the mess is tossed around, upset, or otherwise altered. The difficult part is to discover what in the overall mess may be significant. Are there recent drinks that are spilled, or obscure indications of drug activity? Are the biologics seen of recent deposit, or old and just not cleaned up? The features of the body may point a direction, but in this case there was no blood or biologics or recent injuries seen. The television was on at responder arrival. The bathroom showed evidence of soiled clothing and floor, and the same was seen on the bed in the bedroom. The deceased was partially sitting on the couch and slightly leaned over onto a pile of clothing, dressed in the uniform that would be appropriate to her work at a local nursing home. Law enforcement and coroner deputies were tasked with wading through the mess of the home to try and see what might be significant. The body was recovered and an autopsy planned with the forensic pathologist.

The deceased was discovered when a friend did a welfare check after she did not show up for work, and was last seen around 9:30 pm the night before. The home was not secured when the friend arrived. Police secured the home and sealed it pending further investigation, due to the overwhelming mess of possessions and property. Prescription medications included scripts for codeine and inhalers, muscle relaxants, restless leg syndrome and hypertension meds.

The autopsy report was received after about five weeks. Physical findings included acute multifocal pneumonitis, ascites, cardiomegaly with biventricular hypertrophy, emphysema. tracheobronchitis, and severe generalized atherosclerosis – generally not in good shape for a 54 year old. The kicker was the toxicology, however, showing a codeine level of 44,000 ng/mL (therapeutic average is 134). Boom.

The conclusion of the pathologist was that the extreme levels of codeine and metabolites would make the manner of death dependent on the investigation as to suicide, homicide, or accident – but "the high drug levels indicate mass ingestion and suggest suicide." It is noted in the detailed report, however, that no pills or fragments are found in the stomach. In many cases, an enormous toxicology value like this would indicate suicide, as people rarely accidentally take such large amounts... but certain aspects of this case were suspicious. According to law enforcement, certain friends of the deceased had shady habits. Interviews with friends and coworkers gave no indications of suicidal tendencies (although that in and of itself is not conclusive – many suicides show no previous signs). The deceased was found dressed as if she had just come from work, or was preparing to go to work, although the body condition indicated it was the former rather than the latter. None of the usual medication clues were found in the immediate scene, and in the application of a dose that large, usually there are drugs or paraphernalia nearby. Law enforcement was notified to continue their follow up as this now was termed a suspicious death, and family from out of town coming in to clean the clutter in the home was notified to get a hold of the police if anything unusual was found when they were digging through the residential mess.

A study and analysis of her medications is initiated, and only the codeine scripts were considered, as that was all that was found on the toxicology. Two bottles of codeine in pill form were found at the scene, both had a number remaining, and the amounts gone could in no way account for the tox level based on dosage and metabolism on average studies. The number of pills needed to reach that particular blood level would be 656, an unlikely amount for any one person to consume orally in one sitting – and no fragments were found in her stomach on autopsy. So what are the other possibilities? Codeine is also available in liquid and injectable form, and would be a more likely source, and there were no records of the deceased being prescribed either for her conditions. There was no evidence seen at the location of injection paraphernalia, but the injectable form could also be consumed orally or with another fluid. There were so many partial and open drink containers at the scene, collection did not seem needed at the time, and it was too late now to try and obtain and analyze such fluids after the fact of the tox results, if one could have even determined which of the innumerable glasses, bottles, or cans was significant. It was not anything anyone even thought of in the scene investigation, and even if we had, the condition of the home would have precluded finding anything or everything. On top of that, analysis of all the possible beverage containers would have been cost prohibitive.

Medical or social history did not reveal anything in particular other than her known medical issues. Being a worker in a health care facility did give her possible access to injectable drugs. Law enforcement took over that aspect of the investigation to determine if the facility had anything missing, altered, or otherwise documented to account for as a source. Discussions were held and input given on some of the questions our office needed answered in interviews which would be completed by police. The follow up investigation was open for about three months as these options were completed. Some of the police interviews were anonymously witnessed or reviewed via video tape by our staff. Nothing substantial was found, and law enforcement noted the case would be "inactive" rather than closed in case something turned up long term.

Background and interviews and research indicated attitudes and future plans on the part of the deceased, as well as activities and interactions, did not indicate a conclusion of suicide, in spite of the unusually high drug levels, although that option could not be eliminated. Chronic drug usage has had accidental over dosage in individuals who acquire an unfamiliar medication form, or who are careless with potency while under the influence. The possibility of homicide could be seen if the deceased was unaware of administration in a mixture, or if illegally obtained. None of the three manners could be reasonably eliminated by the investigation, so while there is no doubt about the cause of death, the manner will have to stay undetermined.

Case 72. #210167 (2010) A 59 year old female was discovered face down in bed by a relative, lividity consistent with position and anterior surfaces flattened, including facial features. No major injuries or trauma seen. Last seen one day prior to being found, medical history included respiratory issues, diabetes, and recurrent depression. Nothing suspicious noted, and an autopsy scheduled due to concerns of natural causes versus accidental asphyxia. Note: by this time all autopsies are forensic if not mentioned as such due to policy of the department. Medications found at the scene do not include any of the usual drugs of abuse except codeine. Investigation revealed nothing unusual or suspicious. Autopsy showed obesity, pulmonary edema, mild cardiovascular disease and a fibrotic thyroid, but no anatomic cause of death. Toxicology showed about twice the single therapeutic dose of the codeine, but well below toxic or fatal ranges. All other medications were within therapeutic ranges and not high enough or in combination as to be fatal. The pathologist noted the death as undetermined.

While positioning indicated that asphyxia or closed space restrictions (face down) may have been a factor, there were no physical findings that were definitive, although unfortunately in that sort of asphyxia we do not always see anything on autopsy. Nor is there a way of eliminating the possibility, so we are left with a 50-50 unknown natural cause or complication versus an indeterminate accident. We have to go with the pathologist on the undetermined manner

> At this point it is worthwhile to comment that there were no undetermined cases in 2011. Based on averages in Fremont County, one would expect that at least one or two cases per year would be undetermined in manner of death, regardless of how good an investigation is. This does not include those cases that are anthropology/archaeology finds of a proto or prehistoric age where determining the manner and cause is impossible. Those finds are not a part of this study, but even at that, there were none of those in 2011 either. Nor were there any reports that turned out to be non-human or animal remains. In that regard, 2011 was an unusual year, and atypical for the averages we see in this county.

Case 73. #212094 (2012) Once again, drug cases can be the most difficult to determine the manner on the deceased. Here we have a 39 year old white male found in a trailer home that was known by local law enforcement as a "high traffic area of suspicious nature". In other words, known for suspicious drug activity. That in and of itself causes complications due to the comings and goings of all sorts of individuals, associated conflicts, and dubious situations. Along with the assorted drug paraphernalia and containers, actual drugs and suspected materials at the scene, there were several notes indicating irrational thinking, and the deceased's cell phone had a message that stated (rough quote), "Hello, this is ****, I'm already dead, go fuck yourself". While the general interior was cluttered and an example of poor housekeeping, there did not appear to be any unusual disturbances. Some furniture appeared broken or smashed, but there is a difference between that which occurs as a result of assault or tussle, and that which looks more like individual mishaps. Also, these items appeared to be not current in destruction, and more like something that broke and the property owner simply did not care to move or fix it for whatever reason. Assessing such subtleties mostly comes with experience and time. No prescriptions were found, but numerous filled and empty syringes were located, as well as bindles and other containers of probable drugs. There was a good amount of blood or purge and vomit in the immediate area of the body, but none of any significance elsewhere in the residence. No major trauma or injuries were observed. Obviously this sort of scene calls for an autopsy.

Autopsy showed long term intravenous drug abuse evidence, and a blood level of methamphetamine of 49 ng/mL, with no other injuries or trauma. In this case, a discussion with the pathologist occurred on several days during the investigation. He noted that the meth levels were not at what is usually seen in suicides. While lower or any level of methamphetamine can cause death in particular circumstances, his concern was that some sort of adulteration was involved. In this case, consultation was extended to law enforcement, as they had possession of, and would be testing, the evidence recovered at the scene. The manner of death would be undetermined pending the results of further investigation. The crime lab later noted they do not test for poisons, and suggested the agriculture lab. Samples from the autopsy were then scheduled for testing for some of the newer designer drugs, as well as the crude "bath salt" named preparations, such as mephedrone/MDPV. This case is a good example of the open mind one must maintain, as well as promoting consultations with the various labs, pathologist, and other agencies... each will have its own set of experience and knowledge, and others may be more current on the latest trends in substance abuse in the community.

Nothing significant was found in further testing. Keeping in mind that a drug such as methamphetamine can have long term and accumulative effects, or can in any amount cause fatal arrhythmia, the pathologist phrased the cause of death as "most likely died of methamphetamine abuse/intoxication". Manner he though best left as undetermined. I would agree, as the investigation could not define definitive evidence of a suicide versus accidental overdose by a chronic drug abuser. The tox amount was just not consistent with what a chronic abuser would take if that was what he had in mind. While some of the writings and messages left by the deceased could be interpreted as suicidal, investigation also showed a long term history of that sort of expression and irrationality, rather than just a recent time frame. Due to that, they could be associated with drug habit and personality rather than indication of immediate intent. Also, there still is the consideration that someone supplied something illegal or adulterated with a substance they either did or did not have awareness of, and we just could never find it on toxicology. While the labs have very good general screens, and can test in most any direction indicated if you can tell them what to look for, they still need to be pointed the right way. There is too many options that something could be there, and not found, simply because it was not tested for if we or law enforcement cannot point the right direction. Negative results only mean they did not find any quantity of what they tested for, not that there was nothing there – an important consideration to keep in mind when it comes to toxicology. Poisons and adulterants can be difficult to define or discover.

Case 74. #212120 (2012) A 28 year old Native American female is recovered from a local rural reservoir as a possible drowning victim in late July. The area consists of several access points down slight embankments, mixed in with rocky cliffs that are popular for jumping into the water. Dependent on the water levels, there are numerous hazards for that activity that include underwater rock obstructions and shelves. Water temperature is warm, relatively clear with little current. Temperature is in the 80's with recent periodic showers in the region. Incident is investigated by numerous jurisdictions and assisted by search & rescue personnel. A truck associated with the incident is along one of the access point to the shoreline, deeply stuck in mud and sand. Trash and other evidence in the area ranges from older use to probable recent camping debris. The deceased was located in the water along the shoreline off a rocky prominence and cliff point a ways away from the truck and camp area, floating face up. There are notable bruises to the left side of the face and head, and other bruising consistent with a law enforcement report of an assault a day or two prior to this event. Hands and feet show evidence of 'water-logging' texture, but general appearance does not indicate submersion of more than a matter of hours. No bleeding is noted at recovery, but considerable bleeding occurred from the mouth and nose area during transport from the scene. No major dislocating trauma is observed that would be consistent with a fall from the height of the rock cliffs in the area.

Initial interviews with her camping partners indicate she was last seen in the early morning after midnight, was not around when they awoke later in the morning, and then seen in the water after a short search. Witnesses relate that there had been drinking and obvious drug activity, after which their truck got stuck and all parties had to spend the night. Law enforcement and hospital records confirm the details of the deceased being the victim of an assault earlier in the week. This fortunately included police photos of the injuries at the time of that incident to compare to what was currently seen. All this information is sent along with the body for autopsy.

The pathologist documents the multiple blunt force injuries, contusions, and abrasions, but does not find any internal head injury that would indicate a related cause, such as brain hemorrhage. This was important, as if there was a long term related developing effect of an assault that causes death, even days later, that death could be considered a homicide. Even at that though, in his conclusion, he would not exclude the possibility that the cumulative effect of the injuries may have contributed. Toxicology was negative for alcohol, but showed a level of benzodiazepines (tranquilizer), elevated cyclobenzaprine (muscle relaxant), as well as cocaine. The lungs

222

contained a "frothy fluid", that indicated some effects of being in the water, but not the definitive findings that normally are associated with full drowning. He notes the manner of death as undetermined.

Other investigator reports of interviews with those witnesses in the area, describe having to pull the subject out of the water more than once while alive the previous evening, with some indications of suicidal ideations. Due to the alcohol and drug use, as well as a certain reluctance to those with the deceased to give a clear substantiation or non-conflicting testimony to the previous evening's activities, the death remained suspicious. Medical records document that in addition to the known assault, there was a history of depressive disorder, domestic violence and abuse (as both perpetrator and victim), and doctor shopping related to controlled substance abuse, notably cut off from some providers for that reason. Total time frame for the investigation and coordination with other agencies encompassed about 2 ½ months.

Here there are several possibilities: drug use and behavior could have led to an accidental incident; suicide appears possible but cannot be substantiated with certainty; homicide is more remote but cannot be eliminated, both due to the possible contribution of previous assault, or the unknown circumstances of the immediate incident. Even the cause remains elusive and undefined. It remains a suspicious but undetermined manner.

Case 75. #213018 (2013) ...And now for a case that was ruled undetermined due to no fault of the coroner's office. In this circumstance, a 105 year old white female died in a local nursing home at the end of January. Unless a non-natural death, nursing home cases are considered statutorily as attended deaths and not the coroner's jurisdiction. Procedure is for the attending physician to certify the death to the State. In this certification, the physician gave a cause of chest trauma due to a fall, and marked the manner as natural (obviously illogical). The State of Wyoming just as obviously kicked it back to us, as an accidental death would, or should have, resulted in notification to this office for investigation and certification. So we have to do an after the fact analysis of the incident, starting a month later when the State got ahold of the department.

The basic question here is simple... as one of our forensic pathologists at one time put it, "sometimes people die because they fell (accident), and sometimes they just fell because they were dying (natural)". So which do we have here? Records from the physician and institution are obtained and reviewed in detail. Unfortunately, even if something suspicious was noted in the record, the body had already been cremated, so no autopsy or examination was possible. As it turned out, the incident referred to by the physician was a fall out of bed three weeks prior to the death. And while a fall from a low bed height is not usually a fatal event, we are talking about a 105 year old person here. Then there is the fact that at that age, with the multiple inherent age related conditions, other medical issues and history, and time frame, there was no clear indication of a relation between the incident and the death. The "but for" rule was pretty useless in someone who was 105. Complications from the fall could not be proven as a direct cause, nor could it be eliminated – a basic 50-50 proposition. No choice in the matter but to rule it as undetermined.

Case 76. #213060 (2013) This 29 year old Native American male was found unresponsive by his mother, who he was living with. The circumstances were a bit unique in that he was a paraplegic as a result of a gunshot wound received during a drug deal gone bad three years prior on a Reservation in Washington State. Family reported he had been in and out of the hospital since that time due to complications from that injury. As a reminder, keep in mind that if a person dies from the complications of such an injury, regardless of time frame, the manner would be homicide, and the original perpetrator is subject to possible charges. An autopsy was ordered, and research started on obtaining information on the originating incident that led to his condition.

The autopsy noted the paraplegia and numerous aspects physically relating to that condition. Other physical findings included possible sepsis (MRSA positive), dilated cardiomyopathy, and hepatic necrosis most likely due to acetaminophen intoxication. Toxicology also showed a blood alcohol of 0.278, and an oxycodone level roughly 21 times the average therapeutic level and well into the toxic range. The pathologist's opinion is that he died of multiple drug intoxication, with sepsis and heart disease most likely contributory. He left the manner of death as undetermined with both accident and homicide (complications of a remote gunshot wound) as considerations.

Judging from his social and criminal history, his lifestyle could have accounted for his heart and liver disease regardless of the incident that left him disabled, and the drug use itself should not be considered as caused entirely from the injury, even if it aggravated his previous bad habits. If the current alcohol and drug use or levels are separated from his physical issues, the cardiac and liver disease would have eventually caught up with him at some point (and be considered a natural death) regardless of the issues related to the injury. So in spite of the forensic and background investigations, there are cross-overs and confusion of possible manners of death. Different findings can be applied in different ways to reach a conclusion of accidental overdose, versus natural heart and liver failure, versus sepsis or other complications of remote injury for homicide. At the levels of intoxicants, there could even be a remote consideration of suicide, although there was no anecdotal evidence found to support that other than the levels of drugs themselves. But for the lethal combination of all current factors, he might have lived either a long or short time, even as a paraplegic, but it was difficult to say what ended up as the primary cause of death. Other cases we have had of deaths resulting from remote injuries have usually had clear indications and evidence that added up to accident or homicide. In this case, the subject's own history and habits introduced so many variables that the only thing we felt comfortable with was undetermined.

Case 77. #213077 (2013) Here is another possibility coroners must keep in mind on some undetermined cases: in late May a 39 year old Native American female died at the hospital after being found at home by family members with evidence of seizures. On autopsy the cause of death was determined by the pathologist to be multiple blunt force injuries with secondary exsanguination. The manner of death was undetermined due to the unknown source of the injuries and inability to define accident versus homicide. Jurisdiction of the case was also to the FBI. The case sat as is, until reopened after a meeting with the U.S. Attorney's Office and FBI investigators in 2016. Details of this case will not be presented or discussed other than the previous facts that are publically known, as appropriate to an open case.

When a case has been ruled undetermined due to being unable to rule out a manner of homicide, since there is no statute of limitations for that possible crime, law enforcement can reopen a case at any time down the road. In this county we have had cases that were known homicides but unsolved, then re-opened and investigated even over 25 years later. Some resulted in convictions, others remained cold cases, but one just never knows. Undetermined cases are more difficult as a cold case, as there is obviously doubt and lack of definition of clear evidence even at the immediate investigation time frame. Sometimes time will pass and make things clearer, or more obscure, but in any event, any case can be reopened for the agency of jurisdiction to take a second look. Sometimes it is just an advancement in forensic technology that now allows now what could not be done earlier. DNA is just one example of that for investigations. This is another reason also why I am so adamant on documentation and complete clarity in reports and records. In this office, undetermined cases are treated like homicides as far as record keeping – save everything. You never know when someone will need to take a second look.

There were no medical-legal cases in 2014 that were ruled undetermined (remember we are not counting historical or prehistorical skeletal remains cases).

Case 78. #215098 (2015) The only case for 2015, and the last case for consideration, is that of a 49 year old white female that was found in a decomposed condition in her apartment after police did a requested welfare check. The scene is in slight disarray, cluttered and messy, however, not suspiciously disturbed. The home was secured when found by officers. The deceased had known severe psychiatric issues for which she was being treated, and past history of drug abuse, both prescription and illegal. The autopsy reveals no trauma or injury, or indications of a suspicious death. The cause of death is an acute Oxymorphone toxicity, and the pathologist's opinion is that it is a suicide.

This case is a prime example of the need of the death investigator to do a thorough psychological and sociological background on the deceased, which was completed here. In the wealth of medical and psychiatric records, as well as interviews, it was discovered that the subject was only marginally socially functioning on her own. In addition, with frequent access history to illegally obtained opiates in addition to her prescription drugs, there was a variety of individual dosages available. This made it impossible for the investigator to determine which, and how many, pills she would have taken to reach the toxicological level found at autopsy. Also, with frequent psychotic episodes, there is the possibility that drugs were consumed in a manic or otherwise inadequately aware condition. For all her documented mental issues, suicidal ideation was not prominent. It remained a possibility, but the research also raised the issue of highly possible unintentional accidental overdose. Therefore the cause was known, but the manner was ruled undetermined.

There can be a multitude of factors in an overdose that can cloud or obscure what was going on at the time unless things are at a level that is unmistakably clear to a reasonable certainty. Unfortunately, like many deaths, the only person who knows 100% for sure what happened in an event, is the deceased. Thus we are tasked with coming to a reasonable conclusion that rarely hits that 100% certainty. While to certain degree it is the investigator's or department's discretion, in suicides, due to the devastating effect that ruling can have on those left behind, I believe in requiring a higher certainty than in some other situations. These things are always a moving target, as each situation is different, and can be the hardest choice in manner of death an investigator will encounter.

At his point in 2015, we will end the analysis of available cases. Some of the undetermined cases since that year are generally still considered open in some respects by law enforcement, our office, or other agencies, and thus it would be inappropriate to discuss any details or evidence at the time of the writing of this study. And while individual identification is removed and educational use is permitted by statutes, we must be sensitive to other issues in recent cases. That leaves out of the 83 originally noted, 80 deaths in 78 incidents (three in one fire event), which has given us a wide variety of circumstances and examples of situations the death investigator might encounter.

Analysis of Cases

Out of the 78 cases reviewed over the 128 years, there are 20 cases I would have ruled a specific manner of death rather than leaving them undetermined. That would include 9 accidents, 5 naturals, 2 homicides, 1 suicide, and 3 cases not Fremont County Coroner jurisdiction to even sign off on. While this is an interesting exercise in determining manner of death, unless there is an egregious error, or someone is today legally questioning a ruling and seeking a readdress of the certification, it would not be proper to file an amendment to change what is on file with State Vital Records. Opinions and analysis of the forensics change, and the older the case, the more significant is the fact you were not there at the time. Also, some critical information may not have been in the file, or just not recorded in older cases. Another factor to consider is that not only do standards for rulings evolve, but also the laws and legal definitions change over time. In any case, my objections or observations on cases I disagree with are noted in the discussions, and the reader can choose to agree or disagree with my analysis as they please.

What that does show is that in about at least a quarter of the cases, different investigators may come to a different conclusion. That would be the first point to offer about undetermined cases, so the lesson for a modern investigator is to seek as many resources and opinions on the evidence as they can prior to ruling. This is also a core principle of why the office of the coroner or medical examiner is there... as an independent perspective from other agencies.

While we are talking about 78 cases, remember that one case (#69 in this text) involved three child deaths in a fire, so we are actually considering 80 individuals and deaths. In a multiple death fire investigation, it is also entirely possible to have more than one manner of death among the different individuals, dependent of the circumstances.

A. When the cause of death is unknown or undetermined: Of the 78 cases, 31 fall into this category, or almost 40%. Out of those 31cases, 21 (27% of the 78 cases) are what I would call "pure undetermined", where the cause of death is unknown, leaving no choice in ruling a manner of undetermined death. This may be due to a range and lack of technology, skills, scientific advancement, or trained analysis in the older cases, or be like those more modern cases where even advanced technology and forensic autopsy do not reveal a defined answer for cause.

The remaining 10 of those 31, the cause is ruled as undetermined, but in looking at the cases, those 10 had a possible cause expressed, but not to a certain sure degree by investigation or analysis. Within that doubt, it is best to leave the cause as unknown and the manner undetermined.

B. When cause may be known, but no defining choice exists between different manners: A more frequent situation for the investigator is that an autopsy and investigation can and does determine a defined cause of death, however, the investigator is unable to choose between more than one manner of death as a conclusion. Out of the 78 cases, this is the circumstance of 47 of the 78 cases, or 60%. This can be because the known evidence in a case points different directions relative to manner of death, or the interpretation of that evidence could justify multiple possibilities.

In looking at these cases, the most common inability to choose is between a manner of accidental death and a homicide (13 cases). In three of those I would have ruled an accident, and in one a homicide, but the reasoning for not changing anything is noted above. The next most common incident is a choice between a natural death and an accident (12 cases). In two of those I would have ruled accident, and one natural. The third most common (8 cases) is that it could not be decided between the three options of accident, suicide, or homicide, and I do not disagree with undetermined in any of those. The fourth most common (5 cases) is a choice between accident and suicide, although I would have ruled three of those as accidental deaths, for the reasons discussed in the individual cases.

Of the remaining nine in this category, 6 are other assorted choices between two manners, and 4 are a choice between a possible three assorted manners, different from the most common ones noted above. In any case, if you cannot clearly define the choice between the various manners of death, then undetermined is your only option. These are often hard choices, but that is what we get paid, elected, or selected to do. And remember, undetermined should only be used if at a 50-50 status or less. A qualified reasonable certainty is rarely ever approaching 90 to 100% in many cases, and you never need to be at 100% to make a ruling. Nice if it works out that way, but that is not the usual case when working with cases and death investigations.

C. Common causes of death that may result in an undetermined manner: By far, the largest number of causes of death in the undetermined cases under consideration is the category of overdose, poisoning, or other toxicity – 21 out of the 78 cases presented (27%). If we deduct the cases that have no cause indicated, such as the ones I like to call the "pure undetermined", that would be 21 of 57 cases, or 37%. This does make sense if you think about it... Toxicology has only become well defined in the last decade or two, as far as coming up with detailed quantification and ability to ferret out many of the more obscure substances. Older cases only had the ability to give a presumptive presence or not, which does not lead to any analysis of if the substance was at lethal level or not. Even today, remember that toxicology can only tell you what you test for, and not anything that was not tested for. While basic and forensic screens may point a direction, if the investigation has no clue as to a particular toxic substance, you may never know it is there, since you did not ask the laboratory to test for some substance specifically outside of the basic screens.

One example of this is a case this office had regarding the sudden death of a young woman who was the proverbial "health nut", a fanatic about marathons, supplements, diet, and nutrition. Autopsy showed dilated cardiomyopathy but no other major physical issues. Due to the lifestyle seen, however, and that the investigation showed she relied on vast amounts of supplements, herbal medications, and brown rice preparations rather than "traditional" food sources for nutrition, we had blood samples tested for heavy metals. While some recent studies at the time had shown that the natural levels of the heavy metal arsenic and other impurities in processed brown rice bases and syrups can be harmful to infants, heavy metal poisoning from food sources had been pretty much rarely seen in adults unless it is a contaminant in growing soils. Selenium for example is known in certain areas to be a naturally occurring ground contaminant that some plants will concentrate in their uptake, specifically on occasion causing poisoning in livestock, and more rarely, human toxicity from consumed produce or grains. Due to the individual's lifestyle choices, and almost absurd supplement habits, it seemed reasonable to additionally test for that class of substances. Our focus of concern at the time was the arsenic, but the whole class of substances was a possibility. While most of these metals in very small amounts are necessary for normal body functions, among other issues, large amounts can cause neurologic problems that might include cardiac arrhythmias that would not be seen on a physical autopsy.

Also, a U.S. Department of Health and Human Services study noted an incident in 2008 of an outbreak of selenium poisoning in 10 states where a supplement product contained 200 times the labeled amount of selenium, prompting a recall once the source was defined. Considering the lack of compounding formulation oversight and regulation in these products, it is amazing that there are not more frequent incidents, and I suspect many individual cases go undiscovered. Most of these studies are copyrighted information, so will not be reproduced here in specifics. I encourage any investigator who encounters similar possibilities to do the appropriate research in these areas if needed or interested.

Toxicology in this case revealed a moderate level of barium, and a high level of selenium, which with arsenic is also a known heavy metals contaminant in rice based products. Unfortunately, with the lack of quality control, listed ingredients, and multiple unknowns in the volume of nutritional supplements and products she was using, we were unable to narrow down anything to a specific product. Most likely it was a combination of sources anyway, and to test the hundreds of possibilities individually was monetarily prohibitive for our small office. The manner was ruled accidental, and the cause due to heavy metals toxicity due to overuse of nutritional supplements. We would have never found any of that if the investigation had not pointed the way and specific things tested for. In a normally appearing healthy individual, this might have ended up undetermined. Too much of anything can kill you, regardless of whether it is a "healthy" substance or not.

Another variable on toxicology deaths is that while amounts found can be exact, the ranges of therapeutic versus toxic versus fatal are just that – ranges based on multiple individuals in multiple studies. We deal with individual cases. While you may be lucky and eliminate toxicology as a cause when there is no doubt as to it being therapeutic, or so ungodly high that there is no doubt of a fatal toxic accident or suicide, the 'in-betweens' can confound you. Add to that the illegal drugs, such as variations of methamphetamine, designer drugs, or fentanyl derivatives that can be fatal to an individual in any amount depending on circumstances, tox can be a boggle. Not to mention the un-guessed at impurities along for a ride. Even something as simple as carbon monoxide toxicity can be hard to determine if accidental or suicide. It is no wonder that overdose/poisoning/other toxicity ends up as the cause in the largest number of undetermined cases.

Another example and issue for recent times is cannabis and its by-products. Toxicology results have evolved from just being a presumptive positive for cannabis, which tells you little about the effect on the death, to now getting quantitative results on the various metabolites. This not only can provide levels that can be compared to national studies, but also indicate time frame of usage. And while at the moment there are no recorded deaths due to direct "overdose" of cannabis, the more refined the products get, the higher chance that will eventually occur, especially in child cases where they encounter edibles. These products are more and more relevant to particular deaths whether segments of society like it or not. In particular for driving under the influence, if you end up with a motor vehicle accident or homicide, it is the influence that is significant, not the substance used, whether alcohol, cannabis, or prescription medications. The tools in these cases are always evolving.

The second most notable cause is general trauma (10 cases of 57) at 18%. These are usually situational and circumstantial as to the source or initiation of the trauma being hard to determine. The third most is firearms, which would be another type of trauma (6 cases of 57) at 11%. It is not too difficult to see that in these instances, differentiating between accident, homicide, or suicide can be the question.

Natural processes, such as cardiac or other organ issues and failures, and seizure conditions are found in 9% (5 of 57 cases), and are subject usually to lack of definition with other factors or manners. Close behind are the infections or sepsis at 7% (4 of 57 cases), again undetermined usually due to originating source, or as a complication of accident, or not.

Last are what I would call the 'situational' causes, where the circumstances or originating incident cannot be defined, or are 50-50 with something else. These include birth issues (4), drowning (4), other asphyxia (3), fire (3 in one case), and hypothermia (1). In one case there is reasonable evidence that there had been a body but it was gone when investigators arrived. While not a case for certification, it is filed in the database as undetermined. This would also be the case for most court-ordered certification of deaths, unless the court determines a manner of death.

D. Trends in undetermined cases: While we have considered a number of cases over a 128 year time frame, the sampling of undetermined is still small (78) in relation to the total number of cases during that time – around about 1%. Consider also we are talking only about Fremont County Wyoming, which has its own unique dynamics and tendencies. In addition, record keeping has only been up to a decent standard roughly the last two decades, along with modern standards for investigations and forensics. The one thing you notice if you study the really old cases is that in the 1800s and early 1900s, the coroners were the only death investigators for the most part, especially through inquests. They did a pretty decent job under the circumstances with what they had to work with. In any case, it would be unfair, and analytically unwise or even unscientific to compare too much those old time periods to today. There is just too much that was different.

The years 2010 through 2015 averaged 1.4 undetermined cases per year. The years 2000 through 2009 averaged 2.6 undetermined cases per year. Since this encompasses a majority of the years I worked for this office, I like to think we are getting better at investigations, but that really is too small a statistical sampling to be a supportable conclusion. Anyone who works in this business knows that types and quantities of cases are unpredictable, and the whole business can go south in an instant. The 1980s and 1990s averaged 1.2 and .8 cases per year respectively, but there are serious questions of record-keeping and investigative ability in those periods. Prior to that it would take a serious time investment at the archives and vital records to even determine if our files are reasonably complete, which I would bet they are not, in spite of the volumes of files we do have. Thus, realistically determining a trend cannot be done from this study.

E. Main lessons to take away from this study: Since a lot of the skills in determining manner and cause of death, especially in those cases that have a high possibility of ending up undetermined, depends a lot on experience and encounters of the investigator, it is hoped that these case studies will provide at least some mental exercises in the thought processes needed. Here are some summary thoughts:

> 1. Just as in life, circumstances and experiences in death investigation will be unexpected, unanticipated, confusing, and full of various possible interpretations to sort out.

> 2. While cases that end up as undetermined are only a small percentage of what you will encounter in investigations, they will often be the most challenging, and the most frustrating. Standards and simplified classifications are often not much help in the grey areas.

> 3. Investigation skills, experience, and tools are always advancing and improving, but even the most modern applications and knowledge will not always give a defined answer. While historically the available tools have evolved, the basic logic remains the same in analyzing evidence – use everything at your disposal to define the manner to the highest degree possible.

> 4. Proper and detailed documentation of an investigation is critical

for tracking and justifying your conclusions, as any case that is ruled as undetermined, may be revisited at a later date in court, or by other investigators and agencies. As far as this jurisdiction is concerned, remember that coroner files belong to the State of Wyoming, not the individual department and must be handled according to statutory and regulations guidelines. For other jurisdictions, know your own laws, rules, and applicable regulations that govern your documentation, and how things are handled within the realm of public records.

5. Seek to use all available resources and acquire other perspectives to obtain as complete a picture as possible. Putting a different set of eyes on the case just may help in coming to a conclusion other than undetermined.

6. Consider the inquest process if available in your jurisdiction to place the manner and cause into the hands of an independent jury. Sometimes the logical presentation of the total body of evidence in that forum will allow a conclusion to be reached.

7. Do not be afraid to rule based on a reasonable certainty by accepted standards, rather than insisting on 90 to 100% certainty. "Reasonable probability" is the name of the game here. Consider the totality of the case – the investigator can overrule a pathology conclusion based on the whole end picture. The forensic pathologist is just a resource and one of the tools of an investigation. It is the coroner or investigator's responsibility to make a judgment based on the entirety of the investigation, not just on the results of a forensic pathology exam.

8. Review your own agency's old cases – seeing what was, or was not done, compared to what could be done, gives practice in the logic of case analysis. Seeing the historical progression of methods and circumstances helps in understanding the process of today's investigations.

9. Don't pass off or defer the responsibility to others, the deceased deserve your best efforts, and attempting conclusions is your job. Keep in mind that the focus of other agencies can affect their perceptions of the evidence. For example, law enforcement, or those with that background, look for and try to fit the evidence into criminality. We are here specifically to have a different and independent focus, one based on the facts as they are. Our

conclusions may help arrive at justice in a homicide, but also can prevent an innocent person from undue accusations.

10. While a few manner of death rulings inevitably will leave you no choice, numbers of cases ruled as undetermined should be low per year. If not low, or there is an unusual spike in undetermined numbers, suspect other issues like external public health concerns, hidden or obscure mortality factors, or internal agency problems such as poor analytical skills or lack of training, or lack of broad overview of the evidence and use of available resources.

11. Don't over-speculate on various scenarios, go with the evidence in a logical manner, regardless of other opinions. Any set of facts can be applied or stretched to fit innumerable possibilities with imagination, and can drive the investigator to distraction and confuse the issue. Keep to the most likely and most reasonable certainties. It is what it is.

12. Be aware of how you store your data. Our first photos on file from 1938, almost 80 years ago, are as usable and readable as the day they were printed on photographic paper. Modern digital photos stored on CDs or DVDs may only be readable for about ten years or less before the media decays and is useless. We have blue "Dictaphone" interview records from the 50s, 'reel to reel' audio tapes from the 60s, VHS and Beta video recordings on file from the 80s and 90s, all of which require specific technology to replay that in some cases is no longer available, or hard to find. If you are fortunate to have one of the modern 3-D laser scene scanners, will your office have the software and technology to access those files years down the road? Consult a knowledgeable digital archivist for the best ways to secure and store modern case information.

13. And finally, be prepared for the emotional stress and difficulty of explaining to family, survivors, next of kin, the media, or others, the whys and wherefores of a ruling of undetermined. Obtaining answers and reasons is part of the grieving and coping process for family, and you will not be able to provide that, only explain why there is no specific answer. The same goes for other agencies if your conclusion does not fit what they are looking or hoping for; and the media, who always prefer things in a neat package or adequate sound bite. Undetermined rulings are often tough, frustrating, and hard to swallow, not only for the investigator, but for anyone expecting a solid answer.

Appendix A: Sample Coroner Report Form with Explanation

Since documentation is critical, this is provided as an example of the types of information that could be covered during an investigation into a death, but keep in mind that the needs and policies of various jurisdictions will determine how much emphasis is given to various aspects and evidence. Another excellent source for this type of information on procedures would be *"Death Investigation: A Guide for the Scene Investigator"* as provided by the U.S. Department of Justice, Office of Justice Programs, National Institute of Justice.

Fremont County Coroner Death Report
EXAMPLE

Date of Call: mo./day/year   **Time**: military 24 hrs   **Case #**:
Military time can ease confusion between AM and PM, especially if circumstances occur near midnight.

Scene Location: exact location of the immediate scene. This may include address, GPS, highway mile marker, etc. Note: some cases may have more than one scene, and additional, originating, or related scenes may be noted here, or in the scene description.

Deceased Information: (as complete as possible)
Name:
Address:
SSN: DOB:
Driver License #/State:
Height: Weight:
Hair: Eyes:

Manner of Death: list as "pending" unless you are sure of the manner. Legal options for the death certificate are: 'Natural', 'Accident', 'Suicide', 'Homicide', 'Pending investigation', and 'Could not be determined'. Other listings not official but used as our designation for the database include: 'Non-human' (usually cases identified as animal remains), or 'Not a Fremont County Case', where the jurisdiction was terminated, or in the case of an assist to another jurisdiction. Older historic cases may be found in the database as 'Unknown' due to lack of information.

Scene Description: Includes a physical description of the location, building, room, highway, vehicles, weather, temperature, area immediately surrounding the body, evidence or other pertinent features. This may be as simple as "Hospital Emergency Room, Trauma #1", or a detailed and long description and/or reference to an attached diagram. If diagrammed or including measurements, the report should note the method (steel tape, roller wheel, etc.).

May sometimes only say "originating scene not viewed" if the body was recovered at another location, or your duties did not include that scene (such as transport only). May refer to photos but keep in mind that an accurate and thorough description of the scene written here is what ties various photos together, and is critical to point out details of significance.

Body Description: Location in reference to the scene, position, condition, injury, livor mortis, rigor mortis, decomposition, clothing, jewelry, other property on the body, distinguishing marks or tattoos, race, age, sex, etc. Sometimes this is separated into two parts, one for the description at the scene, one for more detail on external examination after transport. "Not viewed at scene" may also be used here if the incident occurred at a location other than where the body currently is, such as a hospital. If that is the case, always confirm with law enforcement or others (and document) that the originating scene, or other scenes in a case are being investigated. Specific cases may or may not involve supplemental investigation of other locations. Initial observations may be critical as things change over time, even between the first viewing and autopsy. Descriptions at autopsy should be left to the pathologist and his report to not conflict with that medical terminology or view – the pathologist is the only one qualified to justify or defend his observations during the procedure.

Scene Photographs: yes   **Body Photographs:** yes

TRAUMA DESCRIPTION: If already covered in the body description, may say "see above", or separated into more detail here. Avoid medical terminology unless trained and qualified, or specifically referring to medical reports, or the overtly obvious, or considered general usage. The use of medical terminology can be seen as a diagnosis in court, which the investigator will have to justify by qualifications.

INCIDENT DESCRIPTION: Should include a running narrative of the call: when dispatched and by who, what vehicle, when arrived at the scene, what you did, may refer to what others are assigned, how and when the body recovered and secured, when you leave the scene, where transported, how secured, when call ended. Should include who else was on scene when you arrived, and what agencies were consulted. May refer to others to show certain aspects are covered, such as "scene security and access by law enforcement". Also may include additional information gathered at the scene or later. If reported information given by law enforcement or other agency, say exactly that: "so-and-so reported that…", unless you directly heard or witnessed the information. If a personally contacted witness or third party statement or information, identify and record contact information. May refer to other reports by other individuals or agencies. May refer to photos. May give more detail on evidence, medications, or collection and location. May include a scenario of the death event, but be sure to note only <u>known facts</u>, and do not include speculations, assumptions, or hearsay. May also include what you did not do and why, such as "body not examined in detail, pending forensic autopsy", or "evidence retained by law enforcement" rather than collected, etc.

Aside from the running narrative, this section should include all documentation on the evidence and <u>source of identification of the deceased</u>, and any information supporting the conclusion towards determining manner and cause of death. Additional time spent and information gathered should go into a supplemental report, as the office should receive a copy of your first report as soon as possible (usually within a day). The preference may be to mark a report as "preliminary" to allow changes or additions to the information as the investigation progresses.

Autopsy: yes or no   **Pathologist:** doctor, if known

Toxicology: usually listed as "pending", but make sure to note if drawn, either here or in the narrative. It may also be important to note sample source, such as cardiac, sub-clavian, or femoral.

Location of Death: as exact as possible
Date of Death: exact, approx., or unknown
Time of Death: exact, approx., or unknown
Pronounced by: who   **Date Pronounced**: exact
                                  Time Pronounced: exact

Cause of Death: May often be listed as "pending" if not known for sure. Final determination of manner and cause is by the Coroner if there is any question. Often as listed by the pathologist. Should be the actual physical cause, and underlying or contributing causes.

Witnesses: Names, addresses and contact info if any

Medical History/Medication: May refer to medical records requested, or additional medication inventory sheets. Can list reported conditions, but note source and whether or not verified. Note consultations with any physicians, date and time. Summaries of medical records should be added as completed, if necessary, by Supplemental Report and a note as to when they were received.

Law Enforcement Officers: List officers or agencies unless documented elsewhere

Family: Immediate next-of-kin, names, addresses and contact information

Notification: who was notified (next-of-kin) and when

Property Description: May refer to additional property sheets. Detail on what, when, and where secured. By our policy, no retained property released unless signed for by next-of-kin. May simply refer to release at scene to authorized persons, or reference evidence collected by other agencies in general. Always keep in mind the principle of "chain of custody".

REPORT COMPLETED BY: **Date:**

NOTE: all activities performed by an investigator in relation to a call should be documented, either on the original or supplemental reports. All transports for autopsy will be a brief report including when and where body retrieved, how secured, time of departure, arrival, time left for return and when returned, and disposition of the remains. This is to insure documentation of the chain of custody of the evidence and body prior to release from our office.

Supplemental information and documentation may also be added here to the end of the original report, usually in sequence by the date and/or time the information was obtained or occurred. This could include medical records summaries, additional family or other contacts relative to the case.

In all cases, the report as a whole and any additions should justify and document the sequence and evidence that leads to a final conclusion on manner and cause of death.

The important thing to remember in completing the report is that this will be your only documentation to remind you of what occurred, should you ever have to testify in court regarding a case. Since the legal wheels often grind slowly, it would not be unusual to have that experience occur a year or more after a call or event, and the details you record can be crucial.

Appendix B: Records Retention Rules for the State of Wyoming

Since it is obvious from this study that good records are needed to keep the unknowns to a minimum, the Fremont County Coroner policy is presented as an example and suggestion for the application of Wyoming Statutes. Later investigators will not only appreciate your keeping important information, but also the disposing of unnecessary documents. It is no fun to wade through piles of irrelevant and spurious paper.

The basis for most records rules and law resides in the following Wyoming Statute:

W.S. 9-2-410. Records as property of state; delivery by outgoing officials and employees to successors; management and disposition thereof.

"All public records are the property of the state. They shall be delivered by outgoing officials and employees to their successors and shall be preserved, stored, transferred, destroyed or disposed of, and otherwise managed, only in accordance with W.S. 9-2-405 through 9-2-413."

Additional multiple statutes determine how that 'document property' of the State is filed, regulated, disposed of, or retained. Other statutes determine exactly what is, and is not, considered the 'public record' portion of all documentation, including all hard copy, paper, recorded, or digital forms. Other statutes give rule making authority to the Wyoming State Archives governing the retention or disposal of all governmental documentation. Various schedules on how the different records are handled are in place for all agencies, officials, and personnel of the State and all political subdivisions, which includes county coroners. There are criminal penalties also in statute for not following the rules as they exist, so it is wise for any agency and official to study, know, and create internal policies that conform to State regulations. The bottom line is that by law, they are not your records, they belong to the State of Wyoming. Other jurisdictions and States have their own versions of these types of regulations.

So, while the only filed record specifically mentioned in statutes for coroners is that the transcript and associated documents of an Inquest must be eventually filed with the Clerk of District Court, the Archive rules have the effect of statute and also apply to the various types of documentation as indicated in the schedules. There is some leeway in how the rules may be interpreted and applied, but as an example, I created schedules and policies for our office, and had them approved by the Archives to make sure we were in compliance. The good thing is that once you establish such policies, it helps to keep from being overwhelmed by paper files. When I took office, we were able to shred a large number of cubic feet of paper of unnecessary duplicative administrative trash with State approval and save a whole lot of storage space. Creating policies also cements in your mind what are really critical and important files to retain, or not. Future investigators and administrators will appreciate you doing your job in this area.

Fremont County Coroner's Office Records Retention and Management Policy

Introduction

Recent additions in rules for Coroner standards by the State Board of Coroner Standards in 2009, and statutory changes by the Wyoming Legislature in 2011 have added additional requirements for record keeping and management. Retention schedules can not only define what may or may not be disposed of, and when; but also can form guidelines for organization. The following policy and procedures are established beginning January 1st, 2015 for the Fremont County Coroner's Office.

Note: For any title that states the documents need review, that review should be completed by the State Records Analyst or their designee.

Office Administration

1. **Title:** Purchase Orders, Requisitions, Vouchers (Duplicates)
   State Reference: ADM-GMT-26 Transitory Records
   Retention Schedule: Retain one year, then destroy when obsolete or superseded. Originals are filed with the County Clerk.

2. **Title:** Travel Expense Voucher and Report (Duplicates)
   State Reference: ADM-GMT-26 Transitory Records
   Retention Schedule: Retain one year, then destroy when obsolete or superseded. Originals are filed with the County Clerk.

3. **Title:** Inventory Records and Reports
   State Reference: FIN-ASM-03 Inventories
   Retention Schedule: Retain 5 years after the fiscal year end then destroy.

4. **Title:** Personnel Files
   State Reference: EMP-PER-22 (long term) & EMP-PER-14 (short term)

Retention Schedule: Long Term: retain 10 years after completion then destroy. Short Term: retain 5 years after separation then destroy. See State schedules for what this includes.

5. **Title:** Personnel Hiring Records
   State Reference: EMP-SAR-01 Applicants-not hired
   Retention Schedule: Applicants not hired, retain 3 years after calendar year then destroy. Successful Applicants - transfer to Personnel File and subject to Title #4 above

6. **Title:** Time Sheets
   State Reference: EMP-SAR-18 Time and Attendance
   Retention Schedule: Retain 2 years after calendar year end then destroy

7. **Title:** Coroner Policy and Procedure Manual
   State Reference: GAC-PSM-02 Policies, Procedures and Manuals
   Retention Schedule: Retain 5 years after superseded then destroy. One copy retained permanently pending historical evaluation by State Records Management

8. **Title:** Coroner General Correspondence
   State Reference: ADM-GMT-05 General Correspondence
   Retention Schedule: Review for legal, administrative, or historical value. Destroy 3 years after create date.

9. **Title:** Correspondence, Elected Officials
   State Reference: ADM-GMT-04 Correspondence, Elected Officials
   Retention Schedule: Permanent. This includes records related to internal and external communications to or from elected officials of policy issues, concerns and issues, and actions taken. (Considered separate from Title #8 above)

10. **Title:** Budget Worksheets and Records
    State Reference: ADM-GMT-26 Transitory Records
    Retention Schedule: Destroy when obsolete or superseded.

11. **Title:** General Office Files (as defined in WS 9-2-405(a)(ii) only), not otherwise specified
    State Reference: ADM-GMT-26 Transitory Records
    Retention Schedule: Destroy when obsolete or superseded. Be aware that there may be a need for review of some miscellaneous

records for historical value.

12. **Title:** Transitory Records
    State Reference: ADM-GMT-26 Transitory Records
    Retention Schedule: Destroy when obsolete or superseded. If not otherwise specified, this relates to temporary records, of short term value, not required as evidence of transactions, duplicate copies, miscellaneous notices, preliminary drafts, reports and worksheets, and informal communications not identified by another title.

13. **Title:** Training Programs, Materials, and Printed Copies
    State Reference: ADM-EDU-14 Training Materials
    Retention Schedule: Original: Retain 2 years after superseded then destroy. Copies may be destroyed as Transitory Records

14. **Title:** Reference Material
    State Reference: ADM-GMT-20 Reference Material
    Retention Schedule: Destroy when obsolete. This refers to records and other materials which are maintained solely for ease of access and reference

15. **Title:** Complaints and Inquiries
    State Reference: LGL-LAR-49 Complaints and Inquiries
    Retention Schedule: Retain 6 years then destroy. This includes general department issues or information, and not personnel or case issues, which are filed individually.

Summary on Office Administration Files: There is no regulation that says files have to be destroyed at the above minimum retention periods. Longer period may be applicable depending on space availability, possible legal or historical value, or preference of the Coroner. These titles are to serve as a guideline for organization and minimum retention periods.

Operational Files

1. **Title:** Case Files – General: May contain any or all information and documents relating to the Rules for Death Investigations as established by the Board of Coroner Standards, Chapter 6, Section 4, in addition to all correspondence and documentation relating to a specific case, not otherwise listed.
    State Reference: LGL-COU-04 Case Files and Dockets
    Retention Schedule: Permanent, with the exception of Medical

Records, as listed under separate Title

2. **Title:** Case Files – Medical Records (copies)
   State Reference: ADM-GMT-26 Transitory Records (Special circumstance defined)
   Retention Schedule: <u>Homicide or Undetermined Manner</u> – Permanent; <u>Accident or Suicide Manner</u> – Retain 2 years or until all civil adjudication completed, then destroy; <u>Natural Manner</u> – Retain one year, then destroy. <u>Autopsy and toxicology reports</u> – Permanent
   NOTE: the original or supplemental reports of the investigator must include a summary of the review of relevant information from the medical records that were critical in determining the manner and cause of death, prior to the destruction of the records.

3. **Title:** Case Files – Coroner Inquest, Duplicate
   State Reference: LGL-COU-04 Case Files and Dockets
   Retention Schedule: One copy, Permanent [Originals are filed with the Clerk of District Court per WS 7-4-206 and retained to the State Archives]

4. **Title:** Case Files – Verdict and Case Docket, as described in WS 7-4-105(a)
   State Reference: LGL-COU-04 Case Files and Dockets
   Retention Schedule: Permanent

5. **Title:** Public Records Requests
   State Reference: GAC-RCM-07 Public Records Requests
   Retention Schedule: Permanent. Coroner policy is that all requests under W.S. 7-4-105 be placed in the applicable case file when completed.

Legal Summary

Coroners have documentation requirements and concerns unique to the Office. The only currently defined document to be retained by Statute is the Coroner Inquest, and that is statutorily through the Clerk of District Court. The only other statutorily required document is a Verdict and Case Docket, per WS 7-4-105(a), effective July 1st, 2011. Death certificates prepared by a coroner and registrar are already filed with Vital Records, however the Docket contains additional information not found on the certificate. The Rules adopted in 2009 by the Coroner Board of Standards now define the basic (but not necessarily all) documentation that should be in the individual case file on every death that is a coroner case.

Medical and Psychological records are obtained by coroners as authorized by WS 7-4-201(f); and *The Health Insurance Portability and Accountability Act of 1996 (HIPAA). [Code of Federal Regulations] [Title 45, Volume 1] [CITE: **45CFR164.512**]   Subpart E--Privacy of Individually Identifiable Health Information.* Coroners by law cannot issue any secondary release of this information or documentation, and they can be considered part of the Case File. As would be expected, this can often be a large volume of information and paper, sometimes numbering cases of documents for an individual investigation. Therefore this policy defines a retention schedule under special circumstances for these records, even though they are transitory copies. Homicide or Undetermined cases may remain open investigations by law enforcement agencies for years, and sometimes decades. Thus, no matter the volume, all files in a homicide should be retained permanently. Accident or Suicide cases would not have criminal legal implications, but may have civil actions, thus should be retained for a reasonable time, but not indefinitely. Medical records in Natural cases would have no criminal or civil implications, and should only be retained for a reasonable time to ensure there is no change or question on the investigation. It is emphasized that this only pertains to medical records obtained by the coroner that are copies of originals from the originating institution, agency, or facility.

Coroner case files after July 1st, 2011, per WS 7-4-105, are confidential, and exempt from inspection or availability as public records, other than an Inquest, and the Case Docket. This confidentiality statute also necessitates additional responsibility for security and storage, and magnifies the need for a consistent Retention Schedule and management.

Digital Media

For the purposes of Retention Schedules, the Fremont County Coroner's Office establishes a policy whereby all originals or copies of digital media will be dealt with in the same manner as paper documentation as listed in the above Titles. While the minimum standard established will conform to State Reference ADM-ITS-01, ADM-ITS-02, and ADM-ITS-03, the Fremont County Coroner's Office will consider the Coroner Case File Database and Coroner Docket Database as items for permanent retention under the Operational Titles as listed above. This permanent retention also includes all case information, such as digital photos or other media related to an individual case. Permanent and on-going backups will also be maintained per established best practices for digital media.

Records Destruction

The policy for records destruction will conform to best practices as established by the State Records Analyst. All confidential materials, or records that contain confidential materials as specified in W.S. 7-4-105 will be shredded or destroyed irretrievably. Per State Reference GAC-RCM-03 records relating to the destruction of records will be on the approved forms and retained permanently.

Accountability to the State

It is the policy of the Fremont County Coroner's Office to cooperate and interact with the State Archives and Records Management Division to maintain and preserve records as directed and permitted. Any changes to this policy will be transmitted to the appropriate Records Analyst for review prior to implementation. As new programs and technology become available, this office will accommodate the possible transfer of historical records, digital media, and case files, or copies thereof, to the Archives for permanent storage.

Certification of Policy

Per State Reference GAC-RCM-09, the record of this policy, and any changes, will be retained permanently on file at the Fremont County Coroner's Office, and is effective as of January 1st, 2015.

Appendix C: Coroner Statutes for the State of Wyoming

WYOMING STATUTES, TITLE 7, CHAPTER 4
COUNTY CORONERS

ARTICLE 1
IN GENERAL

7-4-101. Election; oath; bond.

A coroner shall be elected in each county for a term of four (4) years. He shall take the oath prescribed by the constitution of the state and give bond to the state of Wyoming, in the penal sum of one thousand dollars ($1,000.00), with sufficient sureties, to be approved by the board of county commissioners, conditioned that he will faithfully perform all duties required by law.

7-4-102 Deputy coroners.

The county coroner may appoint deputy coroners, who shall serve in the absence or inability of the coroner and who shall receive compensation as the board of county commissioners determines by resolution.

7-4-103. Certification requirements; penalty; expenses.

(a) After January 5, 1987, no person shall continue in office as county coroner or deputy coroner unless he has been certified under W.S. 9-1-634 as having completed:
(i) Not later than one (1) year after assuming office, a basic coroner course;
(ii) Continuing education requirements promulgated by the board of coroner standards pursuant to W.S. 7-4-211(c)(iii).
(b) Any person who knowingly fails to comply with subsection (a) of this section and continues in office is guilty of a misdemeanor punishable by a fine of twenty-five dollars ($25.00) for each day of noncompliance.
(c)Each coroner or deputy coroner attending approved classes to receive the certification required by subsection (a) of this section shall receive his present salary or per diem in the same manner and amount as state employees, whichever is greater, and shall be reimbursed for his actual travel and other necessary expenses reasonably incurred in obtaining the required training. The expenses shall be paid by the county in which the coroner or deputy coroner is serving.
(d)After July 1, 2001, no person shall serve as deputy coroner or as an employee of a county coroner who does not meet the employment standards adopted by the board of coroner standards pursuant to W.S. 7-4-211(c)(v).

7-4-104. Definitions.

(a) As used in this chapter:

      (ii)   "Coroner's case" means a case involving a death which was not anticipated and which may involve any of the following conditions:

(I)   Violent or criminal action;

(J)   Apparent suicide;

(K) Accident;

(L)   Apparent drug or chemical overdose or toxicity;

(M) The deceased was unattended by a physician or other licensed health care provider;

(N) Apparent child abuse causes;

(O) The deceased was a prisoner, trustee, inmate or patient of any county or state corrections facility or state hospital, whether or not the death is unanticipated;

(P)   If the cause is unknown, or cannot be certified by a physician,

(L)   A public health hazard is presented; or

(M) The identity of the victim is unknown or the body is unclaimed.

(ii) "Coroner's office" means all personnel appointed and elected to the office of coroner, including the county coroner, deputies and assistants;

(iii) "County coroner" means the elected or appointed officer of the county whose task is to investigate the cause of death in a coroner's case.

(iv) "Anticipated death" means the death of an individual who has been diagnosed by a physician acting within the scope of his license as being afflicted with an illness or disease reasonably likely to result in death, and there is no cause to believe the death occurred for any reasons other than those associated with the illness or disease;

(v) "Unattended" means the deceased had not been under the care of a physician or other health care provider acting within the scope of his license within sixty (60) days immediately prior to the date of death.

7-4-105. Confidentiality of reports, photos and recordings; exceptions; penalties.

(a) After viewing the body and completing his investigation, the coroner shall draw up and sign his verdict on the death under consideration. The coroner shall also make a written docket giving an accurate description of the deceased person, his name if it can be determined, cause and manner of death, including relevant toxicological factors, age of decedent, date and time of death and the description of money and other property found with the body. The verdict and written docket are public records and may be viewed or obtained by request to the coroner, pursuant to W.S. 16-4-202.

(b) Except as provided in subsections (c), (d), (e), (g) and (o) of this section a toxicology report, a photograph, video recording or audio recording made at the scene of the death or made in the course of a postmortem examination or autopsy made or caused by a coroner shall be confidential and are not public records.

(c) A surviving spouse, surviving parent, an adult child, personal representative, legal representative, or a legal guardian may:

(i) View and copy a toxicology report, a photograph or video recording made at the scene of the death or made in the course of a postmortem examination or autopsy made by or caused by a coroner; and

(ii) Listen to and copy an audio recording made at the scene of the death or made in the course of a postmortem examination or autopsy made by or caused by a coroner.

(d) Upon making a written request, a law enforcement entity of the state of Wyoming or United States government, a district attorney, the United States attorney for the district of Wyoming, a county, state or federal public health agency, a board licensing health care professionals under title 33 of the Wyoming statutes, the division responsible for administering the Wyoming Workers' Compensation Act, the state occupational epidemiologist, the department and the division responsible for administering the Wyoming Occupational Health and Safety Act, the office of the inspector of mines, insurance companies with legitimate interest in the death, all parties in civil litigation proceedings with legitimate interest in the death or a treating physician, while in performance of his official duty may:

(i) View and copy a toxicology report, photograph or video recording made at the scene of the death or made in the course of a postmortem examination or autopsy made by or caused by a coroner; and

(ii) Listen to and copy an audio recording made at the scene of the death or made in the course of a postmortem examination or autopsy made by or caused by a coroner.

(e) Unless otherwise required in the performance of official duties, the identity of the deceased shall remain confidential in any record obtained under subsection (d) of this section.

(f) The coroner having custody of a toxicology report, a photograph, a video recording or an audio recording made at any scene of the death or made in the course of a postmortem examination or autopsy may allow the use for case consultation with an appropriate expert. The coroner may also allow the use of a toxicology report, a photograph, a video recording or an audio recording made at the scene of the death or made in the course of a postmortem examination or autopsy by legitimate scientific research organizations or for training purposes provided the identity of the decedent is not published or otherwise made public.

(g) A court upon showing of good cause, may issue an order authorizing a person to:

(i) View or copy a toxicology report, photograph or video recording made at the scene of the death or made in the course of a postmortem examination or autopsy made or caused by a coroner; and

(ii) Listen to and copy an audio recording made at the scene of the death or made in the course of a postmortem examination or autopsy made or caused by a coroner.

(h) In determining good cause under subsection (g) of this section, the court shall consider:

(i) Whether the disclosure is necessary for the public evaluation of governmental performance;

(ii) The seriousness of the intrusion into the family's privacy;

(iii) Whether the disclosure of the toxicology report, photograph, video recording or audio recording is by the least intrusive means available; and

(iv) The availability of similar information in other public records regardless of form.

(j) A surviving spouse shall be given reasonable notice and a copy of any petition filed with the court under subsection (g) of this section and reasonable opportunity to be present and be heard on the matter. If there is no surviving spouse, the notice of the petition being filed and the opportunity to be heard shall be given to the deceased's parents and if the deceased has no living parent, the notice of the petition being filed and the opportunity to be heard shall be given to the adult children of the deceased or legal guardian, personal representative or legal representative of the children of the deceased.

(k) A coroner or coroner's designee that knowingly violates this section shall be guilty of a misdemeanor punishable by imprisonment for not more than six (6) months, a fine of not more than one thousand dollars ($1,000.00), or both.

(m) A person who knowingly or purposefully uses the information in a manner other than the specified purpose for which it was released or violates a court order issued under subsection (g) of this section is guilty of a misdemeanor punishable by imprisonment for not more than six (6) months, a fine of not more than one thousand dollars ($1,000.00), or both.

(n) In all cases, the viewing, copying, listening to, or other handling of a toxicology report, photograph, video recording, or audio recording made at a scene of the death or made in the course of a postmortem examination or autopsy made or caused by a coroner shall be under the direct supervision of the coroner, or the coroner's designee, who is the custodian of the record.

(o) In the event that the coroner, or the coroner's designee, determines that a person's death was caused by an infectious disease, biological toxin or any other cause which may constitute a public health emergency as defined in W.S. 35-4-115(a)(i), the coroner shall release to the state health officer or his designee all information and records required under W.S. 35-4-107. If the state health official or his designee determines upon an examination of the results of the autopsy and the toxicology report that a public health emergency may in fact exist, he shall release the appropriate information to the general public as provided by department of health rules and regulations.

ARTICLE 2
INQUESTS

7-4-201. Reports of death; investigation; summoning of jurors; fees and costs; inspection of medical records.

(a) When any person is found dead and the death appears to have occurred under circumstances indicating the death is a coroner's case, the person who discovers the death shall report it immediately to law enforcement authorities who shall in turn notify the coroner. A person who knowingly violates this section is guilty of a misdemeanor punishable by imprisonment for not more than six (6) months, a fine of not more than seven hundred fifty dollars ($750.00), or both.

(b) When the coroner is notified that the dead body of any person has been found within the limits of the county or that the death resulted from injury sustained within the county and he suspects that the death is a coroner's case, he shall conduct an investigation which may include:

(i) An examination of the body and an investigation into the medical history of the case;

(ii) The appointment of a qualified physician to assist in determining the cause of death;

(iii) An autopsy if the physician appointed to assist the coroner under this subsection determines an autopsy is necessary;

(iv) An inquest; or

(v) Any other reasonable procedure which may be necessary to determine the cause of death.

(c) If the coroner determines to hold an inquest he shall summon three (3) citizens of the county to appear before him to act as jurors at the time and place named. The jurors shall receive the same fee paid jurors in district court as provided in W.S. 1-11-303 and per diem and travel expenses in the same manner as state employees. The coroner may furnish transportation for the jury and witnesses to and from the place of inquest and for the removal of the dead body.

(d) If a coroner determines the injuries which caused the person's death were received in a county other than that in which the body was found, he shall transfer authority for the investigation and inquest to the coroner for that county.

(e) The expense and costs of conducting the investigation or holding the inquest shall be paid by the county in which the injuries were received. The accounts of the claimants shall be attested by the coroner or acting coroner, and shall be presented in duplicate to the board of county commissioners of the proper county. If the board of county commissioners finds that the inquest was necessary and in accordance with law, and the accounts are correct and just, the accounts shall be paid in warrants properly drawn upon the order of the county commissioners.

(f) Notwithstanding any other provision of law to the contrary, the coroner may inspect medical and psychological data relating to the person-whose death is being investigated if the coroner determines the information is relevant and necessary to the investigation.

7-4-202. Impaneling of bystanders as jurors; oath.

If any juror fails to appear, the coroner shall immediately summon the proper number from the bystanders and proceed to impanel them. He shall administer the following oath: "You do solemnly swear (or affirm) that you will diligently inquire and truly present if known or determinable, the time and date of death, and by what means and manner the death of (NAME OF DECEASED) was caused, according to your knowledge and the evidence given you, so help you God."

7-4-203. Issuance of subpoenas; witness fees; enforcement of attendance.

The coroner may issue subpoenas and compel the attendance of witnesses to testify at the inquest. Witnesses shall be allowed the same fees as in cases before a circuit court, and the coroner shall have the same authority to enforce the attendance of witnesses and to punish for contempt as provided by W.S. 1-21-901 through 1-21-909.

7-4-204. Oath of witness; recording of testimony; compensation of reporter.
An oath shall be administered to each witness as follows: "You do solemnly swear (or affirm) that the testimony which you shall give to this inquest concerning the death of the person about whom this inquest is being held, shall be the truth, the whole truth and nothing but the truth, so help you God." The coroner shall insure that all testimony in an inquest shall be recorded. The compensation of the court reporter or of the person transcribing the audio tape shall be as prescribed by the board of county commissioners. Unless specifically requested by the coroner or prosecuting attorney, audio tapes need not be transcribed.

7-4-205. Return of inquisition by jury.
After hearing testimony and making necessary inquiries, the jurors shall return to the coroner their signed inquisition stating the name of the person and when, how and by what means, if known, he came to his death.

7-4-206. Coroner's return to court.
The coroner shall return to the district court the inquisition, the written evidence and a list of witnesses providing material testimony.

7-4-207. Disposition of body and effects of deceased.
    (a) When the coroner investigates the death of a person whose body is not claimed by a friend or relative within five (5) days of the date of discovery and whose death does not require further investigation, he shall cause the body to be decently buried. The expense of the burial shall be paid from any property found with the body. If no property is found, the expense of the burial shall be paid by the county in which the investigation occurs.

    (b) The coroner shall within a reasonable time after completing the investigation, turn over to the appointed personal representative of the estate of the deceased or, if none, to the clerk of the district court of the county, all money or other property found upon the body of the deceased. Personal items valued at less than fifty dollars ($50.00) and items necessary for the convenience of the deceased's next of kin may be released to the deceased's next of kin.

7-4-208. Authority of sheriff to perform duties of coroner.
If there is no coroner, deputy coroner or in case of their absence, or inability to act, the county sheriff of the same county, the state health officer pursuant to W.S. 35-1-241, or the coroner of another county if there is a joint powers agreement pursuant to W.S. 16-1-102 through 16-1-108 between the counties authorizing the coroner to so act, is authorized to perform the duties of coroner in relation to dead bodies.

7-4-209. Postmortem examination; liability limitation.

(a) When an inquisition is being held, if the coroner or the jury shall deem it requisite, he may summon one (1) or more physicians or surgeons, to make an autopsy or postmortem examination.

(b) If it is necessary to obtain or preserve evidence of the cause of death, the district attorney may order that a qualified physician perform an autopsy or postmortem examination of the body of any person who appears to have died by unlawful means, by violence, or when the cause of death is unknown.

(c) No person is subject to civil liability solely because he requested or was involved In the performing of an autopsy that was ordered by a coroner or district attorney.

7-4-210. Fees and mileage, salary.

(a) The coroner or deputy coroner of each county within this state shall receive fees and mileage, if any, as set by the board of county commissioners.

(b) The board of county commissioners shall set the salary of the coroner and deputy coroner. A coroner or deputy coroner shall not be prohibited from receiving other fees for their services unrelated to their official duties as coroner or deputy coroner.

7-4-211. Board of coroner standards.

(a) There is created a board of coroner standards. The board shall consist of one (1) chairman and six (6) members appointed by and who shall serve at-the pleasure of the governor as follows:

    (i)   One (1) shall be a physician with a specialty in pathology who is licensed to practice in this state;

    (ii)   Three (3) shall be duly elected coroners in this state;

    (iii)   One (1) shall be a funeral director in this state;

    (iv)   One (1) shall be a duly elected district attorney in this state;

    (v)   One (1) shall be a peace officer certified under W.S. 9-1-701 through 9-1-707.

(b) The members of the board shall be appointed to terms of four (4) years which are concurrent with the terms of the office of coroner. Board members not otherwise compensated for attending board meetings shall receive travel expenses and per them in the same manner and amount as state employees, and any other reasonable expenses upon board approval. Board members not otherwise compensated shall have their expenses paid from the general fund by appropriation to the office of the attorney general.

(c) The board shall:

    (i)   Meet at least biannually and at the call of the chairman or of a majority of the membership;

    (ii)   Promulgate standards dealing with the investigation of coroner's cases;

    (iii)   Promulgate educational and training requirements for coroner basic and continuing education requirements and review those requirements annually;

(iv)   Cooperate with the peace officer standards and training commission in developing basic and continuing education courses for coroners;

(v)   Promulgate employment standards for deputy coroners and coroner employees. The standards may include the requirement that deputy coroners and coroner employees provide to the employing coroner fingerprints and other information necessary for a state and national criminal history record background check and release of information as provided in W.S. 7-19-106(k)(ii) and federal P.L. 92-544 and consent to the release of any criminal history information to the employing coroner.

(vi)   Promulgate rules and regulations to provide for the review of complaints if a coroner or deputy coroner has failed to comply with any provision of W.S. 7-4-103 or this subsection or has failed to meet any educational or training requirement provided under this section. The board shall make recommendations to the peace officer standards and training commission regarding revocation of certifications based on these investigations;

(vii)   Provide for a system to offer educational programs to assist coroners and deputy coroners in meeting educational and training requirements provided under this section.

(d) The peace officer standards and training commission shall cooperate with the board of coroner standards in establishing course requirements and continuing education requirements required by law.

(e) The board shall contact the district attorney for the county or the attorney general to initiate an action and may serve as complaining party in an action under W.S. 7-4-103 (b) or 18-3-902 to remove any coroner who is not in compliance with W.S. 7-4-103.

(f) In addition to any action under subsection (e) of this section, the board shall notify the county commissioners for the county of any coroner or deputy coroner who has had his certification revoked.

W.S. 9-1-634. Academy to provide coroner training; certification of completion.

(a) The director of the Wyoming law enforcement academy shall provide at the academy or other location within the state a basic coroner's course of at least forty (40) hours. The course shall comply with the standards promulgated by the peace officers standards and training commission and the board of coroner standards.

(b) The executive director of the peace officers standards and training commission shall issue an appropriate certificate of completion to any coroner or deputy coroner who completes a coroner training course offered by the academy or which the board of coroner standards has certified as meeting board standards.

Also changed in the 2011 Legislature:

Section 2. W.S. 16-4-203(d)(i) is amended to read:

16-4-203. Right of inspection; grounds for denial; access of news media; order permitting or restricting disclosure; exceptions.

(d) The custodian shall deny the right of inspection of the following records, unless otherwise provided by law:

(i) Medical, psychological and sociological data on individual persons, exclusive of coroners' verdicts and written dockets as provided in W.S.7-4-105(a); *(previous wording stated "exclusive of coroner's autopsy reports")*

Other above referenced statutes:

W.S. 1-11-303. Amount of fees. (jurors)
W.S. 1-21-901 through 1-21-909. Attendance of witnesses, contempt...
W.S. 7-19-106 (k)(ii). Background checks, criminal history...
W.S. 9-1-701 through 9-1-707. Peace officer standards and training commission.
W.S. 16-1-102 through 16-1-108. Wyoming Joint Powers Act
W.S. 18-3-901 through 18-3-902. Causes for removal from office enumerated, procedure...
W.S. 35-1-241. Safe disposal of corpses in emergency circumstances.

Other statutes indexed as referring to coroners or coroner duties:

W.S. 1-12-102. "Dead man's statute" (testimony)
W.S. 1-14-104, 105. Fees of physicians in testimony and post-mortem examination.
W.S. 2-17-101. Authority to authorize burial or cremation (7 days in this section)
W.S. 6-4-501, 502. Desecration of Graves and Bodies.
W.S. 14-2-708. Court ordered genetic testing of the deceased.
W.S. 14-3-207. Reporting deaths in cases of suspected child abuse.
W.S. 33-16-527. Duty of funeral director to ascertain cause of death prior to disposition.
W.S. 35-4-601 through 35-4-607. Unclaimed bodies.
W.S. 35-4-607. Who may have bodies in possession.

W.S. 35-19-101 through 35-19-103. Determination of death..

APPENDIX D: BOARD OF CORONER STANDARDS

In 2009 the Board of Coroner Standards established as a part of their rules, minimum standards for Coroners and death investigation.

CHAPTER 6
STANDARDS DEALING WITH THE INVESTIGATION OF CORONER'S CASES

Section 1. Definitions. W.S. 7-4-104 is appended to these standards as Appendix A and adopted and incorporated herein.

Section 2. Conduct. Coroners shall act in accordance with all relevant state and federal law. In addition, in dealing with the deceased, the family of the deceased, and the general public, the Coroners shall conduct themselves in a manner consistent with the highest standards of professionalism, compassion, and respect.

Section 3. General.

(a) The Coroner shall work jointly with all law enforcement agencies having jurisdiction in a death scene investigation.

(b) The Coroner has jurisdiction over and shall take custody of the body.

(c) The Coroner shall assume responsibility for the property of the deceased.

(d) Evidence is the responsibility of law enforcement and/or the Coroner.

(e) The Coroner shall protect the chain of custody for any evidence in their custody.

(f) The Coroner shall provide for transportation, security, and preservation of the deceased until released to the next of kin or their designee.

(g) The Coroner shall pronounce death, and record the date, time, and location.

(h) The Coroner shall provide for the notification of next of kin.

(i) The Coroner shall provide the office staff and investigators:

(i) Safe and adequate equipment to perform any duties of the office; and

(ii) Adequate and appropriate safety and personal protective equipment suitable for the circumstances of the investigation.

Section 4. Investigations.

(a) The Coroner shall identify the deceased and determine the Manner and Cause of death as accurately as possible.

(b) In determining the Manner and Cause of death, the investigation shall include:

(i) Scene Investigation;

      (ii)   Toxicology sample on the deceased;

      (iii) Inventory of property, evidence, and medications;

      (iv) Photographs;

      (v)   External Exam; and

      (vi) DNA sample.

(c)   The Coroner shall issue a written report for all death investigations. The written reports may include but are not limited to, data from measuring devices, diagrams, evidence and body labeling, interviews, psychological and social histories, medical histories and consultation with physicians, autopsy, fingerprints, radiology, odontology, or DNA profiles or any other method necessary to determine the cause and manner of death.

(d)   Investigations requiring a forensic autopsy of the deceased shall be conducted by a Forensic Pathologist who has been certified in that specialty by a nationally recognized certification board.

(e) All investigations will be completed in a reasonable time. The term 'reasonable time' is defined as that time period necessary to complete and collect data and information from toxicology, autopsy, or other investigation procedures, to determine with medical certainty a manner and cause of death.

Section 5. Records. The Coroner shall maintain all public records in accordance with W.S. 9-2-405 through 9-2-413.

Suggested Bibliography

These resources are not all that are available, but are just a few of those I have found very useful over the course of investigations, and include some of the resources referred to in this study. Please note that many are frequently available in updated versions beyond the particular edition noted. Some are in the Public Domain, while others are copyrighted and available by purchase from various sources. There are also many specialized organizations and associations for different aspects of medical-legal death investigation not mentioned here that have materials available.

State of Wyoming web site at http://www.wyo.gov : source for all things relative to State government, including statutes, agency rules, and resources.

Wyoming State Archives, Barrett Building, 2301 Central Ave., Cheyenne, WY 82002: (307) 777-7826 – source for archived documents as well as resources and records management specialists. Also accessed via the web through the State site.

National Association of Medical Examiners at http://thename.org : source for standards and publications regarding determination of the manner and cause of death.

Death Investigation: A Guide for the Scene Investigator, National Institute of Justice, U.S Department of Justice, Office of Justice Programs, 810 7th Street N.W., Washington, D.C. 20531 Many other publications are available from the NIJ.

Disposition of Toxic Drugs and Chemicals in Man, seventh edition, by Randall C. Baselt, Ph.D., © 2004 by Biomedical Publications, P.O. Box 8299, Foster City, CA 94404

Ellenhorn's Medical Toxicology- Diagnosis and Treatment of Human Poisoning, second edition, by Matthew J. Ellenhorn, M.D., © Williams & Wilkins, 351 W. Camden St., Baltimore, MD, 21201

Death Investigator's Handbook – A Field Guide to Crime Scene Processing, Forensic Evaluations, and Investigative Techniques, by and © 1993 Louis N. Eliopulos, Pub. Paladin Press / Paladin Enterprises, Inc., Gunbarrel Tech Center, 7077 Winchester Circle, Boulder, CO 80301

Pathology for Death Investigators, by Jay Dix, © 2001 Academic Information Systems, Inc., 5609 St. Charles Rd., Columbia, MO 65202

Crime Scene Staging Dynamics in Homicide Cases, © and by Laura G. Pettler, Ph.D., Pub. CRC Press, Taylor & Francis Group, 6000 Broken Sound Parkway NW, Suite 300, Boca Raton, FL 33487

Forensic Art and Illustration, by Karen T. Taylor, © and Pub. CRC Press, Taylor & Francis Group, 6000 Broken Sound Parkway NW, Suite 300, Boca Raton, FL 33487

Wildlife Forensic Field Manual, Edited by William J. Adrian, Wildlife Researcher, Colorado Division of Wildlife; printed by the Association of Midwest Fish and Game Law Enforcement Officers, 2nd Printing April 1999.

Some of these are good field manuals, others basic texts, and some are special aspects of investigation to show just how detailed available resources can get... The last one may not be of much use in Detroit, but in this part of the country it helps to know the difference between an antelope or bear bone, and a human. For those that specialize, there is a wealth of detailed materials available out there.

Investigators are encouraged to develop their own personal library of resources, some of which you may use on almost a daily basis, others in only specific circumstances. For example, being an artist and sculptor, I took an interest in forensic reconstruction on human skulls for identification. While being a discipline of approximation, it did result in the positive ID of remains in a case, which was very satisfying. Such skills are only rarely called upon, but when needed, are nice to have in your toolbox. Find your own interest and run with it – forensic skills are multiple and varied, ranging in anything from paper and computers at a desk, to the various bugs crawling around a scene in the field. There really is no end to the variety of skills to acquire if interested.

www.ingramcontent.com/pod-product-compliance
Lightning Source LLC
Chambersburg PA
CBHW071253220526
45468CB00001B/106